Renewing Parish Culture

Renewing Parish Culture

Building for a Catholic Future

John J. Piderit, S.J., and Melanie M. Morey

SHEED & WARD

ROWMAN & LITTLEFIELD PUBLISHERS, INC.
Lanham • Boulder • New York • Toronto • Plymouth, UK

A SHEED & WARD BOOK

ROWMAN & LITTLEFIELD PUBLISHERS, INC.

Published in the United States of America
by Rowman & Littlefield Publishers, Inc.
A wholly owned subsidiary of The Rowman & Littlefield Publishing Group, Inc.
4501 Forbes Boulevard, Suite 200, Lanham, Maryland 20706
www.rowmanlittlefield.com

Estover Road
Plymouth PL6 7PY
United Kingdom

British Library Cataloguing in Publication Information Available

Library of Congress Cataloging-in-Publication Data

Piderit, John J.
    Renewing parish culture : building for a Catholic future / John J. Piderit and
Melanie M. Morey.
        p. cm.
    "A Sheed & Ward book."
    ISBN-13: 978-0-7425-5903-5 (cloth : alk. paper)
    ISBN-10: 0-7425-5903-3 (cloth : alk. paper)
    ISBN-13: 978-0-7425-5904-2 (pbk. : alk. paper)
    ISBN-10: 0-7425-5904-1 (pbk. : alk. paper)
    1. Church renewal—Catholic Church. I. Morey, Melanie M. II. Title.

    BX1746.P485 2008
    282'.73090511—dc22   2007038792

Printed in the United States of America

♾™ The paper used in this publication meets the minimum requirements of
American National Standard for Information Sciences—Permanence of Paper
for Printed Library Materials, ANSI/NISO Z39.48-1992.

In Memoriam

Rev. John J. McGinty, S.J.
Pastor and Provincial

Contents

Foreword   ix

Preface   xi

Part I: The Framework

1   The Parish   3

2   Catholic Culture and the Sisterhoods: A Legacy of
    Strong Leadership   23

3   Reclaiming the Sisters' Legacy   39

Part II: Issues for Parishes

4   Mass Attendance   59

5   Eucharistic Culture   73

6   Penance: The Sacrament of Reconciliation   91

7   Divine Intervention and Prayer   111

8   Religious Education of Children and Adults   131

9   Loving Service in a Faith Community   153

Part III: Issues for Parishes and Dioceses

10   Priest Shortage and Pastors   175

11   Lay Leaders in the Parish   197

12   Finances and Growth   219

13   Politics and the Witness Community   239

Bibliography   261

Index   265

About the Authors   273

Foreword

Please allow me this opportunity to personally express my gratitude to Father John Piderit of the Society of Jesus and Melanie Morey, who together authored *Renewing Parish Culture*. At the heart of Catholicism in the United States is the parish. For decades the parish has been the nucleus of formation, education, outreach, and above all a living encounter with our Savior, Jesus Christ, in the sacraments. The following chapters clearly present an accurate account of Catholic culture in our twenty-first century.

The past fifty years reflect a dramatic change for Catholics in America. Catholic parishes in the United States were staffed by a team of priests and religious sisters until about forty years ago. At most parishes, a large thriving Catholic school was part of the community. Many adults in our society recall each grade being taught by a religious. Most of these were religious women who sacrificed their lives in educating generations of Catholics. One of the largest changes is the reduction in the number of religious sisters to minister in parishes and teach at Catholic schools. In addition, most parishes now have only one or possibly two priests. Young Catholics have limited interaction and understanding of a religious vocation. The promotion of vocations is now everyone's business in the parish. A positive development is that laity are more involved in Catholic education and parish ministry as never seen before in history.

In many ways, *Renewing Parish Culture* is like a compass. Each chapter points the direction where renewal is taking shape each day. Nevertheless, true renewal that is guided by the Holy Spirit takes one step of faith at a time in helping to build the Kingdom of God.

Seán Cardinal O'Malley, O.F.M., Cap.
Archbishop of Boston

Preface

THE ISSUE

Parish life in the United States today is part of a complicated narrative that is not entirely reassuring for the Catholic Church. It is quite true that some parishes in the country's suburbs are expanding as more and more families get involved, worship, and serve with a community of believers. It is also true that in economically robust regions, new parishes are being established. However, the traditional pattern of parish growth and development that predominated until the late 1960s is beginning to give way. Over the past forty years, loss and contraction have become a predictable part of the Catholic parish story. That is especially true in urban settings where parishes have come on hard times. It is a real struggle for some parishes to keep the Catholics they know live within their boundaries from migrating elsewhere or to attract them to weekly Mass. For some, the lack of parishioners has been so grave, it resulted in church closings.

Parish participation seems to be waning, and that is a problem for the American Catholic Church. According to most national polls, somewhat fewer than 35 percent of Catholics report they attend Mass two or more times a month. That estimation, in fact, presents a rather rosy picture of what is actually happening. People of all faiths tend to overstate the frequency of their participation at religious services, so it makes sense to look for a more accurate assessment of what is really going on. Many dioceses do just that by asking pastors to do a physical count of actual participants at weekend liturgies, which they report to the diocese as a percentage of registered parishioners. This more reliable data is discouraging because, while the numbers vary, attendance percentages tend to be in the 20s.

To illustrate the magnitude of the challenge, suppose that in some diocese with at least one large city approximately 25 percent of Catholics attend Mass on average two or more times per month. Assume this is the average for all parishes in the diocese and there is a normal dispersion of parishes above and below the average. This means that many parishes in this diocese have an average attendance number higher than 25 percent and many have averages in the low 20s, perhaps even in the teens. This is a dramatic change from the 1960s, when the average percentage attending two or more times a month was in the high 50s or low 60s.

Many things have happened inside and outside the Catholic Church that contribute to this result. In our estimation, however, the most profound has been the dramatic decline in numbers within religious congregations and the priesthood. Particularly important is the falloff in the number of nuns who played such an important role in most parishes. The disappearance of sisters from many parishes meant they no longer interacted with young and old or reinforced the work of the priests. It also meant the disappearance of many of the religious practices the sisters used to cultivate Catholic culture among the young.

American Catholics would welcome a dramatic resurgence in vocations to religious life and the priesthood. Even if such a thing should happen, however, it would have little impact on parishes for years to come. This book presumes nuns will not be around to help in parishes in any significant numbers during the next ten to fifteen years. Nuns the less, the book also assumes laypeople are and will be available to serve parish communities in different ways. It also assumes the need for new ways, first to draw many more baptized Catholics into the regular liturgical life of the parish, and second to encourage their participation in other parish programs.

OUR APPROACH

In any given Catholic institution or set of institutions, Catholic culture is the set of people, practices, stories, and symbols used by the institution to promote the Catholic faith, to assist the Catholic Church, and to explain to non-Catholics why our beliefs and practices make some sense, even though they remain wrapped in the mystery of the triune God.

Our area of expertise is Catholic institutional culture. Together we have over fifty years' experience with Catholic colleges and universities, and recently we wrote a book about the challenges they face.[1] While our primary institutional experience is in the arena of Catholic higher education, we also have extensive contacts with parishes. Father John Piderit has developed a new daily after-school venture in parishes. This program resides in parishes and targets Catholic children who attend public school. As part of the preparation to launch this venture, Father John visited approximately forty parishes and conducted extensive interviews with the pastor at each site. Most of these parishes are in the New York City metropolitan area, but about ten of them are in Chicago. For the past five years, Father John has also been in residence in a parish in the southeast Bronx. During that time, he has interacted extensively with five pastors and parishes in the same area.

Melanie Morey has served as a parish director of religious education and taught religious education in a number of other parishes. As staff member of a ministerial training program, she worked extensively with young adults who served in Catholic schools and in local parishes. She has also done extensive research on religious congregations of women and their institutional legacy. Melanie has long-standing relationships with a number of Catholic institutions where she has served as a member of the governing board.

This book begins with an analysis of the policies religious sisters put in place in institutions. It does so, not as a lament for days gone by, but rather as a way to illuminate effective practice by identifying four principles or characteristics which we believe account for much of the nuns' success. These four principles guide what we suggest parishes might do as they move forward to renew parish culture.

HELPFUL RESOURCES

We gratefully acknowledge much assistance in articulating the ideas for this book. The authors are very grateful to Rev. Joseph Kelly, pastor of St. Anthony on Commonwealth Avenue in the Bronx, for his friendship, support, insights, and graciousness in allowing St. Anthony to be a testing place for a number of the approaches presented in this book. Msgr. Paul Sanchez has been especially helpful in suggesting the principal challenges facing parishes. He and a number of other pastors and friends have provided excellent feedback on various chapters of the book. Special thanks go to Msgr. Thomas Derivan for his wisdom over the years and his extensive comments on particular chapters and also to Msgr. Edward Whalen, Msgr. Thomas Gilleece, Msgr. Lesley Ivers, Msgr. Edward Scharfenberger, Rev. Ralph Starus, and Rev. Vito Buonano. Rev. Joseph Bisignano was outstanding in his openness to new programs and in sharing his approach to pastoring. Rev. William Pape has been especially insightful concerning the flourishing and subsequent demise of parishes. Dr. Mary Byrne Rogan read a number of chapters and offered nuances we introduced into several chapters. Christopher Morrison made an early contribution which helped us clarify our approach. Rev. William Bergen, S.J., as well as Padre José de la Luz Carrasco have offered helpful pastoral and theological insights about parish ministry over the years.

Many other people have provided input along the way. Rev. William Grogan is a colleague, friend, perceptive critic, and source of abundant pertinent information. Marie McCarrick read a number of chapters of the book and provided valuable feedback. Vince and Kathy Cook are perceptive observers and participants in parish life and have provided much help. Most Rev. Joseph M. Sullivan is a source of energy, ideas, and encouragement and was especially helpful on matters relating to personnel policies for priests. Thomas Grizzetti has provided important financial assistance without which this project would not have continued. Lee Kendall, eager for results, has provided very helpful, practical ways to promote Catholic activities at the parish level. Father John is also grateful to Cardinal George of Chicago, who appointed him to the advisory board for Mundelein Seminary. This position provided Father John with deep appreciation for the work of Mundelein and seminaries in general.

Both authors acknowledge the assistance of various people who helped us appreciate the extensive training received by lay ecclesial ministers as well as the important roles they play in parishes. These include Dr. Mary Cross, Rich Shively, Dr. Timothy Schilling, Rev. Brian Bachand, Sister Joan Curtin, and Dr. Zeni Fox.

Finally, the authors are very grateful to Cardinal O'Malley for his general endorsement of the approach taken in this book. Cardinal O'Malley has been a strong leader of the Archdiocese of Boston during a very difficult time. We know how much he wants to promote parish life so that parishes thrive in the coming years.

NOTE

1. See Melanie M. Morey and John J. Piderit, S.J., *Catholic Higher Education: A Culture in Crisis* (New York: Oxford University Press, 2006).

I

THE FRAMEWORK

1

The Parish

The local parish is the cultural home base of American Catholics. It is in these smallest and most basic institutional units where Catholic culture is nurtured, sustained, and transmitted. Our first experience of the community of faith beyond our own families is in our parishes, where we receive the sacraments, practice the faith, and come to understand what it means to be Catholic. The local parish is the setting where we ritualize significant passages in our lives and experience great joys and sorrows. We celebrate baptisms, First Communions, confirmations, and weddings in our parish churches. We also come to the parish in times of sorrow and when we need forgiveness and healing. The sacrament of reconciliation is offered there, and parishioners in dire circumstances often come there looking for the priest or other parish staff when they need counseling and support. And finally in death, the community of faith comes together once again in the parish at the funeral Mass.

Parishes are the primary places where American Catholic life is cultivated and sustained, and the vitality of American Catholicism depends to a great extent on the vibrancy of parish life. Unfortunately, across the length and breadth of this country, regular participation by Catholics in parish life is on the wane. This worrisome trend, if left unchecked, poses a real threat to Catholic cultural life. The purpose of this book is to address this very serious and mounting "crisis of the faith."

The troubling decline in parish participation is real, but in talking about the Church in the United States, diminishment is surely not the whole story. There are many parishes with outstanding programs that attract large numbers of active parishioners. Also, a new wave of ethnic Catholics is refreshing the United States. These groups include a great variety of Hispanic groups, whose growth, size, and influence have deepened, enriched, and broadened parish liturgy. There are also many positive aspects and developments being experienced in practically all parishes, regardless of their size and patterns of growth. Nevertheless, many parishes face serious challenges. A clear indication of the depth of these challenges is the number of parishes which have closed or been combined with other parishes over the past twenty years.

Statistics reveal some of what is happening within parishes and among American Catholics, but a better sense of the problems we face can be gleaned from more particular stories about parish life. One such story comes from the pastor of a prominent parish in the Northeast. This parish has a well-established liturgy committee that has functioned nicely for years. At one of the regular meetings a year ago, the pastor was reflecting on the fact that many Catholics do not feel much pressure to attend Mass every Saturday evening or Sunday. He noted that, once, most Catholics absolutely believed that missing Mass was a sin, and they would feel duty bound to confess it when they went to confession. Now, Catholics rarely think of missing Mass as sinful, and if they go to confession at all, they would not think of mentioning they missed Mass. In most instances, the pastor said, the topic does not come up in confession unless the priest asks them directly about their patterns of Mass attendance. After the pastor made his observation, some lively discussion ensued among the members of the liturgy committee. Most committee members themselves wondered why anyone would confess missing Mass on Sundays. These were good, stable, level-headed members of his congregation, and two-thirds of them saw no reason a penitent would confess missing Mass on Sunday, much less a holy day of obligation. If this is what the active, engaged "leaders" of the parish were thinking, the pastor could only imagine what was going on with the other parishioners. Even more alarming was thinking about what most of the baptized Catholics who lived in his parish but chose not to attend, Sunday after Sunday, thought was expected of them. It was clear that cultural expectations in his parish about going to Mass had radically changed. Once, weekly Mass attendance had been the norm. Now, going to Mass was considered a good but optional thing to do. Regular Mass attendance was no longer a cultural norm.

Many parishes in the United States have Mexican parishioners. These ethnic Catholics bring real joy and enthusiasm to parish life. Many attend Mass regularly and usually do so with their entire families. But even within this community of enthusiastic Catholics, consistent participation in parish life is spotty. A major feast day highlights the problem. December 12 is the feast of Our Lady of Guadalupe, to whom most Mexicans are very devoted. Early on that morning, usually around 5 a.m., Mexicans are accustomed to gathering in church to sing the "mañanitas," which are the morning songs honoring Our Lady. Many parishes arrange to have a mari-achi band present to lead the early morning congregation in the singing of the "mañanitas." During the course of the singing, individual families approach the image of Our Lady of Guadalupe and place beautiful roses in front of her image. The flowers recall the story of when the Virgin Mary appeared to Juan Diego in the winter and roses bloomed at the site. The roses were a sign to the bishop of the Virgin Mary's desire that he build a basilica on the apparition site. This is a beautiful liturgical celebration, and the Church abounds with devout Mexicans celebrating this wonderful feast. Unfortunately, the number attending the "mañanitas" in many parishes far exceeds the number that regularly comes to Mass on Saturday evening or Sunday. Of course, in Mexico itself, the same pattern of large turnouts on the feast of Our Lady of Guadalupe and more modest turnouts for Sunday Mass prevails in many areas of the country. The experience of December 12 dramatizes the limits of Catholic parish culture even within this devout ethnic community.

Neither in the United States nor in other parts of the English-speaking world is Catholic parish life monolithic. There are differences in cultural patterns regionally, and around the world notable differences exist between urban and suburban parish patterns. In the United States, one of the more notable differences between urban and suburban parishes is in the patterns of Mass participation by children and young adults. In urban parishes, consistent participation is much more problematic. For instance, in many urban parishes with Catholic schools, less than half of the Catholic children in the school regularly attend Mass on Saturday evening or Sunday. In some parishes, the percentage of children attending Mass regularly on the weekend is as low as 25 percent. Similarly, in many urban parishes, participation in Saturday evening or Sunday Mass by children who do not attend Catholic school is very low. Children who are preparing for First Communion or Confirmation are required to attend Mass regularly. However, Catholic children not in these grades often do not participate in religious education. Even if they do, many do not come to Mass regularly on Saturday evening or Sunday. Of course, the reason the children do not attend is because the parents do not attend. Finally, many urban parishes see very low Mass participation by Catholics in high school. High school students, whether attending public or Catholic high school, are rare in urban parishes. Overall, it is difficult to imagine parishes thriving over the next twenty years if young people do not attend Mass regularly.

Baptism into the Catholic Church establishes individuals as Catholic, and unless they repudiate baptism, once a Catholic, always a Catholic. However, there are no active Catholics without the Eucharist, and the heart and soul of parish life is the Eucharistic liturgy. For much of the Church's history in the United States and other parts of the developed world, a solid majority of Catholics came to their local parish community for Sunday Mass. That was true for young and old, across all regions of the country, in the cities, suburbs, and in rural areas. The parish community was formed around liturgy and grew strength from worshipping together. Today the trend in regular Mass attendance among Catholics is spiraling downward, and parish life is suffering. Unless and until those trends are reversed, parish life and culture in the United States and elsewhere will be threatened.

When dealing with large cultural movements, reversing a trend can be daunting. Especially in Western society, which places a premium on individual freedom, even modifying the direction of a trend can be a Herculean task. It is our general conviction that simply telling Catholics more consistently and clearly what they have to do is unlikely to change their behavior in matters religious and moral. Current patterns reveal that, rather than attend Mass, many Catholics around the world rather enjoy going to a mall on a Sunday morning, attending a sporting event, or spending time with their family. They may occasionally think of going to church on Sunday, but more frequently other activities enjoy higher priorities. Changing behavior for significant numbers of Catholics requires persuasion and encouragement to try new, more appealing approaches to religious practice. This is the general strategy we pursue in this book.

In the early twenty-first century, Catholics around the world are still adjusting to significant changes in thinking and perceiving which emerged during the prior two centuries. Science and technology play dominant roles in modern society, and they have produced benefits from which the large majority of people in Western society are not willing to walk away. So, religious practice has to fit comfortably with a scientific outlook and expectations about religious practice have to acknowledge the importance Catholics give to a scientific, technological, and even pragmatic approach. Similarly, archaeology and the careful study of manuscripts and documents over the past two centuries have revealed the extent to which the Old and New Testaments as well as the Catholic Church itself have been subject to historical development. That is, there is now good reason to believe that many books in the Old and New Testaments were not written by a single author or even within a single generation by multiple authors. Similarly, we now understand that it took several centuries for the bishop of Rome, who would eventually be known as the Pope, to become the acknowledged, most faithful preserver of the faith tradition that stems from the apostles themselves. Catholics have a more historically nuanced perspective on the development of religious belief and practice. Since Catholics understand more clearly that the Church developed over time, they also appreciate that it can continue to develop, perhaps in some unexpected ways. An important challenge is to show how new ideas, approaches, and practices can emerge within the Church, at the same time that it remains faithful to the central messages contained in the Old and New Testaments.

Canon law defines parishes as stable communities of Christian believers entrusted for pastoral care to a pastor under the authority of the diocesan bishop.[1] In each of these communities, a culture is forged that animates the local parish and contributes to the extensive culture of Catholicism in that country. The Catholic culture forged in parishes and other Catholic institutions is but one of many national subcultures that contend and compete for attention, participation, and influence.

Catholics in the United States are part of the broad American culture, and Catholics elsewhere are part of their national culture. U.S. Catholics, like all Americans, are influenced by it, react to it, and help shape its contours. But Catholics also participate in American Catholic culture, which makes a difference for them and the larger secular culture, as well. When Catholic culture is rich, strong, and compelling, it can influence the mixed bag of national culture and how American Catholics respond and operate within it. In any country, a strong Catholic culture can help strengthen those things in the national culture that Catholics believe contribute to authentic human experience. It can also push back against other cultural components that are wayward, degenerate, or downright evil. A weak or tepid Catholic culture, on the other hand, can have little if any national influence or impact.

The contours of Catholic culture are shaped in large part by Catholic institutions, including local parishes. Broad-based Catholic culture can only be robust if Catholic institutional and parish cultures are strong and dynamic. As we have noted, while there is considerable variety among Catholic parishes in the developed world, almost all parishes face significant cultural challenges. Addressing these common challenges in ways that can revitalize and enrich parish culture is the subject of this book. In addressing these challenges, the book provides no new data about major trends in Catholic parishes. Instead, it explores, adapts, and applies insights from the cultural legacy fostered by religious sisterhoods in the United States over the past two centuries to enrich parish culture in our own time.

COMPONENTS OF CULTURE

Culture in organizations results from the interplay between actions and inheritance. Actions are the present choices people make within a culture about what they will do and how they will behave. Previous choices create inheritance or the given cultural context for present actions. Culture changes as participants act in ways that either confirm or modify inheritance. Three interrelated components influence cultural action—content, symbols, and actors. *Cultural content* consists of attitudes, beliefs, values, and norms that motivate and guide cultural action. *Symbols* are the narratives and stories, practices, rituals, and beautiful images of culture that make it present to itself and its members. *Actors* are the people who sustain culture by accepting, practicing, and modifying its norms, attitudes, beliefs, images, rituals, and stories. Every vibrant culture has two different kinds of cultural actors: *cultural catalysts* who lead by making adjustments that reinvigorate the culture in altered circumstances, and *cultural citizens* who sustain culture by making nearly daily decisions to do things in ways that reinforce the existing culture.

To exist, culture must satisfy two minimum conditions: *distinguishability* and *inheritability*. *Distinguishability* is the readily apparent differences in central activities between one culture and its competing cultures. *Inheritability* pertains to the dynamics of culture. A well-functioning culture operates intentionally to ensure it is authentically assimilated by new generations of cultural citizens. If a culture is not distinguishable to new actors, they cannot be transformed by it. On the other hand, new cultural actors can transform and deform the culture's content with relative ease if it is not inheritable.[2] Organizations may be blind to the need for change. They may also unwittingly change in ways that undermine their existing culture.

CATHOLIC CULTURE AND PARISHES

Catholic culture is composed of beliefs and practices, behaviors and understandings. It is "found" in a context that nourishes the faith of believers and galvanizes them into action. Faith in Christ, participation in the Catholic Church, and Catholic culture are closely connected, but they are not the same. Catholic culture builds upon faith and membership in the Catholic Church. Faith is a freely given gift from God—an invitation. With the help of grace, human beings respond to it by believing and becoming disciples. Genuine participation in the Catholic Church is a manifestation of Catholic faith and the primary means by which we receive grace from Christ to fulfill His mission for us. As we understand it, Catholic culture focuses on the particular ways in which the faith is lived, sustained, and supported in a community of believers. Despite common beliefs and common rituals, structures, and understandings, there can be genuine differences between, for example, American Catholic culture and Mexican Catholic culture. That is because Catholic culture emphasizes the way faith is embedded in a particular context.

Catholic cultural distinguishability concerns distinctiveness. It is perceived through the actions and practices that make it visible. The practice of the faith in a parish makes Catholic culture visible and distinguishable.

Since central activities of a parish are liturgical, that is, the regular celebration of Mass and inviting people to participate in the sacraments, the primary activities are distinctly Catholic. Unless a parish gradually stops offering regular celebration of the Eucharist or offers most of the sacraments only infrequently, it is Catholic in its core activities. The essential actions in parishes are closely related to important Catholic beliefs and they occur regularly and frequently. Therefore, they satisfy the positive criterion of distinguishability. There is, however, also a negative criterion of distinguishability that parishes must satisfy. Parishes should not have practices that confuse people about the Catholic faith. Parishes cannot determine their own moral or theological teachings; these must be compatible with the teachings and practice of the Catholic Church. Overwhelmingly, pastors strongly support official Church teaching. Therefore, the great majority of parishes fulfill the negative side of the distinguishability principle.

While many parish activities have a Catholic profile, not all do. For example, parishes may run athletic leagues or other activities for children which lack any particular Catholic flavor. The activities may be open to all children—Catholic as well as non-Catholic—and be the same as those offered in nonsectarian institutions. There is nothing wrong with these activities, but how important they are for the parish can certainly be questioned. If they attract children or adults to other central liturgical activities of the parish, they could be important. Running an athletic league for neighborhood children who would otherwise not have wholesome opportunities for play is very worthwhile. But, even in this case, some connection to the religious commitment of the parish is important. The parish should seek ways to let children know that the parish's motivation in providing the athletic league is the love of Christ. Making this connection enhances the inheritability of the Catholic culture in the parish.

Inheritability in parishes is about viability. Parishes cannot be vital and vibrant and make a cultural impact if their very existence is threatened. That means that without compromising distinguishability, a parish must necessarily make adjustments to assure it attracts a sufficient number of parishioners to remain a viable entity. In this framework, a parish can sensibly sponsor social gatherings for young adults in the hope they will induce some of the young people to participate in the core liturgical activities of the parish. Parish financial and personnel resources are limited, however. Consequently a parish intent on maintaining inheritability should not squander its resources by spending too much time and money on activities with unsure outcomes. A well-run parish needs plans with specific targets for participation and religious outcomes. They also need to assess performance. For example, a parish might offer social or athletic activities to attract people to participate weekly in Saturday evening or Sunday Mass. If so, the staff should gather appropriate data to determine whether they achieve this goal.

In a parish setting, inheritability applies clearly to programs that educate young people and help adults to grow in the faith. When children
are very young, it suffices for them to attend Sunday Mass with their parents, engage with their parents in some outreach to others, and for their
parents to teach them about the meaning of the Mass and other prayers
and religious practices. As they reach school age, they should start to
learn more about the Catholic faith, and how and why they practice it.
The ambient culture challenges the legitimacy of belief in God and Jesus
Christ as truly God's Son. Children need to be able to answer questions
that arise in their own mind and also to learn how to deepen their practice of the faith.

Having effective programs of religious education is necessary for a parish
to fulfill the inheritability criterion. Fifty years ago in Catholic parishes in
the United States, many children learned about their faith in parochial
schools. Over the past several decades, however, Catholic parents increasingly have sent their children to public schools. That means that parishes
must now make adjustments and dedicate more resources to the effective
religious education of Catholic children in public schools.

Parishes that do not satisfy the inheritability criterion will eventually
close. Sometimes this is the fault of no one. Parishes are mainly geographical units, and if enough Catholics migrate out of a neighborhood or region, a once flourishing parish might have to close. This is a sad necessity
and need not reflect poorly on those in the parish. On the other hand, if the
parish closes despite a large number of at least nominal Catholics who
could be induced to participate in parish life on a regular basis, it may reflect adversely on the parish. In this case, the failure may indeed have been
one of effort or imagination.

PARISH PERSONNEL

While pastors are canonically defined as the essential leaders of parishes,
they do not do this work alone. Some parishes are staffed by more than one
ordained minister, and most parishes have lay assistants. Parochial vicars[3]
are priests whose primary responsibility in parishes is to assist in the pastoral care of the community. There are also priests-in-residence[4] who serve
in parishes. While they normally live in the rectory and assist by celebrating
Mass in the parish on Sundays and during the week, their primary ministerial assignments are outside the parish. Increasingly, deacons are being assigned to parishes to work with the pastor. Deacons proclaim the Gospel at
Mass and distribute Holy Communion. They also are authorized to perform baptisms and officiate at weddings, and they frequently minister to
those who are sick or suffering.

Parishes could not function without an effective lay pastoral team that includes ecclesial ministers and pastoral staff. Lay ecclesial ministers include pastoral associates, directors of religious education, youth ministers, music ministers, and others professionally trained for and directly involved with teaching and evangelizing in the parish. The parish secretary, the bookkeeper, and individuals involved with managing the parish plant comprise the pastoral staff and they round out the pastoral team.

HOW PARISHES FUNCTION

One primary function of any parish is to gather the faithful to praise God the Father through His Son in the Eucharist. Parishes are expected to offer a sufficient number of Masses so the community can join together to listen to the Word of God and celebrate the Eucharist with little inconvenience. Weekday Masses are also celebrated, and the faithful are encouraged to attend. Funeral Masses, religious education, and the sacraments of matrimony, reconciliation (formerly called confession), baptisms, confirmations, and anointing of the sick are all important activities that take place in parishes. Some of these occur almost weekly and others only once or twice a year. Parishes also provide services to the poor and less fortunate, and many have programs to attract and welcome new members.

The services referred to above take place in the parish church. Parish organizations meet in the church, rectory, hall, or school if there is one. Once a parish is established, it has annual expenses it must cover. These include: mortgage payments; heating, cooling, and electricity for the church and other parish buildings; salaries and benefits for priests, nuns, and lay associates, including those responsible for music at Mass and other functions. Parishes are also expected to make annual contributions to the diocese. These contributions are used to cover various expenses incurred by the diocese and, in many cases, are also used to subsidize parishes which have insufficient income.

Parishes should cover their own expenses and make an annual contribution to the diocese. Normally, aside from contingency funds, a diocese has no independent wealth. Some dioceses have foundations that support seminarians, schools, or other particular activities. With the exception of such funds, most American dioceses rely on regular collections to cover their annual expenses. If a diocese has poor parishes, the money it provides to these parishes must come either from special diocesan-wide collections or through taxes levied on more well-to-do parishes. In general, with the exception of the annual diocesan contribution or special support from a national Catholic organization, each parish is expected to cover its own expenses through the weekly and special collections the parish takes at Sunday Masses.

Total annual expenses for a parish depend primarily on its size, the number of people hired, the number of buildings, the age of the buildings and the upkeep required, and the geographical area in which the church is located. A small parish would typically have total annual expenses of approximately $150,000 to $250,000. Total expenses in a large parish with modest facilities would be between $600,000 and $800,000. Very large parishes with an extensive staff and facilities may have total expenses from one to a few million dollars. In all these cases the expenses of parish schools are not included. For ease of reference in what follows, the arbitrary marker of regular Sunday attendance determines parish size. Our criterion for calling a parish a large parish is 1,500 or more parishioners.

A vibrant Catholic Church is a growing Church. This has certainly been the case for most of its history in the United States. Today the number of Catholics in the United States continues to increase, but other key signs of growth are flat or declining. In the past twenty years, we have seen a leveling off in the number of parishes. While there are some parishes that close each year and some new ones that open, the impact of these changes has been minimal. For example, in 2005, only thirty-six new parishes were opened in the entire United States. The closing or combining of some parishes and the establishment of new parishes in high-growth areas, taken together, have resulted in a small overall annual decrease in the total number of parishes in the United States over the past twenty years.

In a large country like the United States, shifting Catholic population patterns are unavoidable. It used to be the case that in the northern part of the United States, urban parishes were large and had at least five and six weekend Masses. During the past thirty years, many of these parishes have been closed or combined. Many of the remaining urban parishes now no longer qualify as large parishes.

In terms of new housing, suburbs and larger areas in the southern and western parts of the United States are the growth areas. That is especially true in new suburbs fairly distant from city centers. In these ex-urbs, new housing developments have been built and many new churches have opened to serve them. The increase in housing in the South and Southwest continues, and along with it, the emergence of new parishes. In areas where growth is negative, parishes have been or will have to be closed. But in a vibrant Church, the impact of growing regions should far outweigh the impact of decreasing regions.

Parishes are definitely not corporations, but every parish faces economic realities. Although we are reluctant to apply economic terms to parishes, there is one concept from the world of business we believe is useful. In business, a corporation, firm, or partnership is usually interested in increasing market share. For example, suppose the Sleek Corporation produces computers. Sleek wants to know the percentage of computers sold in a given year in a particular geographical region in which it produces. That is its market share.

In a parish context, using the term "increasing market share" overemphasizes human activity and underemphasizes the divine initiative. Masses, loving service, religious education, prayer groups, and many other activities of parishes do not take place in a religious market in any normal sense of the word. Nevertheless, while faith is a pure gift from the Holy Spirit, we can prepare the ground by preaching and praying, which are the essential components of evangelization. If a local church is committed to evangelization, and if it is adhering to the principles for institutional success, it should be attracting people to its regular services. Parishes should strive and plan to grow by attracting more people to Saturday or Sunday Eucharist.

LAY ENDORSEMENT

This book relies on the cultural success of religious sisters as fertile ground for suggesting what needs to be done today to renew parish culture. One important reason nuns were able to make such valuable contributions to American Catholic culture in the previous centuries is that they had extensive and deep support from priests and laypeople in the parishes. For the most part, nuns had entered the convent as young women, ready to dedicate their entire lives to Christ by serving the Church. The sisters lived simple and pious lives. Via their habits and their religious activities, they were visible and distinctive among the people in the daily celebration of the Eucharist, and they produced impressive results as educators, nurses, or caregivers. Although they were not clerics and not members of the hierarchy, the sisters had enormous status in the Catholic community. The ways nuns are depicted in today's media are amusing at best and insulting at worst. However, back in the 1930s, 1940s, and 1950s, "Sister" was always right. This attitude was at times exaggerated, but for the most part parents respected the sisters and believed they were attentive to the best interests of those in their charge, especially children. If a sister suggested some course of action, including punishment, parents were inclined to go along and do what was asked. After all, earlier generations of children had submitted to the direction and discipline of the sisters, and as adults they were grateful for the care, prayers, and instruction they received.

Times have changed. In our current environment, parishioners no longer respectfully defer in most circumstances to religious authorities. Even in Catholic schools, parents do not defer to either nuns, if there are any, or lay teachers. In order for a parish to function well, however, structures must be in place so that those with authority generally are able to exercise it effectively and without the burden of crippling suspicion. An effective culture requires trust and buy-in. These are qualities which can grow over time, but for a Catholic culture to be nurturing and transforming, they are essential.

LAY ECCLESIAL MOVEMENTS AND NEW ECCLESIAL COMMUNITIES

The twentieth century saw many outstanding initiatives worldwide to draw lay and clerical Christians into active practice and dissemination of the Catholic faith. Some of the members of these groups associate with one another but do not live together and are designated *movements*. Other groups consist of people who live together, take vows of poverty, chastity, and obedience, but are not members of a traditional religious community. These true Catholic communities are referred to as *new ecclesial communities*. Many of these groups of dedicated lay Catholics emerged in the power and enthusiasm of the Second Vatican Council. Included among these groups are Focolare, Communio e Liberazione, Opus Dei, Regnum Christi, the Neocatechumenate, San Egidio, L'Arche, Schoenstatt, Chemin Neuf, Christian charismatic renewal, Cursillo, and Christian life communities. Hundreds of these groups are very active in the United States.

The lay participants in these movements and communities are a powerful source of renewal in the Catholic Church, and many of these Christians are very active in both their lay movement and also in their local parish. These movements and communities represent outstanding initiatives, and they are worthy of careful study and analysis to understand better the positive impact they are having on the Catholic Church. Since the focus of this book is on parishes, however, and because space is limited, the lay movements and communities are not discussed.

AN INSTITUTION IN NEED OF REFORM

The general assumption in this book is that Catholic institutions help promote the Catholic faith in the current generation and are likely to prove successful in doing so for future generations. Of course, no institution is successful all the time. In order to survive long term, organizations must recognize difficulties and make necessary cultural adjustments that effectively address them.

The sexual abuse scandal in the Catholic Church that came to light seems to challenge this book's positive assumption about the religious effectiveness of Catholic culture. The bishops were negligent in dealing with this issue, which they have admitted. Their lapse in judgment resulted in devastating harm to the abused individuals and to the whole of the Catholic

Church in the United States. What began as a crisis became a full-blown scandal once the public understood its pervasiveness, its duration, and the bishops' role in covering it up. In the aftermath, Catholics are tormented by a raft of "if onlys." If only we had all been more vigilant and less trusting, children would not have suffered. If only the bishops were less concerned about scandalizing, they could have prevented this tragic scandal. If only the bishops had some lay parents help review abuser priests, they might not have been reassigned. If only the bishops had anticipated the outcry and outrage of faithful people, they would have confronted the issues earlier and saved many innocent children. If only the bishops had anticipated the financial ramifications of their approach, they would have taken effective steps to isolate offending priests from children. If only the Vatican had stepped in, requiring bishops to act effectively or replacing bishops who were slow to act, children and the whole Church and society would have been spared terrible suffering and a ghastly ordeal. All of these "if only" statements are expressions of shock, horror, and disbelief that such egregious behavior went on, that people in authority knew about it, and no one did what was necessary to stop it.

Institutions are under constant pressure to change. This pressure emerges from one of two places, either from within the organization or from without by competing institutions or cultures. In most cases, institutional change agents work from within organizations. Parents change parishes, for instance, by volunteering, suggesting new approaches, and pointing out what competing parishes are doing. Volunteering or working within the organization does not guarantee change, but if enough people bring pressure within the organization, it usually changes. In the sexual abuse crisis, the pressure for changing a destructive policy did not come primarily from people within the operational structure of the Church. Not even at the level of the parish priest was there effective action. Many priests who personally have never been engaged in sexual abuse must have known that some of their fellow priests were acting egregiously. But, like the bishops, they kept the matter quiet or were not able to persuade their superiors to take effective action. The real pressure for change came from outside the organizational structure of the Church. It was exerted by abuse victims, their families, rank and file Catholics, and by the media.

Once the abuse became public and the extent of the bishops' failure to act became known, a whole raft of explanations for how it could have happened for so long emerged. It is surely true that the bishops made poor decisions, but this is hardly a full and satisfactory explanation of this tragedy. The pressing question is why so many of the bishops made such poor decisions and failed to confront the issue effectively.

The painful and difficult institutional reality the sexual abuse scandal brings home is how powerfully institutions resist change. They do so even in the face of potentially devastating consequences of inaction that will likely be their cultural undoing. Although resistance to change is a pervasive organizational pattern that threatens the vitality of institutions and in some cases their very survival, it is not inevitable. Denial and self-deception fueled the Catholic Church's tenacious adherence to a misguided policy that produced disastrous results. Since this book deals with Catholic culture in parishes, it is important to acknowledge the tragedy of sexual abuse at the very beginning and probe the underlying realities that block Catholic institutions from initiating the kinds of cultural changes they should undertake.

STRUCTURAL WEAKNESSES

Organizational cultures operate in two realms—the real and the ideal. Ideal culture is publicly articulated and includes the beliefs, values, norms, and practices that represent what the organization hopes to be. Real culture includes the beliefs, values, norms, and practices that actually operate in the institution. There is always some distance between the ideal and the real cultures in an institution. However, by effectively measuring and monitoring that distance, institutional leaders are able to initiate necessary changes when needed to keep the institution culturally on track. If institutions do not effectively monitor significant departures from their ideal cultural norms, things can go seriously awry. Once an organization's real culture has strayed dangerously far from its ideal culture, it is in a crisis, and only dramatic change and cultural revitalization will set things to rights. Failure by those in charge to initiate change in a cultural crisis will further entrench destructive patterns that distort institutional culture. Unfortunately, all too often when leaders finally realize there is a crisis, they feel threatened and motivated by a sense of shame, embarrassment, and fear. As a result, they act defensively instead of moving to make necessary changes.[5]

That is certainly true of the bishops who confronted the sexual abuse scandal. Certain elements of the real culture of the Church in this situation were diametrically opposed to those espoused in its ideal culture. Little was done by bishops to effectively monitor and measure known deviance, and when they were forced to face the reality, they responded defensively. Instead of initiating the decisive cultural changes that were required, the bishops succumbed to denial and self-deception and responded feebly in misguided attempts to protect the Church from scandal.

Priests and bishops were able to keep the abuse quiet and out of the media and this exacerbated the Church's negligence in addressing and dealing with sex abuse cases. In most instances, the abused person felt personal shame. Indeed, victims often believed themselves, rather than the priest, to be responsible for the abuse. Furthermore, many victims were very young children. Neither the abused children nor the parents had any interest in attracting the bright light of public scrutiny, which could easily make their lives more difficult and perhaps impair the healthy development of the child. Also, many parents received the personal assurance of the bishop or the bishop's representative that the matter would be handled effectively. Catholic parents trusted the Church and presumed steps would be taken so the priest could not abuse again. In fact, many priests were simply transferred to a new parish and no attempt was made either to inform the new pastor or protect the parishioners.

In some cases, bishops adopted "rehabilitation" policies to address the sexual abuse of children by priests without having adequate information about these policies' efficacy. The bishops and other staff involved in handling these issues had little idea of how frequently sexual abuse of children occurred in other groups and to what extent perpetrators of abuse could modify their behavior. Bishops relied on the advice of psychologists who maintained sexual abusers could be "cured" and therapists who proved overly optimistic about their own abilities to bring about lasting change in the behavior of abusive priests. This kind of selective analysis of the true dimensions of the problem allowed bishops to avoid disconfirming information that could have led to meaningful change.

One incident should have been enough for bishops to remove any priest from contact with children. However, the abusers were their colleagues, and bishops could not imagine turning them over for criminal prosecution, especially based on information received privately. The Church's central message that Christ came to forgive sins surely gave support to bishops already inclined to be merciful and forgiving to priests whom they knew. Unfortunately, the way bishops chose to support priest-abusers put innocent children in harm's way and dealt a grave blow to the Catholic community.

All institutions are vulnerable to denial and self-deception, which reinforces resistance to change at times of significant cultural crisis. The sexual abuse crisis dramatically demonstrates these vulnerabilities and provides some useful lessons about what can happen in institutions embroiled in a cultural crisis.

1. *Unless safeguards are in place, confidentiality can easily be abused.* Organizations adopt confidentiality practices to safeguard their interests and those of individuals involved with them and to protect both the individuals and the organization from harm or injury. It is unethical for institutions to suppress information that is harmful to others in order to protect certain individuals, the organization itself, or the organization's image. Understandably, victims and their fam-

ilies often brought their accusations about priest sex abuse to the bishops in confidence. Bishops maintained they were protecting all involved by keeping these cases confidential. Only denial and self-deception, however, could have allowed bishops, in the name of confidentiality, to bury accusations in priest personnel files and move the offenders to different parishes without revealing what the priests had done.

2. *Cultural values can be distorted to justify bad decisions.* Value distortions are a form of institutional self-deception. All institutions have ideal cultures comprising an array of beliefs, values, and norms. In a crisis, institutions frequently distort one or more of these values as a way to justify present practice and avoid initiating significant culture change. In the sexual abuse crisis, a distorted understanding of mercy—or false mercy—helped bishops justify maintaining "rehabilitation" and relocation policies for priest abusers. It is false mercy to forgive and then hope and pray that a person will reform himself. Unfortunately, to a large extent that is just what bishops did. While many bishops received professional advice that a priest had gained control of his sexual desires involving children before they relocated him, they still took the risky step of placing these men in situations with little or no supervision. By operating out of a distorted understanding of forgiveness and mercy, bishops were able to continue a policy of rehabilitation and relocation that threatened not only innocent children, but the Church itself.

3. *Misplaced institutional loyalty will undermine an organization.* Loyalty makes institutional life possible, but when it is misplaced, it can easily damage the very institution it is supposed to support. When institutional loyalty is well placed, it allows for problems to be addressed within the institution and avoids public embarrassment or unnecessary damage to the institution's reputation. When loyalty is misplaced, however, it silences dissenting voices that can prevent wrong-headed decisions. It can also encourage destructive and sometimes unethical behavior and puts greater emphasis on how the institution is perceived than on how it behaves. Misplaced loyalty was rife within the Church when bishops and their advisers were grappling with the sexual abuse scandal. In their attempts to protect the Church from scandal, bishops certainly focused more on how the Church was perceived than on what the Church was doing. Decisions to move abuser priests from one place to another without protecting children or informing pastors were wrong-headed decisions at best and immoral ones at worst. While the bishops hoped to protect the Church, their actions and cover-up resulted in even greater damage.

A PRELIMINARY PRINCIPLE OF PROVISIONAL SUPPORT

Prior to the sexual abuse scandal, Catholics in most instances were willing to work within the normal framework of various ecclesiastical institutions to bring about change. For example, in parishes, a parishioner or two might suggest another time for Sunday Mass to the parish priest. If the pastor heard many suggestions calling for a similar type of change, he would usually make the move. If he didn't change the schedule of Masses and people still were pressing for change, parishioners knew they could wait him out and hope for a more positive response from the next pastor. If people thought that the parish school should have a sports program or an after-school program, parents would approach the principal, suggest a feasible way to institute the change, and if the principal thought it was a good idea, the change would be undertaken. Yes, some pastors and principals were difficult, unwilling to take suggestions, and uninterested in how their decisions might be received. But even in these circumstances, committed Catholics rarely went public with their concerns. Some would wait patiently for a leadership change they hoped would bring greater responsiveness. Others would make an institutional change to a different parish or school where they found the leadership more responsive. A few would take their complaints to a higher authority in the Church. Each of these approaches could be undertaken without vocal public complaint, and most were settled discretely.

In dramatic fashion, the sexual abuse scandal revealed the flaws in the quiet approach to settling difficulties in the Church. When presented with convincing evidence that certain priests were dangerous to parishioners, especially young and defenseless ones, Church authorities failed to do the right thing. Because of this dreadful lapse, uncritical support for Catholic institutions is no longer possible, let alone wise. Instead, Catholics should operate under a principle of limited support. That means Catholics should provide general moral support for Catholic institutions as long as every Catholic organization has significant safeguards in terms of three things. First, whenever complaints are lodged and the process is dealt with confidentially, the institution must have a way for the complaint to reach a very high official in the organization. This official then has a solemn responsibility to take appropriate action. He or she must also communicate to the complainant that effective action is being taken to correct the situation. Second, in matters involving confidential proceedings, there should be a person outside the normal chain of command—a type of ombudsman—who reviews all decisions. Optimally, the person would not be appointed by the most senior official in the institution and would work for a different but similar type of institution. This approach would make a truly independent review possible and help assure cultural values are not distorted in rendering decisions. Finally, Catholic institutions need to discourage misplaced

loyalty. They can do this by establishing procedures to measure and monitor how the institution behaves in light of its cultural ideals. They also
should create an institutional problem-solving environment in which a variety of ideas and approaches compete.

Catholics are called to support the Church whether it is prospering or
faltering. Our hope is that our support during difficult times will re-
dound to the benefit of other Catholics when calmer times offer greater
growth in the Church. The outstanding example of this is the role played
by the Christian martyrs in the growth of the Church, especially in the
first few centuries of its existence. But many Catholics involved in
Catholic institutions, including vowed religious men and women, countless volunteers, and many lay professionals, have sacrificed at various
times for the benefit of our institutions. This extra commitment is especially noticeable at times of founding, such as when new parishes or organizations were launched. In these early days, some cultural actors play
essential roles that help bring institutions to a point where they can survive and eventually prosper. The efforts of most individuals who sacrifice
mightily for institutions are forgotten, which is unfortunate. Current
staff and volunteers in any Catholic institution or parish stand on the
shoulders of giants, the generous men and women who suffered and
served so the organization could prosper. It is only fitting to remember
and acknowledge their sacrifice.

MOVING FORWARD

The disgrace of the sexual abuse scandal in the Catholic Church has caused
much pain in the Church, most especially to the victims themselves. With
an assist from massive media microanalysis, the bishops have drawn up an
effective plan to severely limit the potential of sexual abuse in the future. All
the issues we raised above are being addressed through the various preven-
tion programs instituted in dioceses throughout the country. This tragedy of
sexual abuse will undoubtedly have a negative impact on the ability of the
Catholic Church in the United States to attract young men to become
priests. At the very least, it raises considerable obstacles to effective recruitment.

Despite such challenges, the Catholic Church in the United States must
find ways to extend its market share. For this to occur, parishes must find
ways to attract more people to regularly attend Mass, give witness to the
Gospel, and be committed to helping the less fortunate. To make progress
in achieving this goal, we draw on the successful strategies of religious
women over the past two centuries.

NOTES

1. John P. Beal, James A. Coriden, and Thomas J. Green, eds., *New Commentary on the Code of Canon Law* (New York: Paulist Press, 2000), 676.

2. The conditions of distinguishability and inheritability were first derived in a book that explored Catholic culture in Catholic colleges and universities. See Melanie M. Morey and John J. Piderit, *Catholic Higher Education: A Culture in Crisis* (New York: Oxford University Press, 2006).

3. Because the term *parochial vicar* is cumbersome, such priests are often referred to as assistants, assistant pastors, or associates. At one time a parochial vicar was referred to as a *curate*, a term now seldom used in Catholic parishes.

4. The term *in residence* is used because the priest's primary assignment is not the parish but some other apostolic work.

5. Chris Argyris develops this analysis of organizational resistance to cultural change. See Chris Argyris and Donald Schon, *Theory in Practice* (San Francisco: Jossey-Bass, 1974), and Chris Argyris, *Overcoming Organizational Defenses* (Boston: Allyn and Bacon, 1990).

2

Catholic Culture and the Sisterhoods: A Legacy of Strong Leadership

The most effective transmitters of Catholic culture in the history of the United States are Catholic sisters.[1] The dynamic interplay between their own highly effective sisterhoods and their equally effective schools, colleges, hospitals, and orphanages contributed mightily to the breadth and depth of American Catholic life.[2] Religious women were dramatic cultural actors who succeeded in attracting young women to their ranks and cultivating future generations of American Catholics.[3]

Nuns were not alone in the work of Catholic cultural transmission in the United States, but shared it with religious brothers and priests. Doubtless, a discussion of the contributions of both religious men and women in transmitting Catholic culture would portray the American Catholic experience most accurately. For the purposes of this book, however, it seemed both more effective and efficient to focus on only one of these examples of cultural transmission and we chose to attend to the nuns.

Women religious significantly outnumbered religious brothers and order priests in apostolic ministry in the United States. They staffed and ran many more elementary schools, hospitals, and orphanages than their male counterparts. The sisters also established and ran the largest number of Catholic colleges in the United States. While religious men and order priests made a significant impact on the education of boys, particularly in Catholic high schools, Catholic elementary education was almost entirely in the hands of the nuns. All in all, because of superior numbers and the breadth and depth of their cultural reach, we believe the sisters were the primary transmitters of Catholic culture in the United States. Through their apostolic work, nuns had the greatest impact on how American Catholics came to understand themselves.

The sisters were religious missionaries to the American culture. Called to follow Christ in a special way, they committed their lives to attaining personal holiness and helping others to do the same. Unencumbered by wealth or families, entrants to religious life joined communities of like-minded women. They submitted their own wills to the dictates of the religious congregation. And because they believed they could make an outstanding contribution to the mission of the Church, they generously embraced whatever had to be done.

Catholic nuns took to heart the admonition of Jesus, which is captured in Matthew's Gospel: "Behold, I send you out as sheep in the midst of wolves; so be shrewd as serpents and innocent as doves" (Matt. 10:16). Jesus also warned that the children of darkness are more clever and innovative than the children of the light. These were women of the light and they were not going to be outmaneuvered by the children of darkness. They were motivated, savvy, and resourceful. The spirit of excitement and resourcefulness that motivated Catholic sisters was contagious, and it still has the power to impel the Church forward in our own time. The sisters' resourcefulness took advantage of particular circumstances not likely to be repeated and therefore it had limits. The nuns overcame these limits by adopting an organizational approach that combined resourcefulness with effective standard operating principles. The most religiously dynamic of the principles they followed in running the various institutions they founded and managed were those that contributed to both institutional distinguishability and inheritability.

The story of religious congregations of women is an inspiring story of organizational dynamism, resourcefulness, and a good deal of success. It is also a cautionary tale of organizational failure—a story with a darker side. At the height of their organizational success and in response to the Second Vatican Council, women religious embarked on a process of institutional renewal. Filled with optimism and committed to enhancing their own vitality and the effectiveness of their institutions, nuns chose to make radical cultural changes that proved to be their undoing.

The organizational story of women religious is compelling and instructive and serves as the analytic foundation of this book. This chapter takes a fresh look at this story with a particular focus on two things: the sisters' approach to leadership and the power of their own lived witness in their institutions.

LEADERSHIP

The ability of the sisterhoods to attract large numbers of young women to their ranks and keep them for life was surely enhanced by patterns of strong congregational leadership. For much of their history, religious congregations of women were led by remarkable women. These women literally imagined and then built a Catholic institutional network capable of effectively serving and inculturating generations of committed Catholics. By today's standards, the way religious life was structured prior to Vatican II seems designed to create docile and submissive nuns. The sisterhoods were hierarchical institutions, and religious superiors had absolute authority over congregation members, including over their professional development. Certainly humility, meekness, and a willingness to abnegate the self in favor of the community were virtues fostered in religious life. Congregations were also hierarchical institutions, and obedience to the superior was equated with obedience to God. Also, the leadership in these communities did have complete authority to make decisions that affected the personal and professional lives of the women who answered to them. In other words, the institutional situation was ripe to breed repression, authoritarianism, and a narrowness of purpose. These abuses might have existed in religious life, but they simply could not have been the rule. If they had been, congregations would not have produced such an array of outstanding women with courage, capacity, knowledge, and wisdom who literally transformed the face of Catholicism by their work and their wits and their wisdom.

Superiors exercised leadership in a variety of ways. Some did so with an iron hand and some were petty or lacked vision. But most superiors encouraged, supported, and mentored their fellow sisters—including those with whom they disagreed. Novice mistresses were placed in charge of very young women who entered in their teens with little or no real idea of their own capacity for achievement. Many of these young women benefited from wise judgments made about their abilities and vocational potential, paths carved out, and opportunities arranged. These young women received educations over time that allowed them to become respected professionals with significant influence in their fields. Religious women had to be and often were forward-looking pioneers. Their creativity and resilience inspired others to join them in entrepreneurial efforts with far-reaching religious and temporal goals.

CONGREGATIONAL DYNAMISM

The dynamism and effectiveness of religious congregations of women well into the mid-twentieth century is an extraordinary example of organizational success and know-how. At its core, this enterprise was animated by prayer, religious devotion, and loving spirit. The sisterhoods were strongly rooted in the liturgical life of the Church. Along with daily Mass and the Little Office of the Blessed Mother, the spiritual practices of the sisters included a wide variety of prayers, devotions, and liturgical experiences. Their apostolic work was time consuming, but daily community prayer and private prayer were primary defining activities for them. The Eucharistic movement was the most vital spiritual movement of the first half of the twentieth century, and devotion to the Blessed Sacrament was prominent in the sisterhoods. It primarily took the form of forty hours devotions and benediction along with celebration of daily Mass. Because of a deep devotion to the Blessed Mother, communities included the Angelus, the litany of the Blessed Mother, along with recitation of the rosary and celebrations of particular Marian feasts among their spiritual experiences. Congregational prayer manuals included scores of devotions and prayers that only increased in number with each edition.

The rhythms of communal prayer defined the contours of religious life and spilled over into the institutions where the nuns served. In hospitals, they incorporated devotions to Mary and the saints, along with the rosary, forty hours, benediction, and novenas. As was noted earlier, daily Mass was offered in hospitals, and sacraments and prayers for the sick and dying were part of the daily routine. In the schools and colleges they operated, the sisters incorporated many of the same religious rituals, prayers, and practices that were common in hospitals. They also enhanced their congregational devotions within the life of their schools, academies, and colleges, creating elaborate feast-day celebrations that were often the high points of the academic year.

The life of religious women, their prayers, and their work emerged within the context of love—love of Jesus Christ and love of those they served. Because of this love, sisters were willing to endure significant hardships. They also fought tenaciously and worked tirelessly for the salvation of the souls of men and women—young and old—that came to their hospitals, schools, and orphanages. Love of God was the heart of religious life, and that love was cultivated through constant prayer and extended to others in service within apostolic ministries. While the context of their commitment was love, sisters were not themselves always loving. Pettiness and cruelty, jealousy and anger, and other weaknesses certainly were in evidence in congregational life. Despite these lapses in love, the sisters accomplished amazing things. They sustained their communities and provided extraordinary service to the Church, and did so with limited resources and in the midst of great challenges.

Catholic sisterhoods are often depicted as rigid and unchanging bodies. But looking at the record suggests something quite different. By and large, women's congregations were willing to change when shifts in circumstances demanded it—even when those adaptations came at a cost. Upon arriving in the United States, congregations found traditional cloister to be an obstacle in their ministerial work. This realization was painful, and adjustment did not come easily. Saint Philippine Duchesne of the Religious of the

Sacred Heart of Jesus, for instance, realized that many of the practices that were integral to cloistered life could not be accommodated to teaching schedules. After all, in the rough and tumble reality of nineteenth-century America, even chopping wood for fuel necessitated breaking cloister. She grieved the loss of those things and continued insisting hers was a cloistered order, but she moved on and adapted her life.[4] Under new rules created by religious congregations, sisters continued to pray, sleep, and dine with their fellow sisters within convent walls, but they were allowed to leave the convents for periods of time to work among the people. Church authorities saw these adaptations as a significant departure and determined that members of congregations who adopted them would no longer be permitted to take solemn vows. Although they would have preferred it to be otherwise, sisters accepted the new restriction—a price they were willing to pay in order to adapt cloister and minister more effectively.

In order to survive and continue to thrive in the United States, congregations with European motherhouses needed to Americanize. Shortly after arriving in the United States, congregations began recruiting young American women to join their ranks. In order to enhance recruitment and be more effective in their work, most congregations adopted English as their primary ministerial language. They also rewrote their constitutions in English. The congregations were caught for a time between their European roots and their emerging American identity, which strained relationships within local congregations and with motherhouses as well. Some congregations were able to work things out and remained joined to their European motherhouses. Others found it necessary to become independent. While the process was a difficult and sometimes painful one, most European religious congregations managed to successfully Americanize.

Another significant adaptation in religious congregations came in response to changing standards for accreditation in schools, hospitals, colleges, and universities. As the demand for these institutions increased, most sisters were sent out to work in them in apprentice-like fashion right after novitiate. As a result, their formal education was completed on weekends and in the summer over a number of years. Over time it became clear that Catholic institutions could not compete effectively because their staff and faculty did not meet minimum standards set by accrediting bodies. By the 1920s, there was a flurry of congregational colleges and nurses training programs established to address the educational needs of the sisters. As more advanced degrees were required, especially by college faculty, congregations developed various programs to assure their sisters were prepared and their institutions could compete effectively.

Time and again the sisters had to accept that what they had been doing so successfully was no longer useful and effective. Aware of the market in which they operated and attuned to shifts in the environment, sisters realized that without change, their institutional and ministerial work would be at a disadvantage. Changes in cloister, Americanization, increased professional-ization in schools, hospitals, and colleges, and any number of other signif-icant cultural changes came about because women religious were willing to take a hard look at outcomes and measure their performance against stan-dards other than ones of their own making.

HEROIC WITNESS

For much of their history Catholic nuns were able to establish, nurture, and sustain successful institutions that played a dominant role in transmitting Catholic culture in the United States. What happened within the congrega-tions themselves made possible the cultural success of these institutions. Catholic sisterhoods were organizations that cultivated religious culture and transformed young women into Catholic witnesses. Religious life was esteemed in the Church as a life singularly dedicated to loving Christ, giv-ing witness, and serving others in community with like-minded women who lived out vows of poverty, chastity, and obedience. Sisters' vowed lives in community reflected an exquisite and carefully maintained balance be-tween the prayer life of the community within the convent and the service work of the community outside its walls. Clarity of purpose defined reli-gious congregations of women prior to the Second Vatican Council. As Joan Chittister points out, "The strength of the life lay in its unyielding clarity of focus, both spiritual and professional. No one asked what a sister did be-cause everyone already knew."[5]

Religious orders were intergenerational organizations. In them, the best teachers and models introduced young entrants into intense and some-times arduous periods of formation. These years of postulancy and novi-tiate were designed to completely reorient those who entered. During them, all aspects of these young women's lives, including how they prayed, what they wore, and how they comported themselves every moment during ex-tremely regimented days, were precisely structured. In their mature years, sisters clearly recalled the rigors of the years of formation. Many also ac-knowledged these were very happy years. In part that was because they were leading lives of deep spirituality, and in part because they shared so many experiences in common as young sisters. Carefully crafted rationales, rhythms, and rituals cultivated congregational culture and defined the sis-terhoods for much of their American history.

Catholic sisterhoods were courageous organizations with challenging goals. The women religious who shaped much of American Catholic culture were not timid in what they set out to do. The congregational histories of these religious groups abound with stories of courage and bold imagination by women whose esprit de corps emboldened them to take risks for the sake of the Kingdom. They believed they were doing God's work, and their faith sustained them in difficult times and circumstances that would have severely tested the resolve of the most steely eyed entrepreneurs. The sisters were called to a life of self-sacrifice, and superiors did not relax rules or practices just because they imposed hardships on the sisters. Furthermore, leadership among the sisters was extraordinary in terms of overcoming external obstacles. Whether it was the iron will of Sr. Carmelita Manning, R.S.M., picking out forty-three acres of prime real estate in Detroit on which to build a school and then securing the deal,[6] or Mother Augusta Anderson, C.S.C., negotiating for land and raising money in mining camps to build Holy Cross Hospital as well as pioneering a prepaid health insurance plan with the mining companies in Utah, women religious thought boldly and acted decisively.[7]

In the late nineteenth century, religious women also made their mark in health care. Once health care moved from a home-care model to an institutional model, the sisters proved to be successful managers and hospital administrators. According to statistics from the Catholic Health Association, by 1922 there were 675 Catholic hospitals in North America and over 20,000 nuns involved in running and staffing these institutions. While their hospitals were unique in terms of religious mission, they were competitive in all other areas. The sisters understood the positive relationship between sound business practice and their religious and service mission. Because they were nimble and entrepreneurially savvy, the sisters were able to found excellent hospitals, provide Catholic service to new populations of patients, attract and keep physicians, and maintain administrative control over their institutions. They did all this at a time when women enjoyed little public power and in a Church dominated by a male hierarchy.

Unlike the Protestant hospitals of the day, Catholic hospitals were not Church funded. However, they were not pure charity hospitals, either. The hospitals had limited endowments and of necessity relied on patient fees for survival. The sisters understood the market realities of their day and focused time and energy on negotiating contracts with government and business enterprises to provide medical care for large numbers of otherwise underserved individuals. Some congregations, such as the Sisters of the Holy Cross, negotiated with the U.S. Treasury Department to provide medical care for seamen in the late nineteenth century. At that time there was an increasing demand for seamen's hospitals, despite the fact many of them were understaffed and poorly managed. The government realized the sisters could provide more cost-effective and superior care, so they contracted to pay the sisters to provide these services.

The sisters also recognized and took advantage of another opportunity to extend their services and stabilize their finances. Immigrants working on railroads and miners needed medical care but could not easily afford it. The companies they worked for needed healthy workers but were in no position to offer medical services themselves. The sisters negotiated with the mining and railroad interests and developed medical prepayment plans that entitled workers to medical services at the Catholic hospitals. These large long-term contracts provided a direct benefit to mining and railroad companies, helped provide stable financial support for the Catholic hospitals, and assured a hitherto uncared for group of immigrant workers that they would receive excellent medical care when they needed it.

The sisters were able to attract both Catholic and Protestant physicians who brought patients to the hospitals by working with them in a complementary fashion. The sisters ceded power over medical decisions to physicians but kept administrative control and authority for the education and training of nurses in their own hands. Because they owned and administered the hospitals, the sisters controlled staff appointments of physicians. Unlike most hospitals in the first part of the twentieth century, the Catholic hospitals run by nuns did not restrict physician privileges to a small group. Instead, they combined a small group of senior physicians who provided medical leadership in the hospitals with an open-staffing policy that brought new physicians and increased numbers of patients into their institutions.

HARMONY WITH THE HIERARCHY

Not only did women religious execute grand plans, but they did so in relatively harmonious ways. In what they set out to do, most nuns were decisive but never self-aggrandizing. The sisters tended to be humble, yet their endurance outlasted many a more powerful rival. They were unyielding and tenacious in pursuing a desired outcome, but they were also masters of generous negotiation. Women religious were schooled to exercise power, not for the sake of power itself, but for those they served in the name of God. This purpose and their courage and imagination helped them develop an institutional network of amazing breadth and depth.

The Roman Catholic Church was foundational to the identity and character of religious congregations of women. Religious orders were created as spiritual and ministerial extensions of the Church, and in all of their schools, hospitals, and orphanages they evangelized, worshipped, and served in the name of the Church. They were agents of its overall mission. Women religious operated successfully within the ecclesiastical boundaries of the Church. They also wanted to extend both its reach and its effectiveness because the Church's mission was their own.

Nuns were "women who created new roles for themselves without violating hierarchical boundaries within which they lived and worked," Barbara Wall tells us, and "they took control of their destinies and gained a place for themselves in church and society. This translated into increased influence for them, and their stature enabled them to accomplish the tasks they deemed important."[8] Women religious operated effectively within the Church, but it was not always easy. Sometimes nuns did not get along with priests and bishops. The histories of the sisterhoods are replete with stories of protracted battles for autonomy and unwanted intrusions by clergy into their lives. While these battles were real, they could be characterized more as intense rivalries rather than outright rebellions.

Women religious accepted the structure of the Church and considered themselves important partners in the mission of the Church. Within their own communities, they replicated hierarchical structures and held to them unflinchingly. The religious superior had absolute authority in religious congregations in all things. Patricia Wittberg points out that during the 1950s, obedience "was ranked first among the vows—surpassing even chastity in importance."[9] In formulations of the vow, obedience to the superior was likened to obedience to God. Whether wise or unwise, the judgment of the superior was followed. Not only did superiors have ultimate authority, but they exercised authority over everything that happened in communities of women religious. In her book *The Way We Were*, Joan Chittister describes how superiors spent endless hours determining everything that went on in the convent. "Superiors spent their nights . . . making up lists of who should do table waiting, or table reading, or prayer leading or phone duty every week and who should accompany whom to the doctors' offices in town every day and who should walk with whom in funeral processions. And, of course, they wrote a steady stream of letters of correction designed to make fast the customs of the house."[10]

This authority structure could be stifling. However, for much of their history, sisters enjoyed far more opportunity to exercise legitimate authority and power in society than most women of their day. The nuns owned their own hospitals and were responsible for setting policy and operational decisions. The sister administrator at St. Joseph's Hospital in Paterson, New Jersey, for instance, faced down the medical staff over choosing the chief surgeon—a power she believed rested with her on behalf of her religious congregation. Orders also had extensive control in their colleges. They not only staffed the institutions and held many faculty positions but also occupied all positions on the boards of trustees.[11]

Sisters willingly worked within the Catholic system to create a parallel space in the Church that they controlled. In matters pertaining to doctrine and liturgy, the nuns were obedient to directives of the Church and did not resist them. In matters of practical judgment, however, the sisters exercised holy prudence. Depending on circumstances or personalities, some sisters chose to artfully resist decisions made by individual priests or bishops.

Some sisters fought for their rights in institutions when they disagreed with the clergy and hierarchy. Because bishops and priests desperately needed the nuns to run schools and hospitals, they often relented when the sisters threatened to walk out.[12]

In other situations, sisters would avoid directly challenging a decision made by the clergy. Rather, they would choose to view the decision as a preliminary arrangement. With the benefit of more time, closer collaboration, and greater amounts of prayer and persuasion, they expected things could be adjusted amenably. Sisters were also savvy to the normal workings of the Church. Neither bishops nor pastors retained jurisdiction over the sisters forever. On occasion, going along to get along was the prudent path sisters opted to take. Eventually they would have a new pastor or bishop with whom to renegotiate.

Religious congregations of women were also a growth industry in the Church for much of their history in the United States. In 1850, there were 1,344 nuns in the United States.[13] By 1948, there were 141,083 women in religious orders in the country, and by 1965 that number had swelled to 181,421.[14] In a little over one hundred years, the number of women in religious life had increased by 7,160 percent, whereas the population of the United States increased by approximately 825 percent over the same period of time. As the United States grew and expanded territorially and began absorbing waves of immigrants, the Catholic Church also experienced rapid growth. Demand for the services religious women could provide increased dramatically in this market as bishops and priests moved to open Catholic schools, hospitals, and orphanages to serve the needs of their people.

DUAL RECRUITING

Sisters were as religiously committed as the clergy to increasing the market share of Catholics in the United States. They also understood that by expanding their ranks, they would be better able to serve the needs of people within and without the Church. There were never enough sisters to meet the increasing needs of the growing population, and the competition between and among congregations to attract potential sisters was lively in the late nineteenth and early twentieth centuries. In order to assure they had adequate sisters to keep their communities flourishing, congregational superiors made numerous recruiting trips to Europe each year, especially to Ireland, Germany, and France. They would visit sodalities, parishes, and devotional societies to seek possible entrants to serve in the United States.[15] Schools, academies, and orphanages the nuns operated also offered excellent opportunities for sisters to recruit young women to their ranks. In 1917, according to Eileen Brewer, Mother Samuel Coughlin, O.P., of the

Sinsinawa Dominicans began the practice of establishing a vocation director in each convent. Mother Isabella, B.V.M., of the Sisters of Charity of the Blessed Virgin Mary, established quotas of sorts in 1922, instructing that each sister should obtain one or more vocations in order to carry on the work.[16]

The most appealing recruiting tool in the sisters' arsenal was their own witness. The young sisters were particularly powerful role models. They were enthusiastic about religious life and would encourage the best and brightest of their students to consider whether they had a "call" to become a nun. The young women who came in contact with the sisters were impressed by them and intrigued by the mystery of their lives lived for Christ. Frequently, groups of young women in the academies and nursing schools would join the ranks of the young sisters with whom they had developed close relationships and burgeoning friendships. The sisters prayed for vocations and encouraged their young charges and their parents to do so also. They told stories about their own vocational journeys and delighted the young women with heroic tales about their congregational founders and other significant members of their orders. There was hardly a single Catholic woman who did not seriously entertain the idea of a religious vocation at some point in her young life. The sisters knew idealistic young Catholic girls were open to entering the sisterhoods, and they made every effort to recruit them for their own communities.

The women who joined religious congregations did so willingly and with enthusiasm. The Church taught, and they believed, that religious life was a superior religious state. The idea of religious virtuosity, as Sister Patricia Wittberg describes it, appealed to enthusiastic young women who wanted to commit their lives to God and to service.[17] Spiritual idealism was cultivated in all Catholic institutions, and families were often delighted their daughters were joining one of the sisterhoods. Many young women were educated by the sisters, experienced them as mentors, and wanted to emulate their lives in religious community.

As cohorts of young female entrants to religious congregations grew in size, the enthusiasm they brought to the life only increased. While postulancy and novitiate was an arduous period, the esprit de corps that bubbled up among these earnest young women kept their spirits high and their commitment intact. Religious congregations were very successful in keeping their recruits for life, despite the fact their lives could often be difficult. There is much speculation about why women were so attracted to the life. Many suggest that, as difficult as it was, being a nun offered a path toward professional opportunity and away from unwanted marriages and economic privation. That is surely true to some extent, but scholars increasingly point out that it was "the unmeasurable quality of spirituality" that was so fulfilling to so many for so long.[18]

Women religious also played a significant role in recruiting young men for the priesthood. As committed and informed Catholics, sisters understood that vocations to religious life and priesthood come from the Holy Spirit, but they also knew they had a key role to play in initiating and sustaining them. The sisters were frequently the first people to encourage young boys they thought had the requisite qualities to think seriously about priesthood. Because in most cases the boys they hoped to influence were young, their approach was gentle. By asking, "Have you ever thought of being a priest?" or suggesting, "You could be a very good priest if you wanted," nuns planted the seeds that frequently blossomed into priestly vocations.

FINANCIAL REALISM

One of the greatest challenges for religious congregations in the United States was financial. Their institutions started, survived, and thrived without significant financial help from archdioceses or dioceses of the Church. They relied on dowries, gifts from families, and their own wits and willing work to achieve financial stability. In her book *Sisters in Arms*, JoAnn McNamara chronicles the ways nuns went about creating a financially viable situation that allowed their ministerial work to grow and flourish. The Schools Sisters of Notre Dame combined a raft of activities that funded their community and its works. They were cooks and gardeners, gilders and cobblers, bookbinders and secretaries. The Kentucky Dominicans farmed, grew flax, and made linen, which they then sold. In Santa Fe, Sr. Blandina Segale and the Sisters of Charity of Cincinnati were involved with a quarry, lime kiln, brickyard, and lumber mill. Sr. Joseph of the Sacred Heart was an architect and contractor whose professional success made it possible for the Providence Sisters to found hospitals, schools, and other institutional works.

The labor of sisters in the United States was complemented by their willingness to literally beg in order to keep body, soul, and ministry together. The long history in the Church of seeking alms was extended by sisters who adopted the practice in their earliest days in the United States. This practice extended well into the twentieth century, when sisters were still going door to door, seeking donations for building funds. These "alms" complemented the money sisters received from their families as Christmas gifts, which they willingly contributed to assure the growth of their congregation's institutional initiatives.

Sisters were able fund-raisers. They benefited from the generosity of Catholic women and men whose largesse was blessed by accompanying tax exemptions. The nuns had strong links with wealthy women and cultivated alumnae who encouraged their husbands to give generously to the sisters.

Dynamic and wily women religious also impressed businessmen and town fathers with their tenacity and their faith. These prominent individuals—Catholic and non-Catholic alike—often worked on behalf of the sisters to assure their institutional dreams came true. Nuns lived spartan lives themselves, and they invested goodly sums, often purchasing land and buildings, frequently at bankruptcy auctions.

The practice of contributed services was the financial linchpin in the congregational enterprise. This mechanism made it possible for women religious to build and maintain financial stability in schools, orphanages, colleges, hospitals, and within their own congregations as well. Arguably, this financial structure that sustained the sisters was deeply flawed because it undervalued their labor. For a long while, however, this system worked well for them and splendidly for their institutional ministries.

Although the sisters regularly had to find new ways to attract financial support to sustain their institutions, congregational leaders also understood the importance of organizational growth. A necessary requirement for growth was an increasing number of young women entering the religious life. But growth was insufficient, since even congregations that were growing had to close some of their institutions. In most cases, this took place because, even after valiant efforts, the institutions were not financially viable. Despite such closures, rapid growth in vocations during the nineteenth and twentieth centuries enabled the sisters to enlarge the institutions they had, build annexes to schools, and expand hospitals. They also built new institutions in emerging neighborhoods or in rural areas. Each religious congregation wanted to expand, but the sisters were also eager to increase the number of Catholics regularly participating in ecclesiastical institutions. The sisters had a growth orientation focused on increasing the market share for Catholics in whichever type of institution they were running—be they schools, colleges, hospitals, or charitable centers.

CATHOLIC COMPETITION

Many Catholics recoil at the idea of competition among Catholic institutions. The women religious who created the culturally persuasive institutions that shaped American Catholicism did not seem to share this view. Rather, they realized that a form of healthy Catholic competition benefited their own congregations and institutions, as well as those with whom they competed. Not only did religious congregations compete for vocations, but they also competed in the general sense that they wanted the institutions they sponsored to be among the most highly regarded in the particular class of services they offered.

Parishes were geographically defined, and children attended the parochial school in their own parish or in the nearest parish that had a school. As a result, competition among Catholic parochial schools was uncommon. At urban Catholic high schools catering to a large number of mobile Catholic students, things were different. These institutions did compete for students, as well as academic and athletic prestige. Some Catholic colleges also competed for students, and as students were recruited and accepted across broader regions of the country, that competition became more intense. Competition among Catholic hospitals existed in cities with a number of Catholic hospitals but was uncommon in small cities or urban areas. In all of these situations, competition focused on attracting students or patients to a particular Catholic institution.

Catholics have a traditional aversion for direct competition, where "direct" means head-to-head competition for market share. The nuns shared this aversion, and generally speaking, they did not open institutions in close proximity to existing ones run by different groups of religious sisters. In fact, as Patricia Wittberg points out, many superiors refused to honor a local bishop's request to open a girls high school if they thought it might adversely affect another community's school. "The Mothers Superior were not about to let the clergy play them off against each other if they could help it."[19]

GENERAL CHARACTERISTICS FOR INSTITUTIONAL SUCCESS

Nuns gave Christian witness, executed well, made deft dynamic adjustments, recruited effectively, exercised financial realism, and promoted growth and competition within their religious congregations. These leadership characteristics were also in evidence in the ways women religious led their schools, colleges, hospitals, and charitable organizations. All are important and positive, but they are not exclusively or even primarily Catholic characteristics. Indeed, these attributes would contribute to smooth functioning in any institution.

The primary interest of this book is Catholic culture and how the ways nuns successfully cultivated and transmitted it in specific institutional settings can inform cultural renewal in parishes. Recruitment, financial realism, and leadership are important in parishes and are addressed in three thematic chapters in Part III. The general analytic framework applied throughout the book, however, relies on four specific principles for success that marked the institutional approach of nuns, and these are developed in the next chapter. All of these principles strengthened the distinguishability and inheritability of the Catholic institutions the nuns established and contributed to their religious cultural success.

NOTES

1. While there are differences between *nuns, sisters,* and *women religious,* in colloquial speech the terms often are used interchangeably to refer to women who belong to Roman Catholic religious orders. Throughout this book we follow colloquial pattern and use the terms interchangeably.

2. Patricia Wittberg, S.C., argues convincingly that a cultural cross-fertilization occurred between the religious congregations and their institutions. The sisters certainly defined the culture of the institutions, but their involvement in institutions also shaped the self-understanding of the sisters as well. See Patricia Wittberg, *From Piety to Professionalism—And Back? Transformations of Organized Religious Virtuosity* (Lanham, Md.: Lexington Books, 2006).

3. The sisterhoods undertook extensive renewal in response to the Second Vatican Council in the mid-1960s. The revolutionary nature of this renewal created a cultural cleavage within the Church and within the sisterhoods about how to understand the historical import and impact of religious life. Much has been written in the post-conciliar period that denigrates the culture of pre-Vatican II women religious. Palpable ambivalence developed within congregations themselves about their own legacy. Even the harshest critics of the sisterhoods agree, however, that Catholic nuns had far-reaching influence in shaping the culture of American Catholicism.

4. Jo Ann Kay McNamara, *Sisters in Arms: Catholic Nuns Through Two Millennia* (Cambridge, Mass.: Harvard University Press, 1996), 568.

5. Joan Chittister, *The Way We Were* (New York: Orbis Books, 2005), 21.

6. Melanie M. Morey, "Leadership and Legacy: Is There a Future for the Past?" (doctoral dissertation, Harvard University Graduate School of Education, 1995), 159.

7. Barbara Mann Wall, *Unlikely Entrepreneurs: Catholic Sisters and the Hospital Marketplace, 1865–1925* (Columbus: Ohio State University Press, 2005), 60.

8. Wall, *Unlikely Entrepreneurs,* 9.

9. Patricia Wittberg, *The Rise and Decline of Catholic Religious Orders: A Social Movement Perspective* (Albany: State University of New York Press, 1994), 241.

10. Chittister, *The Way We Were,* 56.

11. Wittberg, *From Piety to Professionalism,* 90–92.

12. Wittberg, *From Piety to Professionalism,* 92.

13. Mary Ewens, "Women in the Convent," in *American Catholic Women: A Historical Exploration,* ed. Karen Kennelly (New York: Macmillan, 1989), 24.

14. Rodney Stark and Roger Finke, *Acts of Faith: Explaining the Human Side of Religion* (Berkeley: University of California Press, 2000), 175.

15. In the years between 1872 and 1900, vocations to the Sisters of Charity of the Incarnate Word, for instance, came mostly from Europe, with 45 percent of vocations coming from Ireland, 21 percent from Germany, and only 16 percent from the United States. That pattern did not change significantly between 1901 and 1920, when 47 percent of recruits came from Ireland, 21 percent from Germany, and only 14 percent from the United States.

16. Eileen Mary Brewer, *Nuns and the Education of American Catholic Women, 1860–1920* (Chicago: Loyola University Press, 1987), 102.

17. Patricia Wittberg, *Pathways to Re-Creating Religious Communities* (Mahwah, N.J.: Paulist Press, 1996), 19–32.

18. Brewer, *Nuns and the Education of American Catholic Women*, 22.

19. Florence Jean Deacon, "Handmaids or Autonomous Women: The Charitable Activities, Institution-Building, and Communal Relationships of Catholic Sisters in Nineteenth Century Wisconsin" (doctoral dissertation, University of Wisconsin, 1989), 137, cited in Wittberg, *From Piety to Professionalism*, 93.

3

Reclaiming the Sisters' Legacy

For much of their history, institutions run by women religious operated within a parallel, yet separate, Catholic universe in the United States. The cultural distinguishability of institutions in this milieu certainly contributed to their success, but it did not guarantee it. In order to attract and maintain a steady clientele, Catholic institutions had to compete effectively and prove culturally inheritable. Women religious employed dozens of approaches to realize their institutional goals, but four key strategies are worth noting. What we term *narratives*, *norms*, *benefits*, and *practices* guided the operational approach of sisters and contributed significantly to the religious success of their institutions.

Catholic sisters (1) used *consistent narratives* to help institutional participants make sense of Catholic culture. They also (2) established and enforced *clear norms* or standards of behavior for all involved. The sisters (3) provided real-world *benefits* to those they served and (4) employed countless small *practices* or rituals that reinforced Catholic cultural beliefs, values, and norms.

Employing these strategies, religious women created institutions, most of which not only survived but flourished. That does not mean, however, that in every one of their initiatives the sisters employed all or most of these four strategies. The nuns were, after all, creative women quite capable of genuine innovation. However, for the most part, these strategies helped women religious develop and shape the Catholic culture in their institutions. These strategies are of interest because they contributed positively to the legacy of the nuns. But beyond the purely historical, they are compelling because of their potential, once adopted and adapted, to strengthen today's Catholic institutions.

NARRATIVES

Symbols are the cultural glue that holds organizations together, and narratives are a particularly important part of any symbol system. A cultural narrative tells the story of why an institution exists, how it understands itself, and what it strives to accomplish. The narrative also showcases heroic leaders and exemplars who epitomize the virtues the institution holds dear. These narratives provide cultural coherence, support and sustain institutional standards, and help organizations achieve their goals. In religiously affiliated institutions, a well-understood and consistently shared religious narrative provides institutional coherence. It also helps those involved in the organization understand what it is about, why they are in it, and what they need to do while they are there.

Catholic sisters employed consistent religious narratives in their apostolic work. The Catholic institutions nuns founded and ran provided many of the same services available in non-Catholic institutions. Their distinctiveness emerged from the conviction that what happened in these institutions was rooted in the love of God and neighbor and joined to the saving work of Jesus Christ. This understanding was a personal conviction, but it was not a private one. The religious narrative that suffused the sisters' institutions made what they were doing and why they were doing it available to all.

In the 1950s, Sr. Mary Bernice Beck, a Ph.D. nurse-educator, wrote *Handmaid of the Divine Physician*, a manual of religious directives for nurses. Sr. Bernice reminded nurses that the patron of nursing was the Blessed Mother "who nursed the Divine Physician in His infancy and who, at her shrine in Lourdes, now serves as His chief handmaid as He ministers to the sick and suffering members of His mystical body on earth."[1] The image of Christ the Divine Physician was frequently invoked by the sisters and reminded all involved in Catholic health care that just as Jesus healed people body and soul, they, too, were responsible for both the spiritual and physical well-being of their patients. Nurses and doctors participated in a sacred profession that shared in Christ's healing ministry and that called them to lives of selfless service for the glory and love of God.

The mystery of Christ crucified was at the heart of how the sisters understood and explained the suffering they dealt with and which patients and their families endured. Because of Christ's death and resurrection, human pain and suffering had meaning and purpose, and death was not a defeat but a sacred opportunity. For those on the path to recovery, pain and suffering were considered personally beneficial as well as helpful for the Catholic Church. Women religious did not let their patients suffer needlessly as a form of spiritual discipline. Rather, as Catholics, they understood that suffering is not something to be sought, and in fact is something to be avoided. However, when it could not be avoided by reasonable means, the nuns helped patients to accept it as part of God's passive will. Their model was Jesus in the Garden of Gethsemane, who prayed to His Father that "this cup pass, but not my will, but yours be done" (Matt. 26:39). They saw their patients' suffering as a source of strength for the Church because it was a reminder of the Church's most basic calling, to imitate Christ by doing the will of the Father. In Paul's letter to the Christian community in Rome, he said that the community of believers in Christ are "heirs of God and joint heirs with Christ, if only we suffer with him so that we may also be glorified in him" (Rom. 8:17). When it became clear that, despite the efforts of doctors and nurses, a patient was coming close to the final moment of life, more spiritual resources were made available to the patient in a Catholic hospital. The prayers of the sisters were intensified, prayers for the family were increased, and for a Catholic patient the priest was brought in to hear confession, bring communion, and administer what was then called extreme unction.

Through prayer and ritual, the sisters were able to instill and transmit a culture that gave meaning and hope to those who were suffering and in the throes of anxiety and grief. These narratives about suffering and death from an earlier age do not sit well with our twenty-first-century sensibilities. However, in their time, they were hardly shocking. The hierarchy's emphasis on enduring pain and suffering as a way to strengthen faith was a big improvement over the understanding prevalent in other religious cultures that sickness was a punishment for sin. The sisters certainly understood pain and suffering as something that might be "offered up" to God. In hospitals, however, they focused on alleviating pain and providing comfort to those who suffered—comfort that frequently came in narrative form.

Sisters provided a consistent religious narrative within their institutional ministries. These narratives supported and sustained a coherent Catholic culture that permeated all facets of institutional life. They also helped communicate to all participants just how each institution understood its religious character, which enabled all involved to participate more fully in the institution's Catholic mission. The narratives the sisters shared in schools, colleges, orphanages, and hospitals invigorated idealism and inspired those involved to set challenging goals for themselves in their apostolic work. The sisters' narratives were consonant with the core narratives that defined Catholic culture and reminded participants of their connection to the larger Church reality, the Mystical Body of Christ.

NORMS

Effective institutions have clear norms and standards that are enforced. Religious women understood the importance of institutional norms and had a real talent for managing them in their institutions. Much is made in Catholic lore of the heavy-handed disciplinary approach of the nuns in Catholic schools. In fact they were far more authoritative than authoritarian in how they operated. Religious women were hardly permissive, but they were surely more balanced in setting and sustaining cultural norms than some caricatures suggest. It takes persistence and patience to instill a clear understanding of right and wrong. The sisters certainly emphasized good discipline in their schools and colleges and used disciplinary sanctions to enforce standards. They were even more effective, however, in positively motivating those with whom they worked to strive and succeed. Over and over again, nuns gave clear feedback about things done well, things done poorly, and actions that were totally unacceptable. And because they were first and foremost interested in the souls of those they served, Catholic sisters made it clear what kinds of behavior were pleasing to God and which were not. Although Thomas Lickona uses it in another context, his phrase "a deliberate effort to cultivate virtue" is a helpful way to understand what women religious were doing.[2]

In a 1904 catalog, the Sinsinawa Dominicans declared that the educational goal of their academy was "to instill into the minds and hearts of students those high principles of morality and religion which make virtue and refinement proof against the vicissitudes of life."[3] In their role as virtue educators, religious women employed a number of techniques that established standards of behavior in all areas of school life—academic, extracurricular, and spiritual.

The Religious of the Sacred Heart of Jesus (RSCJ) offer an excellent example of the kind of approach women religious used to manage standards at their institutions. The RSCJs relied on competition, standardized tests, oral examinations, and other rigorous and comprehensive tests as motivators to spur high academic performance in their schools. Sacred Heart schools also made excellent use of rewards and prizes as means to establish adherence to cultural norms. *Tres bien*, *bien*, and *assez bien* cards were handed out each week and indicated how well the students were living out the cultural mores of the school. Each week, one young woman was singled out and awarded a blue ribbon that indicated she was determined by the nuns to "possess good spirit, virtue, leadership, and irreproachable conduct."[4]

The Religious of the Sacred Heart did give stern warnings to young women about unacceptable activity. The sisters clearly told some young women they were disappointed in how they behaved. And sometimes they removed recalcitrant students from their schools. By and large, however, the RSCJs relied on positive appeals to assure the maintenance of institutional norms. Both the clarity of expectations, as well as academic and social rituals that elevated excellent behavior, instilled in the students a competitive spirit. Rewarding academic and behavioral performance with clear cultural bonuses was enough to transform most students into daughters of the Sacred Heart.

The nuns who operated nursing schools were equally effective in transmitting and modeling cultural norms. Along with clearly articulated expectations, student nurses were exposed to a way of life in nursing school that formed them both personally and professionally. Humility and deference were certainly qualities sisters encouraged in their students, but they also graduated nurses who were knowledgeable and decisive in their work. In Catholic nursing schools, young women were ushered into a sacred profession that required the highest levels of character, and their training was infused with religious meaning, practice, and ritual. Graduates of these programs—first the sisters and then the lay women and men who followed in their footsteps—developed Catholic cultural fluency in the nursing schools. These effectively educated and trained nurses provided the backbone of Catholic culture in hospitals, integrated Catholic culture into their work, and brought it to bear at the bedside of patients.

Nurses graduating from programs directed by women religious were expected to be exemplary both in Catholic settings and in nonsectarian hospitals. The standards the nuns enforced in their training programs were professional standards, and they integrated these with a Catholic outlook. Excellent and effective procedures for patient care and for comforting patients, as well as for working with physicians—all these were expected of nurses trained by the sisters.

The cultural norms and codes of conduct in Catholic institutions run by sisters emerged primarily from the Catholic identity of the institutions. The sisters also kept a keen eye on new practices in secular schools, colleges, hospitals, and orphanages, and they strategically introduced cultural adjustments to remain competitive. The sisters embraced the Catholic identity of their institutions and clearly communicated to participants what that identity meant in terms of their behavior and performance. The sisters set challenging goals for themselves and for their co-workers and developed practices and procedures that encouraged everyone to excel in all areas of institutional life. The sisters made sure that the culture in their institutions thoroughly reflected Catholic culture at large. They also insisted that participants become more knowledgeable about the Catholic faith and understand how the work they were doing contributed to the vitality of the Catholic Church as a whole. The sisters monitored trends that could potentially affect their institutions, and they made adjustments to their approaches and their programs when practices became out of date or new approaches seemed more promising. The rituals, rewards, and encouragement that were components of cultural transmission were designed to appeal to the highest ideals of participants who enthusiastically embraced them.

BENEFITS

Women religious were always and at all times interested in the spiritual and religious welfare, growth, and development of the people they served in their schools, colleges, orphanages, and hospitals. Simply put, they cared about saving souls. But they were also practical people and knew that any hope of saving souls was dependent on getting people in the doors of their institutions and keeping them there over time. Women religious created institutions that offered tangible benefits to those partaking of their services. Some benefits were real world and some were more spiritual. Both were sufficiently real to be readily grasped by people using the sisters' institutions. Real-world goals and benefits, such as excellent education or health care, were infused with religious meaning, and spiritual benefits—such as developing a relationship with Christ through the Eucharist—were presented as desirable in and of themselves.

In their day, the orphanages sisters founded, for example, met the needs for care and survival of foundlings and other orphaned or abandoned children. This included providing better educational opportunities than were available to most middle-class families.[5] The orphanages were well staffed by the sisters, who made sure the children developed work skills that helped them be self-sufficient and employable when they left the orphanage.[6]

The education at the sisters' schools competed effectively with public schools and other private institutions. That said, there is considerable debate about how "competitive" Catholic educational institutions really were. Some suggest these schools had little or no interest in providing excellent academic training and focused instead on the religious life of students to the detriment of secular academic learning. Others point out that the pedagogical approaches of American branches of the sisterhoods were remarkably forward looking. They also responded to the needs of their students and the demands of the marketplace by making cultural adjustments. Whether or not religious women were on the curricular cutting edge, they understood that, to survive, their institutions had to compete for students with both secular and other congregational schools. As a result, they diversified and adapted their educational programs in response to what was happening in these institutions.[7]

Religious congregations in the United States were not identical. Rather each had its own unique attributes or organizational culture that was often reflected in the kinds of institutions the order founded and the types of individuals it served. Some congregations developed academies serving primarily a wealthy clientele. These eschewed vocational training and focused instead on cultivating skills appropriate for convent life or life as a cultured wife and mother. Other congregations worked mostly with the poor or lower classes. Sisters in these institutions developed strong vocational programs. Many congregations created separate schools with different educational missions. Still others developed schools offering a variety of tracks from which students could choose: academic, commercial, or domestic.

Catholic institutions also provided tangible religious benefits. The nuns presented these to their students, patients, and clients in ways they could easily appreciate. In hospitals, the sisters prayed daily for their patients and for their families, and they benefited. Priests were readily available at all times to administer the sacraments, especially the final anointing when someone was close to death. At a time when the prevailing culture seemed hostile to Catholicism, children in the schools and their families learned about their Catholic faith and were given tools to defend it.

Catholic institutions were competitive institutions that offered both spiritual and tangible real-world benefits to those involved in them. These institutions would never have thrived and flourished as they did if they were perceived as substandard institutions that only offered spiritual benefits. The sisters always had clear religious goals in mind when they founded institutions. But they also knew the success of their religious goals was tied to their ability to compete successfully in the marketplace.

PRACTICES

Practices were the regular actions sisters encouraged students and patients to partake in as a way to participate more fully in the life of the Catholic Church. Many of these were quite particular actions whose meaning was easily grasped by children. When they were regularly repeated, they recalled and affirmed the sacrifice Christ made for each person. A very partial list includes making the sign of the cross upon entering a church, genuflecting before entering a pew, kneeling for several minutes in prayer when first entering a church, writing "JMJ" (standing for "Jesus, Mary, and Joseph") at the top of each notebook page, kneeling down when being passed by a priest carrying the Blessed Sacrament, saying night prayers, and spiritual bouquets for parents and friends. Most of these actions took only a few seconds to perform, but they were reminders of the overall mission each Catholic had a share in as a member of the Church. For college students at Catholic women's colleges, there were also pageants that linked Catholic conviction to otherwise secular rituals, as we shall see below. Whether the practices were small and contained or on a larger scale and intricate, they linked central Catholic beliefs with ordinary life and activities in the nonreligious world.

Mary Frances Clark, one of the original Sisters of Charity of the Blessed Virgin Mary, declared to her fellow sisters that their ultimate goal as teachers was the "religious training of thousands and thousands of souls."[8] This was the view women religious brought to their institutional ministries, who took every opportunity to impart Catholic culture to those with whom they worked. The sisters who founded and operated Catholic schools and academies, for instance, employed a wealth of practices that impressed on all involved the importance of the religious mission of their institutions. As Eileen Brewer points out, "Whether the season was Lent or the day an ordinary one, the sisters succeeded in investing it with a religious significance."[9] Sodalities played an important role in sustaining the religious mission of these institutions. These student associations met weekly and celebrated particular devotion to Mary, the exemplar of virtuous womanhood. Sodalities were religious counterparts to honor societies, and admittance to them was often more prized than admittance to their purely academic counterparts.

Rituals and practices also played a prominent role in Catholic hospitals. Mass and the sacraments were available in all Catholic hospitals, and particular time and energy were spent instructing student nurses about proper preparations for the distribution of Eucharist or for confession and extreme unction, or the last rites. When nursing students performed extraordinarily well in their work, the honor of accompanying the priest who brought Eucharist to the patients was bestowed on them. Chapels were central components of hospital plants, and capping ceremonies and pinning ceremonies always took place in the chapel. These events were powerful sources of religious inspiration for young nurses who were entrusted with sharing in the healing ministry of Jesus Christ.

Since Christianity's earliest days, Church fathers and mothers reshaped secular practices in light of Christian understanding. Instead of rejecting the prevailing culture, these wise women and men chose to transform it. Sisters understood this principle and were adept at performing a kind of religious alchemy of their own. May Day celebrations were a good example of their approach.

May Day festivities with a rich medieval tone were traditional at many women's colleges, especially at the Seven Sisters (or women's Ivy League). The nuns at Catholic colleges enthusiastically adopted the holiday and many of the secular events that surrounded it, including May baskets and dances around maypoles. However, the secular fun at the nuns' schools took place in the shadow of a far more important devotional event, the May procession or May crowning. These processions were quite elaborate and highlighted the importance of Mary as the model for Catholic womanhood. By joining the event with a common collegiate experience and introducing and elevating a religious component, the sisters were able to establish a tradition with far-reaching appeal and significance. At some institutions, these events were the equal of graduation in ritual import.[10]

Capitalizing on secular opportunities to convey a religious message was common practice. In situations large and small, the sisters found ways to make religious connections or transform secular circumstances into religious ones. They believed that infusing day-to-day practice with religious meaning was essential to making the Catholic tradition sustainable in a secular world.

STRATEGIES IN CONCERT

Looking at each of the four strategies (narratives, norms, benefits, and practices) independently helps demonstrate what was uniquely useful about each. In reality, however, they seldom operated as stand-alone approaches. Generally the sisters linked *narratives, norms,* and *benefits* to *practices* that were simple, direct, and easy to understand—a very Catholic approach. Catholicism, after all, is a religion of practice. When Catholics talk about the faith, we do not talk about having it, but about practicing it. On a very deep level we understand that what we believe in faith must find expression in what we do. The sisters understood this intuitively. By favoring an approach that highlighted *practices* enriched by *narratives, norms,* and *benefits,* the nuns both demonstrated and cultivated a Catholic cultural sensibility.

In developmentally appropriate ways, the nuns helped those they were educating and forming to practice the faith. By means of compelling narratives, they linked principles of the faith to specific activities or practices people would understand. This approach reinforced Catholic norms at the same time it helped individuals develop cultural habits that could be relied on to support and sustain faith for a lifetime. One example that nicely demonstrates the sisters' strategic approach was the practice they encouraged of making frequent short visits to the Blessed Sacrament.

Catholics are called to a deep and loving relationship with Christ, which is an essential part of the faith we hope to pass on to children. It is not easy to effectively convey to small children what exactly this means for them. However, by making good use of the simple practice of "visiting," nuns were able to convey two things to young children in an easily understandable way. First, they communicated to children Jesus Christ's love for the children and His intimate involvement in their lives. Second, they were able to impart to the children that they could and should seek to be closer to Christ. Children have firsthand experience with visiting the important people in their lives, including grandparents, aunts and uncles, cousins, and friends. Children like spending time with the people they love, and they also know intuitively that the more time they spend with these special people, the closer their relationships with them become. Because children already understand "visiting" and the role it plays in their important relationships, they can easily appreciate what visiting Jesus in the Blessed Sacrament means and why doing so will help them have a closer relationship with Christ.

Another example of the "enriched practices" approach helped young people in high schools to internalize the command to love our enemies. Each week before big games, students were encouraged to pray for members of opposing teams as well as for the home team. Although students and the sisters rallied behind their own players, they prayed that the opponents would play well and not get injured. The same lesson was supported again during election seasons when the sisters gathered the students to pray for the country and for those who would win and those would lose and for the families of the candidates.

A myriad of other activities the sisters recommended or required followed this same basic pattern. The nuns took common practices, and by means developmentally appropriate and with compelling narratives, they suffused them with spiritual meaning. By encouraging frequent repetition of the practice, the sisters cultivated religious habits for a lifetime. This strategic approach to education and formation was pervasive in all the nuns' institutions, but it was not without its detractors. Some individuals criticized the approach, suggesting it trivialized Christian faith, reducing it to a series of rote behaviors whose performance became an end in itself. While it certainly is possible for any frequently repeated behavior to become more mechanical than meaningful, it need not necessarily be so. As long as developmentally appropriate narratives accompanied them, many of the practices encouraged by the sisters, such as stopping by the church to pray or praying for political candidates of both parties, had the capacity to grow in meaning over the years and become beneficial lifelong religious habits.

CHOOSING PRACTICES

Whether in elementary schools, high schools, colleges, hospitals, or outreach activities to the disadvantaged, the sisters persuaded their charges to perform many practices. In doing so, they also linked the practices to narratives, norms, and benefits. It is not entirely clear whether the sisters had a systematic approach for determining which practices were better or more appropriate or whether there should be more practices of one kind and fewer of another kind. Nonetheless, it does appear that at the very least, the sisters had an informal approach. We know their main focus was to establish a Catholic culture that would both protect the faith and nourish it. Particular actions taken by a group of nuns in a particular religious congregation were based on their collective experience, rather than data collected in any systematic way. Their experience, however, was constantly changing, and as they compared their experience with their expectations for a strong Catholic culture, they made changes.

The sisters constantly updated their array of enriching Catholic cultural practices, adding new ones if they were more apt to accomplish cultural goals and discarding others that no longer seemed particularly effective. Broadly speaking, this operative array usually included an ensemble of three different kinds of practices that we call *Catholic practices, adapted practices*, and *counteractive practices. Catholic practices* were the mainstays of the Catholic cultural practice ensemble. When they existed in sufficient number and were invoked with suitable regularity, these practices could establish strong Catholic culture in their own right. *Adapted practices* were variations on practices existing in the broader society. The sisters adopted and adapted them to the Catholic milieu because they were like low-hanging fruit, easy to assimilate and redirect. *Counteractive practices* offset or neutralized the increasing encroachment of secular culture in areas sensitive to Catholic faith and morals. The nuns kept their eye on the secular culture and noted places where it led to behaviors either directly contrary to Catholic teaching or possibly over the long run injurious to Catholic culture.

Consider first the *Catholic practices*—those necessary for a vibrant Catholic culture. Catholic life is centered on the sacraments—in particular, the Eucharist. Sisters spent a fair amount of time preparing children to celebrate the Eucharist. Whether children attended the Catholic school or were part of what was then called CCD and released time, once a week the nuns would practice the hymns the children were expected to sing at Mass. The children and parents were also encouraged to attend devotions on Sunday afternoon and to make a short visit to church on their own several days a week. The first and possibly most potent part of this sacramental education and formation experience was the example of the nuns themselves. Every morning during the week, the sisters attended early Mass as a group, and they were always present at the children's Mass on Sunday. The children were regularly encouraged to go to confession weekly. In the course of this book, we will have occasion to point to other specific practices that sisters made part of the daily or weekly activities of their students. For everyone, but especially for the young, repetition is the mother of studies. The three central components of the faith for the sisters were the sacraments, the Ten Commandments, and the precepts of the Church. Practices focused on reinforcing through repetition these norms for both children and parents.

The sisters also made use of *adapted practices*—those existing in secular society whose significance could easily be redirected toward a religious message. Earlier we described how sisters transformed secular May activities, prevalent at non-Catholic women's colleges, and imbued them with a religious message. Patriotic gestures familiar at sports events were easily expanded to include a prayer. Similarly, sisters reinforced waning religious messages in secular society. Thus, Halloween was always the Eve of All Hallows or All Saints. Children were encouraged to dress up as saints, as part of their celebration of the religiously more important feast of All Saints the following day (November 1).

Counteractive practices were part of a defensive strategy the sisters devised. By the late 1940s and early 1950s, adolescent men and women were becoming more carefree in their affections toward one another. Since many of the sisters had recently entered the convent and were well aware of dating and social practices among young women and men, they perceived the changes and noted the inroads being made by a far more morally casual secular society. In response, the sisters initiated programs to curtail displays of affection at social events sponsored by their high schools and colleges. Similarly, they offered narratives to influence the behavior (practices) of their students. One famous one was reminding couples on the dance floor not to hold each other too closely and to leave room between them for the Holy Spirit. While even then and surely now these comments caused eyes to roll, the sisters did not care. In their own way, they were pushing back at what they saw as a dangerous trend. The benefit inherent in this little reminder was the presence of the Holy Spirit and the avoidance of serious sin.

Although we have information, much of which is anecdotal, about the practices of sisters, the data have not been cataloged. Nor have there been studies on which types of practices were deemed by the nuns to be more successful. Any such study would have to include a model of cultural change, a challenging subject. Even without such careful analysis, however, it is clear the nuns introduced practices to strengthen the culture or to counter the effects of the secular culture.

This book is written for parishes in the United States which have already undergone and will continue to face significant cultural changes in the decades to come. Throughout this book, we suggest practices to strengthen the culture in various segments of parish and diocesan life. Without adhering to a carefully stated rule, we follow the general guidelines set by the sisters. Attend first to the main components of Catholic culture—*Catholic practices*. Second, pick low-hanging fruit by refocusing secular practices where plausible—*adapted practices*. Third, where Catholic culture seems especially vulnerable to incursions by a contrary secular culture, develop an effective Catholic practice that at least slows the secularizing trend—*counteractive practices*.

In our view, there are a few areas in which it appears secular culture is making significant advances and displacing traditional strongholds of Catholic culture. Perhaps the biggest challenge is in terms of marriage and divorce. Available data indicate that divorce rates among Catholics are extremely high and approximately the same as among non-Catholics. Although priests and laypeople acknowledge the issue, it appears that more practices reminiscent of the nuns are required to get better results in this area.

A second area of concern is pornography. In one sense, this is a very old area of concern for the whole Catholic community. The difference today is that the Internet makes pornography more easily available to the young and harder to control for parents. Parents can limit access to various sites on their home computer, but students have access to various electronic PDAs (personal digital assistants) that allow them to access the Internet without parental supervision. In addition, society is much more tolerant of pornography, so long as no one gets hurt. Catholics, of course, have a much broader notion of what it means to hurt or damage an individual; the deep damage which can occur requires extra vigilance in this area. Developing effective practices with appropriate narratives to counteract this pernicious reality is a serious challenge.

The third area is one of general concern. In fact, it embraces the two specific areas of interest mentioned previously, while nonetheless warranting separate treatment. Ethical lapses in professional settings, in business, in politics, and in the private lives of individuals figure prominently in the news. These lapses pose real threats to the common good and the flourishing of individuals as well. What is at issue is not simply a failure to do what is right or avoid what is wrong, but rather that so many people have no strong feelings or convictions about what is right and what is wrong. In order for any culture or society—especially Catholic culture—to function, the young must be taught what is right and what is wrong. The ethical "dos" and "do nots" have to be reinforced by regularly pointing out to children and adults what behavior is beyond the pale and why that is so. Strong cultures clearly transmit cultural norms. Unfortunately, by that definition, the prevailing Catholic culture appears not to be sufficiently strong.

OBJECTIONS TO THE NUNS' CULTURE

Our description of what the nuns accomplished can reasonably provoke the accusation that we are being Pollyannish. In other words, we might be accused of praising a golden age that never existed. After all, the nuns' culture was at times painful, and by and large, it did not accomplish what it set out to achieve.

To be fair, the jury is still out on how effective nuns were as transmitters of Catholic culture. If they were so good at it, how was it possible that so much of the content of Catholic culture in America, including its practices and norms, unraveled so quickly after the 1960s? The same can be said of their ability to support and sustain the culture of their own religious life, which surely seemed to be a thick and rich culture. If it was so strong, how could the culture of Catholic sisterhoods cease to be either distinguishable or inheritable in such short order after the Second Vatican Council?

Simply put, things were not as straightforwardly positive as our broad-brush treatment might suggest. The nuns themselves would admit to failures in different areas. Sometimes they were disappointed that some of their practices did not have the desired effect, and other times they acknowledged they failed to implement their programs effectively. Furthermore, there were hundreds of congregations of women religious, each of which had distinct experiences in their various undertakings, be they schools, colleges, hospitals, or charitable endeavors. Some congregations were better at establishing, changing, and sustaining Catholic cultures than others. Any overall, but nuanced judgment of the effectiveness of the sisters awaits many more individual studies of the various congregations.

Another point we concede is that at some point prior to the 1960s, something went seriously wrong within the congregations of sisters. Most likely it had to do either with the sisters' formation or the way they lived their life in community. What we do know is that within about twenty-five years—from about 1960 until about 1985—the religious culture of the nuns collapsed. It moved from what appeared to be a vibrant culture, attractive to many young women, to one which had little appeal to new entrants and decreasing appeal to the existing rank and file. Changes in the predominant nonreligious culture certainly played a role. However, it also appears that the narratives and practices of the nuns no longer fit the society for which they were being prepared. So, something must have been seriously amiss for some time prior to the 1960s for such an apparently vibrant culture to pass so quickly from the scene.

All these things are true. The cultural story of religious congregations is certainly not perfect. However, the perfect should not be the enemy of the good. For all these difficulties, religious congregations of women remain the best exemplars of Catholic cultural maintenance and transmission we have. And for that reason, we abide by our general claim, that we present a fair portrayal of the effectiveness of the sisters in creating and sustaining a general Catholic culture for about a hundred years, stretching from the mid-nineteenth century to the mid-twentieth century. We also think it is important to refute four general popular criticisms of the various Catholic cultures instituted by nuns that distort their cultural contribution: first, the practices the nuns employed were simplistic, not just simple; second, the practices may have been effective or reasonable for children, but they did not carry over well to adulthood; third, nuns lacked nuance, seeing things only in black and white or as right or wrong, with very little in between; fourth, the nuns were cruel and reveled in humiliation and corporal punishment.

The claim that the practices sisters imposed on the young were simplistic, as opposed to simple, implies children quickly dropped them once they were no longer under the direction of the nuns. For example, the nuns usually would have children write JMJ (for Jesus, Mary, and Joseph, perhaps adding a cross as well) at the top of each page of their notebook. This might be considered by some to be a simplistic practice. Many children, however, continued this practice long after they were required to. Furthermore, many of those who dropped it did so because their public high school teacher told them not to write such things on their papers. Making the sign of the cross when passing a Church, making the sign of the cross when an ambulance or fire engine passed, remaining silent in church, being neat, being courteous, being prepared with books and papers and a sharpened pencil, being orderly—all these were individual practices but, in our judgment, not simplistic. By and large, children perceived them as sensible, even when they were no longer required to perform them. In short, some practices even the nuns might agree were simplistic. But by and large, they were simple ways of getting important realities across to children.

The second charge, that the nuns' practices did not travel well into adulthood, is also based on a misperception. Many children only had nuns in elementary school and afterward advanced to a public high school and a public college. However, many children continued on in the predominantly girls-only Catholic high schools and Catholic colleges established and run by the sisters. Girls who attended these schools generally had positive experiences. One reason was that sisters changed their practices and, to a lesser extent, their narratives, as the young women matured. That is, they treated the young women as maturing adults. They not only expected more from them but also gave them clear advice about how to function in the future as single women or as Catholic mothers and wives.

Many people resent the simple narratives or story lines about heaven, hell, sin, and purity taught by the nuns—the third objection. People point out that nuns should not have implied that not going to Mass on Sunday put one in jeopardy of going to hell. This was a frightening and unrealistic message for young children. We acknowledge the aspect of fright, but in Catholic society at that time, fear was big and hell was too. The nuns were not alone in communicating this message. Parents, pastors, and much of the Catholic community saw the world and God in much the same way. Furthermore, most families were going to Mass on Sunday, and the fear narratives served to keep things going on an even keel. Generally speaking, the sisters did not impose impossible burdens on children. Furthermore, as the children grew older, the sisters delivered more nuanced messages. The annoyance some had, and in some cases still have, stems from the belief the nuns imposed a culture very appropriate for ten-year-olds but not for thirty-year-olds. The problem here, however, is that the sisters were largely giving the information to ten-year-olds. Those who never heard another, more nuanced message can hardly blame the nuns in grade school for lapses in more appropriate religious education on the high school and college level.

The final objection is that some nuns were sadistic and enjoyed making young children cry. In 1960, there were approximately 160,000 nuns in the United States. It is highly likely that some of them were not well-balanced psychologically, and some of these may have been sadistic. Some students may have had the great misfortune of encountering two or three psychologically maladjusted nuns in their elementary school and the greater misfortune of having had all of them in class. There is, however, no evidence the nuns had an above average percentage of disturbed people in their ranks. Also, there is no evidence that many nuns imposed severe physical punishments on children or relished in humiliating the young people with whom they worked. While teachers rapping knuckles and parents spanking children are seen as unacceptable in our day, they were not uncommon practices in the 1950s. With the benefit of hindsight, we might well wish the sisters had never meted out physical punishments, but their doing so at the time was far less culturally outrageous then than it appears today.

GUIDED BY THE SISTERS' STRATEGIES

In this chapter, we highlighted four strategies religious sisters used to strengthen Catholic culture: the relaying of *consistent narratives*, the establishment and enforcement of *clear norms*, the articulation of *real-world benefits*, and the adoption of numerous small *practices or rituals*. These comprise the distilled essence of an approach which powerfully influenced Catholic culture in the United States for more than 150 years. Although the sisters were not always successful, their story overall is one of great success, at least to the extent success is measured by the spread of institutions.

Catholic culture faces substantial difficulties in the coming decades, and many issues have to be resolved. Our approach in this book is to take the essential strategies the nuns employed and apply them to what we argue is the unfolding reality in parishes. Part II brings this analysis to bear on five central activities of parishes: the Eucharist and regular participation in it (chapters 4 and 5), reconciliation or confession (chapter 6), prayer (chapter 7), religious education (chapter 8), and loving service (chapter 9). Part III then uses these same strategies to analyze those parish issues on which diocesan policy has a large impact.

NOTES

1. Bernice Beck, *Handmaid of the Divine Physician* (Milwaukee: Bruce, 1952), iv.
2. Thomas Lickona, *Character Matters* (New York: Simon and Schuster, 2004), xxv.

3. *Sacred Heart Academy Catalogue* (Madison, Wis., 1904–1905), cited in Eileen Mary Brewer, *Nuns and the Education of American Catholic Women, 1860–1920* (Chicago: Loyola University Press, 1987), 45.

4. Brewer, *Nuns and the Education of American Catholic Women*, 66.

5. See Nurith Zmora, *Orphanges Reconsidered: Child Care Institutions in Progressive Era Baltimore* (Philadelphia: Temple University Press, 1994).

6. Carol K. Coburn and Martha Smith, *Spirited Lives: How Nuns Shaped Catholic Culture and American Life, 1836–1920* (Chapel Hill: University of North Carolina Press, 1999), 209–210.

7. In the 1860s, for instance, the schools added science curricula and upgraded their offerings in mathematics. In the early twentieth century, Catholic schools felt the pressure of competition from public schools that had expanded offerings, and in response, many adopted practical and vocational educational programs.

8. Brewer, *Nuns and the Education of American Catholic Women*, 37.

9. Brewer, *Nuns and the Education of American Catholic Women*, 87.

10. At most of the colleges, young women in formal gowns processed with candles to a Lourdes-type grotto where a highly honored young woman crowned a statue of the Blessed Mother. The Marian events at some institutions were even more extravagant. At Immaculata College, for instance, students with lighted candles formed a "living rosary." At Emmanuel College, students collected gold and silver jewelry from their families, which was melted down to make the crown for the Virgin Mary. See David R. Contosta, "The Philadelphia Story," in *Catholic Women's Colleges in America*, ed. Tracy Schier and Cynthia Russet (Baltimore: Johns Hopkins University Press, 2002), 134–135.

II

ISSUES FOR PARISHES

4

Mass Attendance

Regular Sunday Mass attendance among American Catholics has fallen dramatically over the past forty years. Reversing this trend is the biggest Catholic cultural challenge facing parishes today.[1] Gallup poll results indicate that in 1965, approximately 70 percent of Catholics attended Mass at least once a week. By 2003, that number had fallen to 40 percent. Over the past five years about 30 percent of Catholics report that they attend Mass at least once a week. Some dioceses, however, have seen an even greater slippage in the percentage of people in the pews on Sunday in that period. Two dioceses in the Northeast report actual (not self-reported) average Saturday evening and Sunday Mass attendance at approximately 19 percent of registered Catholics.[2]

NO MASS APPEAL

The Eucharist, the sacrifice of the Mass, is the central liturgical experience of any parish, and the falling number of people regularly attending Mass is a disturbing trend. To reverse it, the Catholic Church in America needs a prepared and willing cadre of very committed lay Catholics who are themselves devoted weekly Mass goers to transmit Catholic culture to the next generation. Some parishes are already sustained and invigorated by a good-size group of such individuals who form the Catholic worshipping community at the Mass on Saturday afternoon or Sundays. At many other parishes, Mass attendance issues are a nagging problem that becomes even more pronounced over holiday weekends and during the summer months.[3] Without some significant intervention, the trend of falling Mass attendance is likely to continue, both during the academic year and especially during the summer.

Because Eucharist is the central liturgical celebration at the very heart of parish life, low Mass attendance is a sign of a weakened or weakening parish culture that needs rejuvenation. By employing the four principles the sisters used successfully to instill Catholic culture, a parish can analyze its own cultural weakness and begin to make necessary cultural adjustments.

At present, the American Catholic Church has no consistent and compelling narrative that both entices participation and justifies the need for weekly attendance at Sunday Eucharist. Without such narratives, attendance rates will simply not improve. There are other issues that affect Mass attendance, but the lack of any compelling narrative is critical. Consequently the rest of this chapter is dedicated to developing three such narratives. Chapter 5 takes a more comprehensive look at Sunday Mass and addresses some of the challenges parishes face. It also invokes the three additional principles of benefits, norms, and practices to suggest ways for parishes to strengthen Sunday Mass attendance.

NARRATIVES AND BENEFITS

The post-Vatican II Catholic Church has not developed a sufficiently persuasive rationale for why Catholics should attend Mass and receive Eucharist on a weekly basis. Many modern Catholics do not understand why weekly Mass is such a big deal or what, if anything, they get from attending. An earlier age had a simple, consistent, and in those days understandable and credible narrative about obligatory Sunday Mass. Failure to attend Mass, Catholics were told, was a mortal sin that could result in an eternity spent in hell. Priests and nuns frequently reminded parents and children of this serious obligation and the consequences of failing to meet it. If Catholics failed to attend Sunday Mass, it was a sin and they had to confess it in the sacrament of reconciliation before they could again receive Holy Communion. This pre-Vatican II narrative was clear and persuasive and coercive.

Eucharist is Jesus Christ's gift to His Church, and Catholics have a serious obligation to attend weekly Mass.[4] Persuasion has replaced coercion as the Church's preferred approach in encouraging Mass attendance, but our current narrative and approach are not getting great results. Any new narrative needs to explain what Catholics might get from going to Mass each week. Compelling narratives today, therefore, will have to focus on some personal, real benefits accruing not only to the community but also to the individual by faithful attendance at Sunday Mass.

Over time, the downward trend in Mass attendance will have a stultifying effect on the religious culture of Catholic parishes. Adopting coherent and compelling narratives that might actually persuade Catholics of the importance and benefits of weekly Mass is a reasonable first step in addressing this challenge. In this spirit, this chapter presents three consistent, coherent narratives for regular attendance at the Eucharist. The first tells the story of the Eucharist in the life of the Church in terms of a living legacy for all Catholics down through the ages. The other narratives illuminate what Catholics can get from actually going to Mass regularly. The second narrative tells how Catholics can learn to love for a lifetime by participating in the Eucharist, while the third narrative relates regular Sunday Mass attendance to gaining true self-knowledge.

NARRATIVE 1: EUCHARIST IS A LIVING LEGACY

From the letters of St. Paul and the Acts of the Apostles, we know that believers in Christ met once a week on Sunday to celebrate the memorial of the passion, death, and resurrection of Jesus Christ. In the first years after the resurrection, Christian believers were Jews or people interested in following the Jewish religion. In these early years, the Jewish followers of Jesus would attend the regular Sabbath (Saturday) services in the Jewish synagogue because they considered Jesus to be the Messiah, the fulfillment of what had been promised to the Jews. The believers in Christ considered themselves blessed by God because He had given them the understanding to realize that Jesus is the Messiah and the only Son of God. By attending Jewish Sabbath services, they were being faithful to their commitment as Jews. They also hoped to convince their fellow religionists that Jesus is the Messiah and, even more, He is God's only Son.

The early Christians were very attentive to the words and actions of Jesus. One of His central actions, vividly recalled after the resurrection by the apostles, was the Last Supper. This supper was either the paschal meal itself or a similar meal which took place the day before the prescribed day for the paschal meal. In this meal, when the time arrived to bless the bread, Jesus took it and said the startling words, "This is my Body, which will be given up for you." And then later in the same meal, He took a cup of wine, and before passing it around, He said, "This is the cup of my blood, the blood of a new and everlasting covenant, which will be shed for you for the forgiveness of sins. Do this in memory of me."

Although the apostles did not realize the full significance of the words at the time, they readily recalled them after the terrible passion and death of Christ and then His glorious resurrection. They understood that Jesus was the new Lamb of God. Jesus, at the very meal which recalled that first Passover, took the cup of wine and said it was the cup of His Blood which was about to be shed for all people so that their sins would be forgiven.

After Jesus ascended to heaven, the apostles, Mary the Mother of Jesus, and the other disciples gathered in the Upper Room and, with frequent prayer, began a process of sorting out what the life, death, resurrection, and ascension of Jesus meant for them and the way they were going to live their lives.

The impact of the passion, death, and resurrection of Jesus was the dominant reality for the disciples. They experienced this drama with their whole being: heart, mind, soul, imagination, will, and emotions. This description is accurate even though neither they nor anyone else other than the soldiers were reported to be present at the actual resurrection of Jesus. Even though they were not present at the resurrection itself, they did experience the resurrected Jesus. Jesus appeared to them! He was alive; they knew that, and they wanted to tell it to others. The gospels tell us that Jesus appeared to all the apostles as well as to larger groups of His disciples. The impact of these appearances convinced them that Jesus was alive and with the Father. It confirmed that the things Jesus told them were all true. The disciples were sure Jesus had overcome both sin and death for them. They also knew that they, too, would live beyond death if they just remained close to Jesus. These insights and convictions became part of their being once they experienced Jesus Christ risen from the dead. They affirmed these convictions in words, but the convictions were also in their hearts, souls, imaginations, emotions, wills, and memories.

The experience of the resurrected Jesus was a total experience for the disciples. Consider a mother who receives a call from the police informing her they have found safe and unhurt her three-year-old child who was abducted three days earlier. At once she knows what she will do when she is rejoined with her child. She will hug and kiss her, keep her close to her. In the future, the mother will be even more protective of the child. Although the mother may be overcome with emotion, her mind is still working. She is not all emotion. She anticipates the reunion with her child with her whole being. The communication from the police is not primarily an intellectual event for that mother. The same was true for the early Christians to whom Jesus appeared. No, they did not get a telephone call from the police. Much more convincing, Jesus appeared to them. This appearance was an event that influenced their whole beings.

Given this intense experience of Jesus risen from the dead, the disciples did not lack motivation. What was missing was a plan and some courage. In the Upper Room at Pentecost, the courage was supplied and the plan emerged. With the power of the Holy Spirit, the once confused and shaken group of disciples went out and started to preach the good news of Jesus Christ.

Sometime before or after Pentecost, the small band of disciples developed a pattern that was consistent with what Jesus had taught them and asked them to do. On Saturday, the Sabbath, they would join with the Jews in the temple or synagogue for regular prayers. Then on Sunday, the first day of the week, they gathered to celebrate the Eucharist, repeating the action that Jesus had asked them to do. These words are given by Paul, Luke, and Mark. From John's gospel (John 6 and 14–17), we know that, when the early disciples celebrated the Eucharist, they understood what Jesus said in the Last Supper in a literal way: they were truly partaking of the Body and Blood of the Christ. From John, it is also clear that when the early Christians gathered to hear the Word of God and pray to the Father by reciting the words of Jesus in the Eucharist, the Christians were participating in the sacrifice Jesus made on the cross. Just as His Body and Blood are made present in the Eucharist, so the once and for all time sacrifice of Jesus is made present and effective in the Eucharist.

This is the witness of the early Church, which is our best guide for understanding how to interpret the momentous events surrounding the passion, death, and resurrection of Christ. It also should be noted that the Gospel message was communicated by the early Church before any one of the four gospels had been written. This demonstrates that the practice of the early Christian Church is both the primary source for the New Testament as well as the norm for our understanding of it, and of the Old Testament as well. The faith of modern Christians is built on the faith of our early fathers and mothers in the faith.

Thirty or forty years after the resurrection of Christ, Christianity had spread throughout the eastern Mediterranean world. At first, those who accepted the gift of belief were fellow Jews or admirers of the Jews. Over time, many non-Jews, or Gentiles, embraced Christianity. As the number of Christians increased, the Jews who remained Jews were less tolerant of having apostates or "competitors"—that is, Christians—worshipping with them. Because the Christian Jews were no longer welcome at synagogue with the non-Christian Jews, the practice developed that many Jewish Christians no longer attended the Jewish Sabbath services. They did, however, still join together with the local Christians for the celebration of the Lord's Day on Sunday, the first day of the week. This was a significant move, since it demonstrated that Christian Jews had the confidence to modify the meaning of the commandment which had been given to Moses and the Jews by God himself, "Keep holy the Sabbath." They recalled Jesus saying He is Lord of the Sabbath. They were certain they were fulfilling God's will by meeting on the first day of the week, when Jesus rose from the dead and began the new creation that results in eternal life through the Church of Christ.

From the letters of Paul, the gospels, and the Acts of the Apostles, we know that Christians were expected to participate in the Eucharist every Sunday. In meeting to listen to readings of both the Old Testament and the not-yet-complete New Testament and by gathering to celebrate the Eucharist, the early Christians were following the path Jesus had trod. In the new covenant established by the words and works of Jesus, the Lord's Day became Sunday, the first day of the week. The reason they expected all Christians to attend Sunday worship is that they considered themselves a new people of God, like the Jewish people. God's gift to them was belief in Jesus Christ, and with the gift of baptism came the responsibility to spread the good news. They were part of the new covenant in the Blood of Jesus.

By joining in the Eucharistic sacrifice, Christians joined with other Christians in the known world, eventually explicitly acknowledged by mentioning the Pope and local bishop by name in the Mass. In the Mass, Christians were also united with the saints in heaven, and with those who had died but had not yet entered the Kingdom of Heaven. Their prayer was not primarily a private undertaking. The Christians were the new community of Israel formed by Christ, and they met together to worship as those who had been saved by His blood. Today's Catholics are part of the centuries old community.[5] In celebrating Eucharist we are joined to them. We are part of the new people formed in the image of Christ, and we publicly witness to that each time we celebrate Eucharist as a believing community. *Eucharist is a living legacy.*

NARRATIVE 2:
THE EUCHARIST TEACHES AND FOSTERS LASTING LOVE

The Gospel according to John emphasizes that God is love and Jesus came to share with us the love of the triune God. A central component of Jesus' message is that true love is often demonstrated at times of great suffering and that true love often requires a willingness to suffer. By invoking Sacred Scripture and by making present the sacrifice of Christ on Calvary, the Eucharist teaches us the path of love. The reception of the Body and Blood of Christ nourishes, strengthens, and expands our love.

Too often people acquiesce in offering and receiving a convenient love, a love that "works" for a time but is not definitive. It lasts as long as a couple finds it convenient or helpful. But Jesus calls us to a transforming love. For modern Christians, this is an especially difficult kind of love. It runs contrary to core convictions of our dominant "secular" culture. Three qualities of Christian love are both distinctive and assimilated in part through regular participation in the Eucharist. Christian love is sacrificial, patient, and, because it integrates the loved one into the community of believers, communal.

The most convincing action that revealed the power of Christ's love in the Church of the first three centuries was the strength of the Christian martyrs. The martyrs willingly gave their lives in order to remain true to Christ. Roman society did not think it was asking too much of Christians to demand they "respect" the Roman gods and just make some sacrifices to them. But the Christians knew there was only one God, and His Son had promised to receive them into the Kingdom of Heaven if they were loyal to Him. The number of Christian martyrs in the first three centuries was likely not greater than one thousand. Although relatively small in number, the early Christian martyrs made a mighty impact.[6] The witness of the martyrs confirmed the faith of other Christians and was a signal to non-Christians to consider the power of the Christian faith. As the second-century Christian theologian Tertullian expressed it, "the blood of the martyrs is the seedbed of the Church." The martyrs, adhering both to the words and example of Christ, set a high bar for sacrificial love among ordinary Christians.

The vast majority of Christians are not called to witness their faith by dying at the hands of persecutors of the Christian faith. However, all Christians are expected to witness to the power of Christ by loving others as Christ loves them. This call to witness is especially strong in our society in the sacrament of marriage in which Christians vow to love their spouse until death parts them. Yes, divorce and annulments are all too frequent among Catholics, but Catholic spouses are called to undying, unselfish love, and most Catholics aspire to love their spouses in this way. But loving unselfishly over the many decades of married life requires training before marriage and "inservice training" during marriage. There is no better training than regular participation in the Eucharist, listening to Christ's words and imitating Him, and asking Christ, in the community of the faithful at Mass, for the gift of loving one's spouse unselfishly until death.

Experience has taught that achieving such love in modern society requires extraordinary commitment. But making a commitment to unselfish love without having trained in it is foolhardy. Unselfish love until death does not flow automatically or even easily from the experience of falling in love with someone. Much more is required. The discipline of weekly participation in the Eucharist is a training course before and during marriage in the sacrificial love expected of all Christians.

Patience is a necessary virtue in adulthood, but it also plays a vital role in relationships, particularly one like marriage. What makes marriage so different is that, in a certain sense, spouses may legitimately take the commitment of their spouse for granted. Each spouse has promised to love and cherish the other until death parts them. All couples have squabbles, but squabbles outside of marriage are different in kind from those in marriage because of this lifelong mutual commitment.

One of this book's authors, Father John, has had the privilege of working with many young couples as they prepare to marry. Most priests have questions they pose to the couples. Some are intended to get at a thorough discussion of underlying issues. Others convey important information about Christian marriage itself. Father John has a series of questions he poses to engaged couples as part of their marriage preparation. He starts off by asking, "After you have had a disagreement or quarrel, how long does it usually take for you to make up?" Most couples reply that the longest they would be annoyed at one another before making up would be a week. The next question Father John poses is "Could you imagine that, once you are married, it may take longer for you to make up and resolve things?" The couple usually understands why it might take a bit longer, probably because they have in mind married couples who get annoyed at one another. Finally, Father John asks, "About how long could you remain annoyed at or angry with your spouse before you conclude that the situation is intolerable?" In countless interviews with couples, the answer to this question has never been more than two or three months. Father John points out to the couples that there are various reasons why a spouse can be upset. In marriage, not everything has to be resolved in a short period of time. In fact, some disagreements, either with a low or high level of engagement, can last for years without destroying the marriage.

Many modern couples have totally unrealistic expectations of how much harmony they will enjoy in marriage. Put negatively, they have very low tolerance for discord. The idealistic views of these couples pose a real danger for the success of their marriages. Should they encounter a fair amount of friction in their marriages, many of these couples could easily conclude the marriage had failed.

Christian love is patient, and all Christians, whether or not they are married, get training in this in two ways, both of which involve regular attendance at the Eucharist. Regular participation in the Eucharist helps us understand our own faults and, despite our faults and sins, Christ's constant love for us. By listening to the readings from the Old and New Testaments, we appreciate God's patience with His people and with those who are called to follow the Son. In listening to and praying over the New Testament, we appreciate the patience of Jesus. We also recognize our own sins in the failings of people described in the parables Jesus used to challenge us. Regular participation in the Eucharist teaches us how to be patient with ourselves and others.

The other training component embedded in regular attendance at the Eucharist is incorporation into a faith community that prays and cares for its members. Two Catholics are usually married at a nuptial Mass. The sacrament of matrimony consists of their promises until death parts them, but their commitment is then blessed by having the newlyweds and their families participate in the Eucharist, which is a reenactment of Christ's sacrifice of love. Married couples need the support of their families, but they also need the support of a community of people who believe in Christ the way they do. By regularly attending the Eucharist as a couple, they both make themselves ready to assist other members of the community and they also get to know other married couples who strive to faithfully live out their marriage vows. Successful marriages require a commitment to a larger faith community as well as support from that community. Weekly attendance at Sunday Mass creates bonds that help sustain a marriage, and for those who are not married, it instructs and forms them in true love for their family, friends, and acquaintances.

Learning how to love as Christ wants us to love requires a regular regimen of prayer and worship in community. Only by participating in a worshipping community and thereby maintaining close contact with Christ do we learn to love. In sum, Sunday Eucharist is the school of sacrificial, patient, communal love. It enables us to grow in love. Sunday Eucharist both prepares young people realistically for marriage and trains them during marriage in love that is unselfish, that is tolerant of faults and disagreements. It both contributes to and benefits from a faith community. *Eucharist teaches and fosters lasting love.*

NARRATIVE 3: EUCHARIST ENGENDERS SELF-KNOWLEDGE

A person who lacks self-knowledge cannot love consistently over a long period of time. Equally troubling, a person who lacks self-knowledge is more likely to make a poor judgment about committing to love another in marriage. A lack of self-knowledge does not necessarily mean someone cannot accurately evaluate another person. It does suggest, however, the real possibility of making important mistakes when assessing the possibilities of living and loving another person for a lifetime.

Self-knowledge means understanding one's own most important strengths and weaknesses as well as the minor ones. Many people think self-knowledge focuses primarily on understanding talents—learning, playing a musical instrument, managing things, and so on. Though certainly talents are aspects of self-knowledge, the most important part of self-understanding is the capacity to evaluate one's own ability to give and receive love. People who do not understand their limitations in this area, and how these deficiencies might develop over time, have limited self-knowledge.

Developing self-knowledge regarding the ability to give and receive love is notoriously difficult. Certainly parents want their children to acquire self-knowledge, and they try to help their children understand their own limitations and potential by regularly pointing out the children's strengths and weaknesses. Most adults acknowledge, however, that true self-knowledge comes only after many long years of effort. People also realize by experience that self-knowledge is not related to abstract intelligence. Some very intelligent people appear to have little self-knowledge, while many less intellectually blessed are wonderfully self-perceptive.

How much self-knowledge is required to successfully negotiate life is unclear, and the requirements may differ from culture to culture and even person to person. Perhaps using the image of quantity (how much?) is misleading and, instead, we should focus on quality. Whichever is more accurate, it is very clear that people who lack sufficient self-knowledge are likely to make very poor choices about whom to marry and love for a lifetime.

All Christians are called to love, but not all Christians choose to marry, which is a special sacramental calling. Self-knowledge can help people make better decisions regarding their married lives. It can also help those who marry and those who do not in the cultivation of lasting friendships that are strong, faithful, and mutually enriching.

For genuine self-knowledge, people need some sense of what they are called to be and where they stand in relation to that goal. Furthermore, this "sense" has to be incorporated into a regular perspective on many different tasks, issues, and challenges. Only by frequently reviewing various activities and considering those activities in the light of a tentative calling do individuals develop a clearer understanding of who they are and where they are going.

A Catholic is called by Christ to holiness, and through His Church, Christ provides the motivation and means to attain this holiness. This is perhaps the most elemental aspect of Christianity. Understanding the call to holiness, appreciating the obstacles, and developing skills to overcome setbacks are all tasks and skills of self-knowledge. The goal of holiness, the reality of obstacles, and the skill of overcoming obstacles all are honed in listening to Scripture, being united to Christ in the sacrifice of the Mass, and in receiving Christ in Communion. Participating in this weekly Eucharistic regimen provides strength and insight, but it also helps people be consistently holy in the various activities they undertake.

In a stirring talk to young people gathered outside Krakow in 2006, Pope Benedict XVI addressed a theme related to lasting love and self-knowledge as consistent narratives for weekly attendance at Sunday Mass. He encouraged the young people to build a house constructed on the foundation of Christ. Jesus invites us, said Pope Benedict, to build on a firm foundation of crucified love. The foundation is a hard love, tested by suffering. Jesus encourages us to build our house on rock, because the rock can withstand the heavy rains or sufferings we must endure. The Pope explicitly acknowledged that most people have many sorrows in their lives. But Pope Benedict reminded the young they are asked to build with someone who knows them better than they know themselves. All of us are asked to build the house, which is our life, with someone who will teach us about ourselves. Christ is our co-builder as well as the foundation. He who is always faithful calls us back even when we lose focus. Our co-builder extends His arms from the cross and tells us, "I gave my life for you because I love you."

Pope Benedict said: "In short, building on Christ means basing all your desires, aspirations, dreams, ambitions, and plans on his will. It means saying to yourself, to your family, to your friends, to the whole world, and above all to Christ: 'Lord, in life I wish to do nothing against you, because you know what is best for me. Only you have the words of eternal life' " (John 6:68). If Jesus is the only one with the words of eternal life, we have to know these words, ponder them, and integrate them into our lives by receiving Jesus' Word completely and participating fully in the Eucharist.

There is a danger, however, that we will merely pay lip service to Christ, relegating Jesus to a king of the past who is not for us today and certainly not for us tomorrow. He can be safely be put off to the side, even some Catholics think, to be consulted in times of crisis or on major feasts such as Christmas, Ash Wednesday, and Easter.

Since Jesus is always willing to welcome us back, what's so terrible about neglecting Sunday Mass for many years? There are at least two major difficulties with this way of thinking. First, saying that Jesus can be put off suggests we do not really think He has the words of everlasting life. Second, it is only by engaging Jesus in Word and sacrament that we actually work with Him to build the house that is our life.

Self-knowledge is attained in a variety of ways and from a variety of sources, including advice from experienced adults, interaction with peers, actually loving and being loved by others, and experiencing failure in loving and being loved. Growth in self-knowledge is similar to growth in the knowledge and love each of us develops for our mothers. As adults, our love for our mothers is very different from what it was when we were children. As adults, we have much more experience, know more mothers, and also through bitter personal experience understand better the deceptions and opportunities in life. Most adults continue to love their mothers and continue to deepen their relationship with them over time. As children grow older, their relationships with their mothers develop and they begin to gain a more mature understanding of their mothers' strengths and weaknesses, their commitment, love, and faith. This knowledge stems from love and an ongoing relationship. Adult children surely recognize their mothers' weaknesses and limitations, but they accept them more lovingly than critically. The relationship that eventually emerges between mothers and their adult children takes time, and it develops in the context of appreciation and love. Children learn how to love their mothers more deeply and differently in incremental steps over time as they gain greater self-knowledge.

A similar dynamic happens at an even deeper level as we develop our relationship with Christ, who is in human form the fullest possible revelation of divine love. Since self-knowledge includes awareness of the limitation and potential of loving, for a Christian believer it necessarily includes developing a relationship with God through His Son, Jesus Christ—a lifelong learning process. We contend that the longer this relationship develops, the better able a person will be to give and receive love that is long lasting. Weekly participation in Sunday Eucharist is an experience in love—a training ground for cultivating the skills of heart and mind and soul that gradually result in self-knowledge. *Eucharist engenders self-knowledge.*

THE POWER OF THE NARRATIVES

Sunday Mass is the central liturgical act of any parish. Parishes cannot be culturally vibrant if parishioners do not regularly celebrate Eucharist. Fortunately, in the post-Vatican II years, Catholics moved away from relying almost entirely on a narrative of compulsion and sin to get Catholics to go to Mass on Sundays. In discarding that narrative, however, we also seemed to stop telling the story of the Church's Eucharistic heritage in any compelling fashion. Consequently, for many Catholics there is no reasonable justification for why the Mass is a weekly obligation. So, we now watch with worry and wonder as increasing numbers of Catholics absent themselves from celebrating Eucharist—that ritual moment when we most fully realize who we are as Church. Unless we craft new and compelling narratives and once again find our voices to share them, this trend with all its corrosive cultural effects will continue unabated.

This chapter outlined three narratives about the importance and value of Eucharist to Catholics that can be summarized in headline fashion: *Eucharist Is Our Living Legacy. Eucharist Teaches and Fosters Lasting Love. Eucharist Engenders Self Knowledge.* The legacy narrative tells the two-thousand-year history of Eucharist in the life of the Church. But it is more than just a history; it is a story that makes real the treasure of the past entrusted to us in our time. We receive this living legacy within the Church, come to understand it more fully over time, and graciously pass it on to the generations of Catholics who follow after us. The practice of Sunday Mass attendance joins Catholics to the central mystery of our salvation and helps us grow in our faith. The lasting-love narrative explains how the weekly discipline of listening to the words of Scripture and participating in the sacrifice of the Mass schools Catholics in a love that is sacrificial, patient, and communal. And finally, the self-knowledge narrative reveals how self-knowledge is gained and deepened by our joining in the weekly ritual of listening to the call of Christ in Scripture and by our participation in the Eucharistic meal as a community of faith. In this way, Catholics come to understand more fully their calling and their potential, as well as their weaknesses and faults.

The wisdom gained by handing themselves over to the transforming grace of weekly Eucharist truly prepares Catholics to make better choices in life, including in the most important arena of relationships.

These three narratives represent our contribution to developing a more compelling story line that can help persuade today's Catholics not only to accept their responsibility to "keep holy the Lord's day" but to willingly embrace it. No matter how persuasive these or any narratives are, however, by themselves they cannot generate a culture strong enough to induce and sustain weekly participation in the Eucharist. Cultivating that kind of culture can only happen when powerful narratives are combined with norms, benefits, and practices that strengthen individual and corporate convictions about weekly Mass attendance. It is to these equally necessary cultural components we now turn.

NOTES

1. For ease of reference, we will use the term "Sunday Mass" to indicate fulfilling the Sunday obligation by attending Mass on either Saturday evening or Sunday itself and to fulfilling a similar requirement for holy days of obligation.

2. Poll results concerning Mass attendance vary widely, and it is important to distinguish between polls that ask people to report how frequently they attend Mass or whether they attended the previous Saturday or Sunday and, on the other hand, actual counts of parishioners in the pews. Polls in which people self-report their attendance give higher percentages for average attendance than actual counts of people in the pews. In general, when compared with the actual number of people in the pews, Catholics and other religious practitioners tend to overstate the frequency with which they attend religious services.

3. Typically, when attendance at Sunday Mass is mediocre to poor during the school year, the attendance turns poor to abysmal during July and August. To a certain extent, parishes located in attractive vacation spots experience the reverse phenomenon. But the increase in attendance in vacation spots in many cases is much lower than the decrease in Sunday attendance at regular parishes during vacation months. In fact, most people take relatively short vacations, but many still stay away from Sunday Mass as long as the children are not attending school in the vacation months.

4. Fulfilling the Sunday obligation is the first precept of the Church, and attending Mass on holy days of obligation is the fourth precept of the Church. The Catechism identifies the six precepts of the Church as the indispensable minimum in the spirit of prayer and moral effort, in the growth in love of God and neighbor (2041). The Code of Canon Law (1983), canon 1247, says: "On Sundays and other holy days of obligation, the faithful are obliged to participate in the Mass. Moreover, they are to abstain from those works and affairs which hinder the worship to be rendered to God, the joy proper to the Lord's day, or the suitable relaxation of mind and body."

5. Many American Catholics are confused by the words "Catholic" and "Christian." In Catholic circles, the terms appear at times to be used interchangeably. But

then, in some situations, the preference is for "Christian," while in others only "Catholic" seems to be acceptable. "Christian," as we first learn from the Acts of the Apostles, was an early name given to the young group of believers in Antioch. Over the succeeding centuries, as Christianity became the official and most pervasive religion in the Roman Empire, people would refer to the Church as catholic, which means universal, since the Church was everywhere in the known world. When the Orthodox Christians broke off from the Roman Catholic Church in the twelfth century, the Catholic Church was increasingly referred to as the Roman Catholic Church, while the Orthodox churches in the east were simply called Orthodox. The big change in usage of "Christian" occurred at the time of the Protestant Reformation. For the first time in Western civilization, there were Lutherans, Calvinists, Presbyterians, Anglicans, and Baptists. These new groups were Christian, but they were distinct from the Roman Catholic Church. Thus, until the twelfth century, Christian and Catholic could be used interchangeably. From the twelfth century on, it was necessary to distinguish between the Orthodox and the Roman Catholics, though both groups were Christian. From the sixteenth century forward, the Protestants and Catholics and Orthodox were all Christian churches; any reference to the group that had remained loyal to Rome during the time of the Protestant Reformation required using the term "Catholic" or "Roman Catholic."

6. See Rodney Stark, *The Rise of Christianity: How the Obscure, Marginal Jesus Movement Became the Dominant Religious Force in the Western World in a Few Centuries* (San Francisco: HarperCollins, 1996), 163–189.

5

Eucharistic Culture

A complex set of factors contributes to the alarming downward trend in Mass attendance that challenges parish life today. This chapter deals with three of these: canonically irregular marriages, growing liturgical ennui, and a shift in cultural expectations about Mass attendance in Catholic families. The first two are relatively straightforward obstacles to robust Mass attendance and are discussed in the first part of the chapter. The third issue is more complicated. As long as Catholic parents are at odds with Church teaching about the importance of Eucharist, Mass attendance rates will decline. While the result of this trend is serious in the present, it will be culturally debilitating for the Church in the future if it continues. Understanding and addressing this widespread and complex issue is the main focus of this chapter.

IRREGULAR MARRIAGES

One of the most painful obstacles to regular Mass attendance is marriage irregularities that effectively render some Catholics sacramental exiles. Civilly married couples who have not married in the Church are not permitted to receive Holy Communion. Catholic couples validly married in the Church who get divorced are also excluded from receiving Communion. Both types of couples may well feel uncomfortable attending Mass regularly. Catholic couples in the first instance can with relative ease reconcile their circumstances by remarrying in the Church. Remarried couples, however, face greater challenges and can only be fully reconciled to the Church if they seek and secure an annulment for the first marriage—a complicated and time-consuming process with a cost attached.[1]

There are options for many couples who are married outside the Church to reconcile their marriages, but most couples either do not know about them or are reticent to pursue them. These are painful and sensitive issues for couples trying to sort out their own relationship with the Church while still hoping to pass on the faith to their children. In our society, pastors can be sure a good number of parishioners fall into this category. Programs designed to give couples clear information and pastoral support can help resolve difficulties that keep some couples from attending Mass and receiving Eucharist. For other couples, it will not be possible to set things to rights in terms of their marriage and Church law. This is a painful reality that requires careful pastoral attention and concern. Ministries to divorced Catholics offer some ecclesial refuge, but those involved remain marginal members of the community of faith. They have a responsibility to attend Sunday Mass, but the Church does not let them receive Communion. It is not surprising that many such couples do not go to Mass or sustain ongoing involvement for their children. A prayerful and compassionate response by parish leadership to the pain of these individuals' circumstances can, however, help some of them remain connected to the Church, albeit on the fringes of its sacramental system.

LITURGICAL ENNUI

There are other Catholics who feel that regularly participating in the Eucharist is more of a burden than a benefit. These individuals understand they are supposed to attend every Sunday, but meeting one more obligation on weekends is less than appealing to them. Like most people in American society, Catholics find themselves increasingly burdened on weekends by all sorts of commitments—family commitments, athletic commitments, volunteer commitments, spillover work commitments, and long lists of chores that have piled up over the course of desperately busy workweeks. When they know few of the people they will meet at Church, are bored by the homilies, find the liturgies lackluster, or do not want to be asked to volunteer their time or give money to one more thing, they will likely avoid going to Mass.

When people are not invested in a community—any community—it is far easier to be critical of what it does or does not offer. While homilies at Mass can always be better and liturgies can easily be improved, it is often the issues of "belonging" that are more troubling and difficult for a parish to address. Only parishes with effective outreach initiatives can actually engage these peripheral Catholics and thereby encourage their regular participation in Eucharist.

An easy first step a parish can take is to position some greeters or hospitality ministers as people enter the various doors of the church. Another step requires more effort and organization, but it would surely have more impact. Parishes have many goals, and it would not be too difficult to include outreach goals among them. A group of volunteers, perhaps from the perceived "insider group of the parish," could set as their goal attracting five or ten new people a month to the parish church for Sunday Mass. The parish could identify one Sunday a month as outreach Sunday and encourage parishioners to invite a Catholic to church who has not been at Mass in some months. Of course it will take more than a one-time invitation to bring these new arrivals into the community of faith. Part of the hospitality ministry of a parish should be ongoing, systematic inclusionary efforts that reconnect with new parishioners, giving them information about what is going on and inviting them to participate more fully as time goes by.

Marriage difficulties and creeping liturgical ennui are thorny issues, but as the first part of this chapter demonstrates, they can be addressed in a more or less straightforward fashion. The problem of declining parental support and engagement in cultivating Eucharistic habits among children is a more complicated and widespread phenomenon. The unique and complex challenges this dramatic erosion of cultural norms poses for the Church is the primary focus of this chapter and the one to which we now turn.

A WINDOW ON THE PROBLEM

In the confessional, priests learn a lot about what motivates or fails to motivate Catholics in the practice of their faith. What penitents say can be a window on what at least some Catholics think is normative. Father John has heard a good many confessions over the years. His impressions provide some interesting insights about the attitudes of Catholics concerning Mass attendance, especially the attitudes of children and teenagers.[2] Admittedly the fraction of young people going to confession is small, but they do still go, and what they share or do not share is often illuminating.

Young children who come to confession often talk about difficulties they have in their families, such as not obeying their parents and not getting along with their brothers or sisters. They also mention sins or faults related to school or their friends. But in Father John's experience, children seldom mention missing Mass on weekends. When gently asked if they go to Mass, their responses vary, but many acknowledge that they do not get to Mass regularly. After making that admission, they frequently add that their parents do not go either. Now, children who participate in confession at least occasionally are probably more religiously sensitive or involved than many

Catholic young people. And no doubt they have heard more than once in their lives that Catholics are expected to attend Mass weekly. Yet even these young people do not perceive weekly Mass as an important responsibility of faithful Catholics.

There is no doubt that many of our Catholic children do not regularly attend Sunday Mass. Furthermore, if they do not attend with their parents, it is highly unlikely their patterns will change, despite any advice they may be given in the confessional or elsewhere. Unless parents reinforce the norm of regular Sunday Mass attendance, it will not be a priority for most Catholic youngsters. That is true even for those who participate in religious education classes or who go to Catholic schools.[3] This goes to the heart of the predicament facing the Church today. How can parishes thrive and Catholicism survive in this country if commitment to Eucharist dissipates? But before we can address that critical issue, it is important to offer some explanation of how we have come to this.

ROOTS OF THE PROBLEM

Consistent with the discursive approach of Vatican II, some priests, theologians, and other influential Catholics stopped emphasizing the "obligation" part of Sunday Mass during the 1960s and 1970s. Most Catholics stopped repeating over and over again that Catholics are required under pain of mortal sin to go to Mass every Sunday. Unfortunately, they did not develop a better rationale in its stead. As a result, many young Catholics who at this time were trying to figure out what it meant to be a Catholic did not get the message that weekly Mass attendance was part of the faith and cultural package. Rather, they got the unfortunate impression that Mass and Eucharist were nice, but not necessary. These same young people now have school-age children of their own. Because weekly attendance is not a cultural norm for them, they are hard pressed to instill it in their children.

The post-Vatican II Church talked about Eucharist in a new way and also focused its message on a different primary group—adults rather than children. For much of its history in the United States, the Roman Catholic Church focused on children as the primary targets of religious cultural education. That did not mean the sisters and the clergy were uninterested in adults; it merely meant they believed the most effective way to get their religious message heard in families was through children. This bottom-up strategy worked extremely well for many years. Primarily through schools, but also in religious education programs and sacramental preparation efforts, children were taught the beliefs and cultural norms of their faith, and parents were more than willing to cooperate with the sisters and priests in this process. In this intergenerational approach, adult Catholics learned along with their children what was expected of Catholics, and they in turn supported what the sisters and priests were teaching.

After the Second Vatican Council, this bottom-up approach was replaced with a more adult-centered process. In this new approach, the baptismal call of the laity was more fully appreciated and parents were seen as the primary teachers of children. Energy and resources were invested in preparing adults whose cultural knowledge would then "trickle-down" to children. Trickle-down is surely a questionable economic strategy and it has proven to be an equally questionable approach to Catholic education and acculturation. Catholic parents have not been as effective as anticipated in passing on Catholic culture to their children. This does not suggest that parents are indifferent to this responsibility. Rather, as more and more women entered the workforce and the pace of daily living picked up during the 1960s and 1970s, fewer parents had the time to continue their own religious education. As a result, they did not always feel they had the requisite knowledge and competence or even the time to assume a more prominent role as religious educators in their own homes. Also, the Church focused on developing a more "adult" understanding of the faith that built on the elementary foundations of generations of catechism learning. This meant the basics necessarily took a backseat and were no longer as effectively and efficiently transmitted to young American Catholics.

PRACTICES FOR ENGAGING THE CHILDREN

Catholic nuns had a successful strategy for Catholic cultural transmission that focused on children and the "practice" of their faith. This approach pulled parents and other adults into the process as willing and supportive collaborators. The children learned, the adults were included, and an opportunity for ongoing conversation about the faith was established that could benefit children and adults alike. The sisters also carefully included a vast array of experiences that reinforced important beliefs, values, and norms. Adopting and adapting this approach can help address the critical problem of Mass attendance we face today. The first step in doing that is twofold: focus on practices and engage the children.

The general strategy we are suggesting has children as the primary focus. The approach more common in parishes today emphasizes involving the whole family in religious education and practice. Both strategies, however, serve the same goal. Our strategy is designed to draw children by giving them enhanced roles at Sunday Mass. It is reasonable to expect that, if children are performing in some way at the Mass, their parents will attend. Rather than simply dropping their children off at the door of the parish church, parents more likely will actually participate in the Mass themselves, because they want to see their children perform or do something special. This assumption provides the foundation for seven specific strategies, which can be summed up as follows:

- Get children involved by having them perform.
- Promote theme Sundays.
- Acknowledge and affirm good attendance.
- Arrange extended First Communions.
- Encourage more than the minimum.
- Have parishioners invite people to special Masses.
- Clearly articulate what is expected.

GETTING CHILDREN INVOLVED

Children would rather participate than observe. Parishes have been building on this notion for years, and most have formal ways that involve children directly in liturgy as altar servers, as lectors, in choirs, or in recitation groups. Membership in these groups certainly enhances children's interest in the liturgy. If it includes a commitment to attend Sunday Mass, their participation would also reinforce an important Catholic cultural norm. In the case of altar servers, for instance, that would mean servers would go to Mass weekly, regardless of whether they are assigned to serve a Mass on a particular Sunday. Maintaining a list of servers' names with dates covering perhaps a month or two of Sundays can be posted in some convenient space. Servers can then come and initial the list for each Sunday they are present at Mass. If the list is in the sacristy, it also gives the priest an opportunity to say hello to most of the servers before or after Mass. Children also like to connect with each other. Giving them a reason to sign their names or initials before or after Mass makes that possible. Letting servers know they will be assigned to serve more often if they regularly come to Sunday Mass provides another incentive for regular Mass attendance. Similar approaches can be used with the children's choir and the children lectors.

Because the goal is to involve as many children as possible in Sunday Mass, a less familiar group has been inserted in the above list of children's groups, namely, the recitation group. Not all children are disposed to singing. However, practically all children like recitation groups. This group can be trained by a volunteer to recite prayers, poems, or important pieces at Mass, perhaps after Communion or even before the entry procession at the beginning of Mass. Initially the pieces they recite may be quite brief, appropriate for the age and background of the children. The recitation group can also retrieve some lost customs that are part of their Catholic cultural heritage. For example, they might learn to recite the "Gloria in Excelsis Deo" in Latin.

These groups should meet regularly. They actually need practice, so ideally they should meet once a week or at the very least twice a month. If they do, the children will feel better prepared and the rest of the community will be more appreciative of what they are doing. Involving the children is, of course, an extra commitment for most parents. It also adds to what are already burdensome schedules for many families. But if we respect Catholic culture, it is also important to offer valuable experiences that will advance the children's interests and the interests of the parish or the universal Church.

In order to retain the interest of the children over several years, it is normally necessary to enhance their experience and responsibilities over time. Providing symbolic cues about their varying levels of experience can also be both effective and appealing. The pride with which children wear sports uniforms and display badges or other marks of accomplishment underscores how positive this approach can be. Servers at Mass, for example, wear a cassock and surplice. It is relatively easy to arrange for more experienced servers to wear a different color or style than the younger ones. Similar distinctions in clothing or accessories can be adapted for children in choirs or recitation groups.

The involvement of children's groups is often confined primarily to the children's Mass. Spreading the wealth to other Masses can be a good idea. This will make the children's involvement a more vital part of parish life and probably attract more participants. If these initiatives prove successful, there may be different choirs or recitation groups for different parish Masses. Of course, such success would require a sufficient number of adult leaders who are willing to train and direct the groups. Nevertheless, the more children who participate, the more delighted the pastor and other pastoral leaders should be.

Choirs and recitation groups can absorb large numbers of children without difficulty. In fact, more participants are better than fewer in these kinds of groups. It is not always as easy to accommodate large groups of altar servers, but with some creativity, it can be done. Prior to Vatican II, a solemn high Mass on Sunday usually had, in addition to other servers, six young servers called torchbearers.[4] They walked in with their candles and otherwise did not do much with the candles until the end of Mass, when they processed out with the other servers. Many parishes today have a similar somewhat modified practice. Generally two servers process in with candles; then, before the Gospel, they take the candles and process to the place where the priest or deacon reads the Gospel, forming an honor guard with the candles. It is relatively easy to increase the number of these servers either by design or to accommodate as many servers as show up, and a number of parishes do just that.[5]

This strategy or "practice" is based on increasing the size and number of children's groups directly involved in some way at parish Masses. For this strategy to succeed, all the activities must encourage Mass attendance. It is important to make sure those youngsters who are most faithful to group norms (including weekly Mass attendance) have a greater opportunity to participate or a higher profile or more responsibility. Children easily understand and accept this dynamic, and parents respond appropriately to the interests of their children.

Strategy 1: Get children involved by having them perform.

THEME SUNDAYS

Theme Masses are attractive to children and their parents and can help create greater enthusiasm for participating in the Eucharist. Possible themes may revolve around sports, musical instruments, or family members. Local or regional celebrations that might warrant a link with Sunday Mass are also appropriate. A Mass for godparents, for example, might be an excellent theme Mass for almost any parish. Godparents have a responsibility to assist parents in educating and forming children in the Catholic faith. A theme Mass offers a way for godparents to do just that. It would also give children an extra opportunity to spend time with their godfathers and godmothers.

In order to assure good participation by godfathers as well as godmothers, it makes sense to have separate theme Sundays for the two groups. In announcing the theme, the pastor could indicate the desired activities, which can become more particular as the years go by. Suppose initially the pastor speaks about a special theme for godmothers at one or more of the Sunday Masses. All children in grade school and high school would be invited to attend Mass on the designated Sunday with their godmothers. At first the emphasis might be simply on godchild and godmother attending Mass together. Over time, suggestions could be made to enhance the experience. Godmothers could use the occasion to give their godchildren something special that has religious significance. They might also add a social dimension, such as an excursion to get ice cream. If they use the outing to share something about their own spiritual life—a particular prayer they like or a saint they are especially devoted to, for example—the event will have religious significance and still be great fun. Most godmothers would be delighted to do this, and all godchildren would be delighted to participate.

If the first Godmothers Sunday is a success, the pastor should let parishioners know of its success and thank the godmothers who participated. He could also announce that the experience would become an annual parish tradition and tell parishioners when it will take place the following year. Over time, the event can develop by adding other opportunities for shared religious experiences, such as a special opportunity for reconciliation before Mass. The same format can be adapted for godfathers or grandparents.

The point is to establish special times when children are encouraged to invite other important people in their lives, besides their parents, to join them at a particular Mass. The goal of this strategy, after all, is to get more family members attending Mass together. One less intuitive family group might be cousins. Some families, especially in the ethnic communities, enjoy living together or in close geographical proximity to one another. As a result, many cousins are in frequent contact with one another. For Cousins Sunday, children can be encouraged to invite one or more of their cousins to attend Mass at the parish with an agreement to reciprocate.

At theme Masses, it is important to give visibility to those participating. For example, godchildren and godparents can be invited to sit in a special section for the Mass. Finding ways to heighten the visibility of the participants in subsequent years will assure this special Mass continues to be memorable and attractive.

Theme Sundays can be scheduled at regular intervals or as befits the occasion, and they can be repeated. For example, if there were a Mothers Sunday planned for some Sunday in October, one could easily repeat this in the spring, perhaps on the country's celebration of Mothers Day. Similarly, for many reasons, it would make sense to have a godmothers Sunday in the fall and a second one in the spring, and similarly for godfathers.

A few times a year, a parish might announce a dress-up day for church. Clothing always conveys a message, and sometimes that message is a far cry from what the wearer actually intends. Because clothing is important to children and adults, it is a type of low-hanging fruit that can be picked for Catholic purposes. Children like wearing special clothes for particular activities such as martial arts, sports, dance, and even in after-school jobs. A parish can designate one or two Sundays a year as dress-up Sunday, dress-professional Sunday, or some other variation on the theme of church attire. Children and adults are then invited to wear clothes that fit the theme. As an example of a theme clothing Sunday, one can request parishioners to wear something purple on a particular Sunday in Lent. Such days can be fun and informative, since they help children understand the message clothing transmits. Admittedly, girls might like this idea more than the boys, but the boys might be more interested if they are encouraged to wear a specific piece of clothing that is unusual or interesting for them. This gives them an excuse to wear something special without, at their age, feeling like total geeks.

A wide variety of themes can be used appropriately in parishes and will encourage greater interest and participation in Sunday Mass. Determining what makes the most sense in any given parish is important, but exploring possibilities and making the choices can be an interesting and creative experience for all involved.

Strategy 2: Promote theme Sundays.

ACKNOWLEDGE AND AFFIRM

Acknowledgment and affirmation are important for all of us. They are essential in the transmission of culture and cultural norms. If we want young people to go to Mass more regularly, we have to find ways to acknowledge and affirm them when they do. Religious sisters were masters at this. They understood that young people respond to affirmation by adults whom they admire and respect. By merely pulling children aside and complimenting them on something well done or pointing it out to a class or other group of children, nuns were able to provide excellent reinforcement for the children's positive religious behavior. Sometimes they had a little gift, such as a holy card, for the children, but other times the recognition alone proved both generally illuminating and personally rewarding for the children involved.

In terms of Mass attendance, establishing a type of attendance honor roll is one useful approach. Given holiday commitments and children visiting relatives in other parishes, tracking attendance over fairly short intervals will provide many more children a chance to achieve perfect or near perfect attendance. Children might be awarded a pin, badge, ribbon, or star—depending on their age. Their names could also be printed on an honor roll, which might be in the vestibule of the church or printed in the parish bulletin. The honor roll could be a general one or it might be distinguished by the child's school. Listing high school students separately from grade school students would also be important. Having special awards for the older students could also be useful, in part because it would encourage younger children to continue to be faithful to regular Sunday Mass in their teen years.

Strategy 3: Acknowledge and affirm good attendance.

EXTENDED FIRST COMMUNIONS

First Communion can be joyous or fraught with disappointment for parish leaders. The pastor and the catechists are delighted for the children on First Communion Day and are often surprised by the children's attentiveness to receiving the sacrament for the first time. The disappointment comes the following Sunday when the first communicants do not return to Sunday Mass. Many priests privately lament how many months it takes to receive Communion the second time. First Communion is, after baptism, the first big step children make in their faith lives, and it should begin a weekly tradition. Unfortunately, for many first communicants, Eucharist becomes less of a weekly ritual and more of an occasional opportunity. There are ways, however, to keep these young people at least partially on track.

Due to the large number of children involved, some parishes have multiple Saturdays or Sundays on which children receive their First Communion.

Whether this complication exists or not, most parishes arrange to have First Communion shortly after Easter, usually close to Pentecost. The Sunday following Pentecost is Trinity Sunday, and the Sunday after that is Corpus Christi, when a procession of the Blessed Sacrament is traditionally held in church. This convergence of important feasts enables a parish to plan a month of Masses for first communicants.

Six months before receiving First Communion, the children could be told to think of this event as lasting four Sundays: the actual Sunday they receive Communion for the first time, Pentecost, Trinity Sunday, and Corpus Christi.[6] On each of these Sundays (or some other suitable combination), all first communicants would be asked to wear their First Communion attire and sit in a special place in the front of the church. As part of their extended experience, the first communicants might learn a special prayer to recite together after Communion as they kneel together at the Communion rail or some other place close to the sanctuary.

Wearing their special clothes more than once will delight children and parents alike. Providing them an opportunity to extend the special day for four almost consecutive Sundays will also be attractive to many. But the most important thing is that the children will receive Communion four times in rapid succession, starting a pattern of weekly Eucharist. This approach also brings the parents to Mass and gives them other opportunities to invite friends and family to a special Eucharistic celebration.

Strategy 4: Arrange extended First Communions.

MORE THAN THE MINIMUM

People frequently perform better when we raise the bar rather than lower it. If we want young people to regularly come to Mass and receive Communion, we should consider expecting more of them. Asking older students to deepen their devotion to the Eucharist by extending their own involvement beyond regular weekly Mass attendance is worth trying. Some Catholics participate in liturgy one or more times during the week. Such weekday Masses rarely last more than a half hour, so usually a teenager or a working spouse can fit one or more additional Masses during the week into an otherwise busy schedule. The liturgical seasons of Lent and Advent are great opportunities to encourage more frequent Mass attendance. Visits to the parish church and adoration of the Blessed Sacrament can also be encouraged.

The straightforward goal here is to inspire young people and adults to more frequently draw grace and strength from the Eucharist. A related goal is to redefine upward what devotion to the Eucharist entails. Due to circumstances and family or job commitments, some Catholics can only attend Mass once a week. Others could attend more frequently and yet do not. There are young Catholics who are called by the Holy Spirit to a closer life with the Lord. One possible activity for them is participating in at least one extra Mass each week.

Young people like group activities. For this reason, a pastor should encourage a group of young people in the parish to attend Mass more frequently, make a visit to church during the week, or participate in adoration of the Blessed Sacrament. Finding out which day and time might be attractive for young people to attend Mass would make sense. Involving the young people in the planning of events and encouraging them to participate together as a group will help any effort succeed.

For security reasons, many churches close their doors after the morning weekday Mass, and the doors remain closed most of the day. A pastor who encourages young people to make a visit to the church during the week would have to change this practice. Just as young people are hired to answer the door and phone at the rectory in the evening and on weekends, teenagers might also be engaged to sit in the vestibule of the church, perhaps accompanied by an adult volunteer, from 5:00 p.m. until 7:30 p.m. During that time, the doors to the church could be wide open once again. This would provide a degree of security without dampening a welcoming approach.

Many churches have weekly adoration of the Blessed Sacrament. Including young people in this devotion is important. One way to do that is to designate a half hour or hour interval when young people in particular are invited to pray before the Blessed Sacrament. If this proved popular, it might be because young people wanted to gather with their friends. It could also be that they truly wanted to pray before the Blessed Sacrament. Who knows? In most cases a little bit of both is probably in play. So it has been for generations. Motives are seldom pure for any of us, but making the most of whatever brings young people to the altar is more than worthwhile.

Strategy 5: Encourage more than the minimum.

BY INVITATION

Many Catholics today find themselves standing uncomfortably at the threshold of the Church. Who knows if they ever will come in? One thing is for sure, however. Unless we invite them in, they will remain outside longer. Creating "Invitation Sundays" is a way to say: Please come back. Either for some or all the Masses on these Invitation Sundays, parishioners, both young and old, would be urged to invite one "occasional Catholic" to join them at Mass. Christmas, Ash Wednesday, and Palm Sunday and Easter are perfect opportunities for extending this invitation. This strategy is designed to double the number of times these "occasional" participants attend Mass each year. This is an incremental policy which does not aim high;

it merely seeks to move people from one religious comfort level to a slightly higher one.

Most Catholic families have a member or a close friend who is somewhat estranged from the Church. Children usually are the best messengers for approaching these adults who have fallen into a sporadic pattern of Mass attendance. Youngsters can easily explain "Invitation Sunday" to these individuals and request they join them for the liturgy. The children might also sweeten the deal by including an outing after Mass. In a sense, this is a reverse variation of godparent Sunday where the godparent treats the child.

Ideally, the invitation would be repeated for each of the three or four Invitation Sundays during the year. There are no guarantees these invitations will be accepted, but making the effort is important. Even if a person who attended very irregularly in previous years now comes to Mass six times a year as a result of Invitation Sundays, significant progress has been made.

Strategy 6: Have parishioners invite people to special Masses.

ESTABLISHING NORMS

The Catholic cultural norm is that Catholics attend Mass every Sunday. For over a thousand years, this expectation was expressed as a serious obligation, under the pain of mortal sin. We no longer threaten eternal consequences for noncompliance with this norm. Without that stick, however, we must develop more carrots to entice the faithful—adults as well as children—to come to Mass. This includes both positive reinforcement for attending Mass regularly as well as some criticism when the obligation is ignored. To be clear, now the feedback must be as regular but more varied than it was during the time the nuns provided their own carrots and sticks to make sure that both children and parents attended Sunday Mass.

One of the fruits of Vatican II is a deeper theoretical appreciation of the centrality of the Eucharist for the life of the Church. Unfortunately, this has not translated into greater practice. The sisters were able to enforce the norm of Sunday Mass attendance both because of their dedicated lives and because faithful Catholics accepted them as moral guides and critics. Without the nuns as a strong force in most parishes, the priests and laypeople must assume more active roles in promoting regular Sunday Mass attendance. Norms are strong behavioral motivators in any culture. If they understand what is expected of them, most people try to live up to the expectation. Unfortunately, at this point, many Catholics are very unclear about Catholic norms regarding Mass attendance on weekends and holy days. If Church leadership fails to clearly establish norms, they cannot expect parishioners to feel obliged by to meet them.

In our experience, even when Church norms about Mass attendance are communicated these days, they are seldom reinforced on any regular basis. In the previous section, we indicated a practice—recognizing students for perfect Sunday Mass attendance over an interval of approximately six to eight weeks—that provides positive reinforcement, along with some implied criticism of those children who do not receive awards. Adults also need positive and negative reinforcement, but this topic is not usually discussed at Masses during the year. A priest may take advantage of a Midnight Mass at Christmas or an Ash Wednesday Mass or service to encourage people to attend Mass regularly. Parishes, however, need to address this topic more consistently and effectively.

In parish bulletins, the times of the Mass are clearly stated. There should also be a sentence or two about the expectation that faithful Catholics attend Sunday Mass every Saturday or Sunday. Similarly, a sentence can remind parishioners and others that, as Catholics, we prosper better as a community when each Catholic joins the community for the common Eucharistic sacrifice on Saturday afternoons or Sundays. Without the participation of all, the group is weakened. Pointing this out to parishioners will likely have little impact on those individuals who attend services only a few times a year. However, it may have a considerable impact on people who attend sporadically, perhaps once a month. The benefits the sporadic attendees receive by participating in Mass are not foreign to them, and they can also appreciate how much better it would be for the community if most Catholics worshipped together each week.

The more particular the message shared with parishioners, the more likely it is to make a positive impact. Similarly, the more frequently (within reason) information is reinforced, the greater the chance it will make an impact. Finally, the better the message is integrated into the Catholic culture itself, the more likely the impact will be lasting. Reinforcement can be personal, communal, or both. Pastors can relay to the community particular experiences of individuals that underscore the benefits of going to Mass. This might be a conversation with a young adult about how regular participation has helped them grow in self-knowledge or a conversation with a married couple who felt better prepared for marriage because of their regular participation in Sunday Eucharist over many years.

Linked to regular attendance at Sunday Mass is cultivating respect for Mass and the Blessed Sacrament. Respect for the Eucharist comes through both positive and negative reinforcement. For this reason, it should be explained to both children and adults that, if they miss Sunday Mass for no good reason other than convenience, they should express sorrow for this sin in confession.

Establishing and supporting cultural norms is difficult and it makes people uncomfortable in many situations and even more so at church. That is not surprising, considering that norms are about who is "out" and who is "in."

While rigidity in terms of norms is destructive, clarity is not. People cannot honestly decide if they want to be part of a culture if they do not know its boundaries. Failure to communicate them for the sake of some misguided sense of inclusion does everyone a disservice.

Clarity about the Eucharist helps everyone, Catholics and non-Catholics alike. It also promotes a greater appreciation for religious pluralism. Catholics recognize that not every Christian community believes that the bread and wine of Eucharist have become the Body and Blood of Christ. To receive Communion in a community means both the community and the individual accept that belief. Asking others to affirm a belief that is not theirs is disrespectful and disingenuous.

It is important at Masses with many non-Catholics in attendance for Catholic cultural norms about Eucharist to be explained.[7] It is also helpful to explain that Catholics who have been away from the Church for a long time must first be reconciled with the Church before receiving Holy Communion. Although the bishops' statement on this matter is contained in the Mass booklets provided in most parishes, no doubt it will be news to some Catholics in the congregation. It is also important to explain why non-Catholics are not invited to receive. Including a written piece in the program for the liturgy allows for a rich and careful explanation. It also does not detract from the liturgy itself.

The leadership of the parish must be on message, and the pastor can legitimately expect that his staff use various occasions with children and parents to reinforce the main themes he sets at the parish. We know there are millions of Catholics who do not regularly come to church on Sunday. Our approach should be that, if we get them involved in the culture and teach them to respect it, the Spirit can move them to a much closer worshipping relationship with the parish community.

Strategy 7: Clearly articulate what is expected.

OBLIGATION AND FREEDOM

This chapter has placed significant emphasis on the obligation of Catholics to attend Mass weekly. Of course, the Catholic Church is famous (or infamous, depending on your point of view) for imposing obligations. But in many circumstances, the Catholic Church invites rather than imposes. In so doing, it offers considerable freedom to its members. Consider the following examples. Ash Wednesday is the beginning of the penitential season of Lent. The Church imposes no liturgical obligation on Catholics this day, and yet they come to church in droves of their own accord. They come to affirm their faith, receive ashes, acknowledge their finitude before God, and begin the penitential season of Lent.

The Church also encourages rather than commands participating in the liturgies of the Sacred Triduum, which are the three days before Easter Sunday. These three liturgies commemorate the central events of the institution of the Eucharist, the passion and death of Jesus Christ, and His resurrection. And yet, the Church does not oblige Catholics to participate in them. Rather, the Church urges participation, and many Catholics respond, because these liturgies are inspiring and grace-filled events in every parish.

Cultural practices and norms help individuals understand what a community of faith believes and values, accepts and prohibits. This chapter focused on how parishes can attend to the issue of declining Mass attendance. The suggestions offered are designed to attract a greater number of individuals to be more regular participants in weekly Eucharist. The Catholic Church and each parish are not, however, simply Eucharistic communities. Nor are they just collections of individuals who come together for Eucharist. Rather, the Church is a community of faith with faults and concerns. In faith, hope, and love, we pray for ourselves and others. We do the same by acknowledging our faults and seeking reconciliation with the community of the Church, the subject of chapter 6.

NOTES

1. The cost of an annulment, which is determined by the diocese or archdiocese, depends on a number of factors and is generally about $1,000 in a large urban archdiocese. The fee is used by the diocese to cover various legal expenses and other costs. However, most pastors make sure that a couple desiring an annulment does not abandon the effort due to the cost. Both the parish and the diocese work to make the expense affordable to people of modest means.

2. These confessional observations do not reveal anything against the seal of confession. Although priests can never disclose anything heard in confession that could possibly be traced to a single person, they are allowed to mention general things as long as no names are mentioned and nothing in what is said can even remotely be connected to any particular individual.

3. Most parishes have programs that require children who will be receiving the sacrament of the Eucharist for the first time or the sacrament of Confirmation to attend Mass regularly. Children either report to an adult at the Mass or get a card signed after the Mass by the priest or some designated layperson proving they were indeed at the Mass on the indicated Sunday. These are worthwhile programs, but for the most part, they only engage students who are preparing to receive a sacrament at the end of the year or the following year. (Most parishes require two years of preparation for Confirmation and some parishes require two years of preparation for First Communion.) Some parishes also require Catholic parents preparing to have their child baptized to attend a number of Sunday Masses prior to the baptism.

4. This group usually comprised those who had not yet learned the necessary Latin Mass responses.

5. There is a limit to the total number of servers who can be appropriately deployed during a regular Sunday Mass, but the limit certainly exceeds ten.

6. This will, of course, depend on how early Easter occurs in a given year.

7. Some churches have had the terrible experience of finding hosts in pews and hymnals after weddings, funerals, or baptisms held during Masses. The problem here is common to these various events. To be polite or because they do not know what to do, many non-Catholics who attend these events follow the pattern of everyone else. They approach the priest at Communion time, take the host, and then, either not knowing what to do with it or now realizing that they are not supposed to consume this because they are not Catholic, they place it somewhere after they get back to their pew. Explaining to the assembly of Catholics and non-Catholics what is permitted and what is not can prevent violation of the Eucharist.

6

Penance:
The Sacrament of Reconciliation

Human beings are wounded and sinful people who experience alienation from God, themselves, and each other. We harbor resentments and are petty. We are cruel or indifferent in our most intimate relationships. We avoid taking responsibility for the wrong we do and the pain we cause, and we blame each other in relentless accusatory rounds. We walk away from those in need, seeking to protect our privacy, our possessions, and our prerogatives. We live in a world rife with devastating poverty that cripples the lives of millions. Daily we find ourselves facing our sinfulness writ large in banner headlines about genocide, war, murder, rape, and mayhem. Confronted with all these terrible realities, we shake our heads, claiming the problems are too big and are hands are tied.

In our communities, our families, and our Church, we often nurse feelings of anger, jealousy, and selfishness. All this is happening at the same time that most of us desire in our hearts to be good, kind, and loving. We are desperately seeking, in the words of a classic spiritual, the "balm in Gilead that heals the sin-sick soul." In our need, the Church offers a great gift in the sacrament of penance. In this sacrament, Jesus Christ, who heals and forgives and "makes the wounded whole," is disclosed. In the sacrament of penance, Catholics also encounter the Church at its most tender. Penitent itself, the Church discloses itself as a healing and forgiving community that has suffered with us in our sins. The Church calls us home in the sacrament of reconciliation and stands ready to rejoice when, like the prodigal, we return. The Church "holds high the lamp of hope and reveals itself as the universal sacrament of salvation, the community which gives up on no one and no situation, no matter how seemingly hopeless."[1]

The renewal of the sacrament of penance called for by the Second Vatican Council was intended to clarify the nature, purpose, and effect of the sacrament. It was hoped the availability of the sacrament in four different forms would make it more inviting and less intimidating and encourage even greater participation. However, that is not how things turned out. Disagreements about when and where and how these new forms should be made available created confusion in the minds of many about what really was "new" in the new rite of reconciliation. That combined with a sense of dread about the sacrament that some Catholics experienced, and which popular lore surely heightened, created a climate over the past several decades in which the sacrament is more often ignored than embraced. As professionals in the Church continue to discuss and disagree about how best to incorporate this sacrament into the life of the Church, relatively few Catholics embrace the ritual as an important part of their relationship with God.

This chapter focuses on the sacrament of reconciliation or penance. It offers a detailed discussion of the sacrament and explores the subject of confession—sin—in some detail. The chapter also addresses the challenges parishes face in trying to encourage parishioners to avail themselves of the graces of the sacrament of reconciliation. Using the strategies of narratives, norms, benefits, and practices identified in chapter 3, this chapter outlines approaches parishes can adopt in their efforts to encourage greater participation in this often neglected sacrament.

NARRATIVES

In our post-Vatican II experience in the Church, we seem to have lost a compelling narrative that persuades Catholics that participation in the sacrament of reconciliation is a great gift. (To present our approach succinctly, "confession" and "penance" are sometimes used, rather than the more correct designation "sacrament of reconciliation.") We must develop better stories about why penance is important and share these narratives well and frequently. What follows are two different narratives crafted to persuade Catholics of the importance of the sacrament to their spiritual lives. The first focuses on forgiveness as a necessity for long-term love. The second narrative talks about the holiness of each individual as being key to the faith of the whole community and the role penance plays in that journey to holiness.

NARRATIVE 1:
CONFESSION CELEBRATES LOVE AND FORGIVENESS

For love to last, it must forgive. In the regular interaction between couples, in the rough and tumble of our professional lives, in tense relationships in which police, physicians, or nurses protect our security or heal life-threatening ills, in all these situations and many more there are abundant misunderstandings, deceptions, shortcuts, instances of taking people for granted, of focusing more on failures in others than shortcomings of one's own, and simple but devastating pride. For people to proceed in love rather than mere toleration or professional respect, forgiveness is required. In the sacrament of penance or reconciliation, we encounter the intimate reality of love and forgiveness that comes from God and is revealed in the life, death, and resurrection of Jesus Christ. God loves us unconditionally despite our weaknesses, flaws, and sinful behavior. God loves us completely and forever. God's love for us is suffused with forgiveness, and that forgiveness keeps open always the possibility that we will grow in our love of God, ourselves, and our neighbors. God's forgiveness means that despite what we do, love has a future. Because we are forgiven, we will not forever be defined by our sins, but rather by the possibility of love and our orientation toward God. Because we have known God's forgiveness, we are not doomed to despair, but we live in love and in the hope of full reconciliation with God and with our fellow human beings. Forgiveness allows us to love and be loved again in relationship even when we have failed miserably. Forgiveness is also a welcome back statement made by the Church. After being reconciled in confession, a person resumes again the path toward holiness in community.

Love entails a nearness or proximity that we desire in many ways. However, there are times that nearness can feel more like intrusion or invasion than intimacy. When that happens, people take offense and often create difficulties, conflicts, and misunderstandings. With the people we love the most, we share the greatest interpersonal proximity, and that intimacy often can breed discontents that cause us to push back. In our most cherished loving relationships, we experience many tiny moments of alienation.[2] Sin is alienation from God, from ourselves, and from others. It is estrangement or disaffection that distances us from the natural state God intended for us. We were made for love, and when separated from love by sin, we are wounded and in need of healing. Only when forgiven can we hope to breach the estrangement that afflicts us and begin the process of reconciliation we both need and want.

The conversation with God that is at the heart of the sacrament of reconciliation helps us understand more clearly why we are alienated and what stands between us and full reconciliation with those against whom we have sinned. Sin is primarily an offense against God, although it often harms family, friends, or neighbors. The forgiveness we experience from God and our reconciliation with the community of the Church make it possible for us to be reconciled and to love again, but it does not make it easy. The sacrament of penance does not erase conflicts and difficulties. It is a conversation with God that takes place in the heart of the Church that can sometimes bring these painful tensions into greater relief as we become clearer about what is really going on.

Communication and conversation are touted in our society as the paths to setting things right. Books like *Men Are from Mars, Women Are from Venus*[3] suggest that if we could just communicate better, we would resolve our difficulties. Unfortunately, that is not always the case. In some instances, greater communication does not result in a meeting of the minds, but rather makes abundantly clear how far apart our minds truly are. Conversations can also bring us to painful realizations about what we need to do. Because doing what is necessary will be so hard, we squirm. Communication, especially as we spend more time with a person, requires a greater investment in figuring out what they are experiencing. Love presupposes that the lover will spend some time analyzing what is happening with the beloved. Without this reflective exploration, the lament "Honey, just tell me what you are thinking" evokes resentment and a feeling of being taken for granted.

We encounter Jesus, who heals and forgives, in the sacrament of penance. As we do so and also experience the Church as a forgiving and healing community, things become clearer to us. For instance, we might come to understand that the tensions we experience in our relationships are more deep seated and dramatic than we had assumed. This sacramental insight brings us greater clarity, but it does not magically make everything all better. Sometimes we come to understand through the grace of the sacrament that we have to be more active and imaginative lovers in the sense of helping those we love understand what is going on inside them. But, for a variety of reasons, we may be reluctant to make this investment. In this case, we surely have greater clarity as a result of our prayerful conversation, but in the process, no magic wand was waved that made the problem disappear. After receiving the sacrament of penance, we still must go back into our relationships where tensions exist, and we still have to struggle to do better in the way we live and relate and love. So we might well ask, why bother?

The sacrament of penance gives us hope. God forgives the wrongs we have committed against Him, and by confessing our sins, we once again embrace Christ, who saved us from our sins. In many cases, through forgiveness granted by the priest, we attain a more sharply defined understanding of how we must change. Because we have known God's forgiveness, we are no longer defined primarily by our sin and forever alienated. In the act of contrition said in confession, penitents say they intend to avoid sin and whatever makes it more likely they will sin again. The removal of our past sins gives us clarity for avoiding sin in the future and for being a Christian who better follows in Christ's footsteps.

Because the Church is itself sinful and filled with sinners in need of reconciliation, Christians are part of a community that both forgives and knows forgiveness. Although our sin alienates us from God, God never ceases to love us, because God never fails to forgive us. If we forgive, we too can continue to love and not define others in terms of their offenses against us. We can live and love each other in the midst of tension and difficulty and the ebbs and flow that characterize the way we love. Forgiveness makes committed love that lasts a possibility. The sacrament of penance is the grace-filled place in the Church where we can profoundly encounter God's tender mercy and forgiveness revealed in the suffering and death of Jesus. *Confession celebrates love and forgiveness.*

NARRATIVE 2: CONFESSION FOSTERS HOLINESS

Christians are called to be holy in their daily lives, and they are called to be different. More is and should be expected of Christians, because they have experienced the grace of believing in Christ and participating in the life of the Church. Since people are persuaded more by deeds than by words, one of the most evangelical things any Christian can do is to lead a holy life. The deeds of a Christian are similar to what John the Evangelist calls signs. Consistent good deeds pose the question to the nonbeliever or the tepid believer, "What makes this person so good and impressive?"

Being a Christian means primarily believing in Jesus Christ and being part of a community of believers who worship together, evangelize together, and demonstrate Christ's love for all people in some appropriate way. The primary emphasis is on community, but the holiness of the Christian community also depends on individual responses to the graces offered by Christ. In a mosaic, careful attention is paid in choosing the shape and color of each individual tile that will be used. Yet the message and beauty of the mosaic emerges only when a myriad of such tiles come together in a carefully and harmoniously arranged display. Each tile is beautiful, but even greater beauty and meaning unfold when the tiles are joined. The same can be said for Christianity. What is arrestingly beautiful and appealing about Christianity is the faith and love of the community as a whole, but it can only be such a stirring community if individual Christians are themselves committed to holiness, repentance, and outreach.

The sexual abuse scandal in the American Catholic Church has been widely covered in the media, as have various instances of financial malfeasance by parish staffs. While only a small percentage of people have been involved in such activities, the media coverage suggests the result has been a falling from grace of the entire Catholic Church. In framing the issue this way, the media pay the Church a compliment and provide some unwitting theological nuance. Their unwritten assumption in these types of reports is that anyone involved with the Church—priest, bishop, or layperson—should adhere to a higher standard and their failing to do so would damage the whole Church. The media are correct that each person who proclaims the faith should be changed by it in ways that make our lives a witness to what we say we believe. The reporting also underscores how important each person is in the Church and how the Church suffers when members sin. The concept of the Mystical Body of Christ is one way that the Church has traditionally taught what the media reports suggest.

Another way to make the point is to go back to the idea of the mosaic. If the Church is thought of as a complex mosaic involving millions of members who operate much like colorful tiles, the importance of each member is evident. In this ecclesial mosaic, if some member-tiles are damaged by, say, the sins of sexual abuse and fraud, the whole ecclesial-mosaic is impacted. If there are enough damaged member-tiles or if they are prominently located, the whole message of the ecclesial-mosaic becomes distorted. The Christian faith is defined in the world much more by practice than theory or dogma, and when the practice is distorted, damaged, or untrue, the entire Church suffers.

In the fall of 2006, six young Amish girls in Pennsylvania were shot and killed by a disturbed parent in the community, who then killed himself. The forgiveness and love of the Amish, and the loving, peaceful way in which they lived through this devastating event, shone through the media coverage of the tragedy. The horses and buggies, the men's and women's attire, and their plain way of talking were part of the background. In the foreground were their faith, simplicity, forgiveness, and kindness. These qualities elicited words of praise for the Amish from many thoroughly modern Americans, as well as for their compelling faith in Christ and their communal way of life. In the midst of devastating tragedy, the actions and reactions of these Amish men and women gave witness for all the world to see that their faith had indeed transformed their lives. And it was enormously attractive and persuasive. In the same way, if Catholics want to restore the beauty and attractiveness of the Church in the wake of devastating scandal, they can only hope to do so by living equally exemplary lives. Because we confront our sins in confession and seek forgiveness from God through the Church, *confession fosters holiness.*

NORMS

The Church expects Catholics who have committed a serious sin to receive the sacrament of reconciliation at least once a year. In establishing its penitential norms, the Church is responding to a great need we have as human beings to be released from the burden of sin—which distorts our relationship with God, ourselves, and others—and to be reunited with the whole

Church community. Sin is the subject of confession. However, until we are clear about how the Church understands sin, we are not in a position to fully appreciate or effectively participate in the sacrament of reconciliation. With that in mind, a discussion of sin precedes a further exploration of norms that structure the experience of reconciliation for Catholics.

SIN

Sin is a "dreadful, tragic mystery" that confounds even the saints.[4] Struggling to understand the power of sin in his own life, St. Paul gave words to what haunts us: "I do not understand my own actions. For I do not do what I want, but I do the very thing I hate" (Rom. 7:15).

All human beings experience evil and failure in their lives, but few would call it sin. The whole idea of sin is largely out of fashion these days. Even in Catholic parishes, sin as a reality to be confronted is usually not given much attention. However, sin is central to the Catholic understanding of human experience and redemption in Jesus Christ, and fashionable or not, it is an important and useful framework to give to parishioners. The simple fact of the matter is that people sin, and sin is the subject of the sacrament of reconciliation or confession. If parishes hope to encourage greater participation in the sacrament of penance, they will have to spend time explaining the Church's teaching on sin, in ways that correspond to people's experience of themselves and others.

Sin disrupts and distorts our relationships with God, with others, and with ourselves. Human beings want to live virtuous lives that deepen our relationships with God and with our neighbors, the world, and ourselves, and yet we get sidetracked and engage in behaviors that absolutely derail achievement of what we most desire. We sin and fail, and then, for reasons hard to identify, we have difficulty admitting to ourselves that we have sinned. Human beings are up to our ears in the "dreadful, tragic mystery" that is sin, and we share St. Paul's deep confusion about how we come so often to betray our own best interests.

Part of the very definition of what it means to be human is to be free. Freedom is a capacity we have to orient our lives with and toward God, others, and ourselves. This capacity is not unlimited as it is in God, but is mediated by our experiences, our place in time and history, our friends and family—our cultural reality—and it plays a part in shaping who we are. Limited though it might be, human freedom allows us to say yes to God or no to God.

Human beings have feelings, desires, emotions, and reason (also called understanding or intellect) that are to some degree culturally shaped.[5] All of these play a roll in the formation of moral conscience, which "is a judgment of practical reason about the moral quality of a human action [that] moves a person at the appropriate moment to do good and avoid evil."[6] Human feelings, desires, emotions, and intellect (including practical reason) often compete with one another in making claims on the will, which is the faculty human beings have that decides which action to select among an array of possibilities. Virtuous people accomplish moral good, and they do so because they align their wills with the judgment of their consciences. When their conscience says something is wrong, virtuous people avoid it. When their conscience says something must be done, such as feeding a starving person, virtuous people act to do so. Virtuous people are not perfectly virtuous, however, and even they sometimes act contrary to their consciences. Free action that is contrary to conscience is what we mean by sin.

Ideally, we take note of our feelings, desires, and emotions, and then pay careful attention to the judgment made by the intellect about which actions are acceptable, which actions morally ought to be undertaken, and which actions must always be avoided. The will resolves any conflicts between the intellect, on the one hand, and the feelings, emotions, and desires, on the other. Emotions, desires, and feelings arise within us. For the most part, we do not control when they arise, though once they appear, we do determine the extent to which we attend to them. We can, for instance, choose to distract ourselves from our emotions and redirect our focus, thereby paying little attention to what our emotions, desires, or feelings suggest.

Emotions, feelings, and desires are affective elements that operate within all of us and often, unbidden, get our attention and motivate us. As wonderful as they are, however, they are difficult to manage, constantly competing, looming large one moment and fading the next. Because these elements are so unruly, taken alone, they do not serve us well as a guide to behavior. Reason is the balancing faculty that allows us to evaluate and interpret what we experience affectively.

Desires are part of this unruly package, but they are more complicated than emotions and feelings. Desires may be elemental, in the sense they proceed from or are directly linked to an emotion or feeling. They can also be complex rather than simple. Complex desires are linked to plans of action, which should always be subject to review by reason. For example, at any given time, people may desire ice cream, comfort, or sexual activity, each of which, as an elemental desire, is neither good nor bad. However, if those desires motivate a particular plan to maybe steal ice cream, to seek comfort by missing Sunday Mass, or to have sex with another's spouse, the desire is bad because it is linked with a plan to do something wrong. Each complex desire we have has to be interpreted and evaluated by reason because it involves a plan of action. Consequently, for the purposes of this book, we consider complex desires as engaged in reasoning. When we refer to simple desires, apart from any plan, we will be pointing to an undeveloped wish or yearning proceeding directly from an emotion or feeling.

With these elements in place, it is possible now to discuss how sin occurs and how it can be avoided. First, however, it will be helpful to simplify terminology by combining three things—emotions, elemental desires, and feelings. For simplicity we use the term "sentiment" to refer to the confusion of feelings, emotions, and elemental desires that we all experience. The words "reason" and "intellect" are often used interchangeably. Judgment is an action of reason or the intellect. Practical reason is part of the intellect or general reason and refers to decisions of the intellect with respect to actions to be performed. It is contrasted with speculative or theoretical reason, which sorts out arguments or approaches concerning general positions or claims.[7] In referring to actions, "practical reason" is the term we will use.

Sentiment deserves our careful attention because it is one of the means God uses to communicate with us. However, as we noted earlier, sentiment alone is an insufficient basis for action. Our actions have to be balanced and reviewed by practical reason, which makes an evaluation whether they are morally acceptable or not. If practical reason judges that actions are not morally acceptable, the will should turn away from them and they should not be performed. Practical reason considers whether actions are good or bad. If, on the other hand, actions are deemed acceptable, the will is under no moral constraint and can choose how to proceed. In this latter case, the will can either favor sentiment or practical reason. Favoring sentiment, which sometimes merely reflects a passing whim, may result in actions that, while morally acceptable, do not further a person's own best interests.

Most of us have made hundreds of decisions to act in accord with sentiment and against a practically reasoned understanding that our action was not morally permissible. In doing so, we sinned. Committing "a sin" refers to a particular act, and the sin may either be a lesser offense or a serious offense.

The Church teaches that we can commit a serious sin only if the three following conditions are fulfilled: the action being considered must be seriously wrong, we must know it is seriously wrong, and we must freely choose to perform the action. In the traditional language of the Church, these three conditions are known as grave matter, full knowledge, and complete consent.[8] Stealing $100 from a person is a serious violation of the commandment against stealing. If a person understands stealing $100 is seriously wrong and still freely steals the money, absent any external compulsion, the person commits a serious or mortal sin. If one or more of the three conditions is not fulfilled but the action is still wrong, it is called a lesser or venial sin.

This approach to sin generally follows the classical Catholic framework worked out by philosophers and theologians over many centuries, and it is also the one used implicitly by many modern Catholic parents and educators. Consider, for example, how parents might approach children who have done something dangerous. The first words of a typical parent, often uttered in an anguished tone, are, "What were you thinking?" From that first utterance, parents are reminding and trying to teach their children to think before they act, to apply reason as a balance to the pull of sentiment. In order to be safe and sound, children have to put proposed actions in a larger context. When children go into the street after a runaway ball, they are responding to sentiment. Only when they do so after making sure there are no cars coming is their action reasonable.

When parents admonish their children for doing something morally wrong, their tone and message are different. Parents remind the children in disappointed and dismayed tones that they did something even though they knew it was wrong. The parents emphasize the disjoint between what the children knew—the act was wrong—and their decision, made by the will, to disregard their true judgment and go ahead and do what they knew they shouldn't do. If for instance a child steals some candy when no one is looking and hides it under a coat or in a backpack, the parent will make a point of stressing that the child knew before doing it that taking the candy was wrong and yet went ahead. In doing so, the parent in his or her own way is telling the child to align will with reason or intellect and not to be swept away by sentiment.

In making decisions about what to do or not do, human beings are supposed to manage their wills so that, at least in moral matters, they follow the judgment of practical reason. We often find ourselves in situations where sentiment urges us in one direction and our practical reason clearly indicates that doing so is wrong. In these circumstances, practical reason and sentiment are in conflict—one urging action and the other restraint—and we feel torn. It is our will that operates as the final arbiter in these tumultuous conflicts. If the decision of the will follows sentiment when reason judges an act immoral, we sin.

An example taken from a typical collegiate experience illustrates the point. Consider a college student who finds himself alone with a young woman in her room in the wee hours of the morning. They have spent the evening together seeing a movie and then getting a few beers in a local bar, and they are "mellow" not "tipsy." At this point, sentiment is strong for the young man to have a sexual encounter with the young woman, but his well-trained reason judges, we assume, that to do so would be morally wrong. What happens next—whether sentiment or reason "wills out"—is determined by an act of the young man's will.

Now, when many young people find themselves in these circumstances, their reasoned judgment is clear but not as compelling as the very strong press of sentiment they are experiencing, and they opt for sexual intimacy. If they do so, in the eyes of the Church they have committed a serious sin. More formally expressed, the three conditions required for serious sin are:

(1) grave matter, (2) full knowledge, and (3) complete consent. In the scenario under consideration, sexual intimacy outside of marriage is seriously wrong; thus the condition for grave matter (1) is fulfilled. We presume the young people are educated Catholics and have full knowledge that sexual intimacy outside of marriage is seriously wrong (2). Finally, while knowing that going up to her room would make it far more difficult to resist a more intimate encounter, they freely decided to do so and eventually become sexually intimate. Condition (3) was fulfilled.

The young man in the room with the young woman is, to be sure, in a very difficult situation. Sentiment is pushing strongly toward sex and yet, if he was raised Catholic, practical reason dictates the action is not permissible. Reason might have stood a better chance in this encounter if it took place at the front door and not in the young woman's room. This is precisely why the Church warns young and old alike of the danger of what it terms "the near occasions of sin." Some circumstances simply weight the odds too heavily in favor of sentiment over reason. Those types of situations are dangerous to our well-being and best interests, and we should avoid putting ourselves in them. That is especially true for younger people whose wills are not sufficiently developed. Parents are well aware of all this and make sincere efforts to keep their children away from people or situations in which they know sentiment is intense, reason easily overwhelmed, and responsible adults are not present to run interference.

All adults mature in different ways, and we all gradually understand weaknesses in the way we confront various realities or situations. Previous occasions in which we yielded to sin give us the experience to realize what kinds of situations put our reason at severe disadvantage to sentiment and thus put our will to the test. Wisdom and maturity help us to recognize and avoid these personal near occasions of sin.

A great gift that we have as Catholics is that we know we are not alone and on our own as we struggle with sin. In the Church, we have the opportunity to reconcile ourselves with Christ and the whole Church through the sacrament of reconciliation. When we do, we are relieved of the burden of guilt and can leave the sins of our past behind us. This means we can look with hope to the future as we make every attempt to make better decisions in our lives. As part of the Church, we can also rely on Christ's presence in the Eucharist as a source of strength, as well as on the support, witness, and wisdom of other members of our parish communities who themselves struggle to avoid sin and live lives of holiness.

As unpopular as Church teaching on sin is in some circles, it is a very realistic portrayal of how people end up, as St. Paul says, not doing what they want, but instead doing what they hate. Even the most virtuous people are at times swayed by their emotions, feelings, and desires and convince themselves, against their practical reason (better judgment), to do the wrong thing because it seems so appealing. Human beings are called by God to goodness both in the long term and in the short term. Many Christians readily acknowledge the validity of the long-term calling and yet succumb to sin in the short term. In that process, we wound ourselves, harm others, and act contrary to our own calling as children of God.

CHILDREN AND RECONCILIATION NORMS

Most Catholics experience the sacrament of reconciliation for the first time as children, just before first Eucharist. Preparing children for the reception of the sacrament is delicate. Clearly seven- and eight-year-old children are not capable of committing serious sin that alienates them from God and the Church. On the other hand, even at this young age, children know they do things that are wrong. They also realize they should forgive others, even though it can be hard. Although they would not express it this way, children wrestle with understanding moral evil in themselves and others, and it is important for adults to help them in this process. Encouraging and assisting children in acknowledging their own failings, in becoming more willing to make efforts to do better, and in understanding the importance of seeking God's forgiveness and forgiving others who hurt them will help children to grow and mature spiritually.

As they approach the sacrament of penance, children need help figuring out what they should confess, and their parents are among the people who will give them the best advice. Unless parents are clear about rights and wrongs and communicate the information wisely in ways that do not burden the young with unnecessary guilt and shame, children will be confused. Parents will sometimes let their children know when they do something wrong that they should tell the priest about it the next time they go to confession. If the children are unkind or disrespectful, or are involved in any of a number of other lapses, they are reminded that the behavior is material for confession. Telling children they should confess this sin helps them understand what things are really wrong. Actually confessing these lapses during the sacrament of reconciliation underscores that they must also make a commitment to do better in the future. By encouraging children to confess these lapses, parents help them develop patterns of behavior that are more loving and honest and virtuous. This in turn helps children avoid more serious lapses as they grow older.

With respect to their children's wrongdoing, parents have a "correctional role." Sometimes it is difficult for parents to decide how authoritative and particular they should be with their children in handling lapses and infractions of family rules. A helpful comparison is with community action policing, an approach which has been used very successfully in urban areas. Community action policing creates an environment supportive of positive civic life by setting strict limits around small infractions. This same focus on details can be helpful for children. Many children are motivated to more virtuous ways by clarifying how their relatively innocent behaviors can be hurtful and should be brought to the sacrament of reconciliation. It is, of course, unhealthy to force young children to confess and see themselves as grave sinners. It is helpful, however, for them to develop a clearer sense of right and wrong, to understand how their behavior impacts others, and to want to love God more fully. Providing children with indicators of what behaviors need attention is important. Hearing these suggestions from their parents who love them and forgive them and want the best for them will also help children to understand a bit better what the sacrament of reconciliation is all about—God's love, forgiveness, and desire for our happiness.

In earlier days, penitents were expected not only to confess their sins but also to indicate how many times they had committed each of them. For many reasons, most people receiving the sacrament of reconciliation in our day do not innumerate their sins. For one thing, most people who go to confession only do so once or twice a year. If they were to include the number of times they committed each of their sins as part of their confession, they would have to do some ongoing bookkeeping to keep it straight, which is hardly likely. Requiring people to specify how often they sinned can turn penance into a numbers game that trivializes the sacrament. Avoiding all reference to numbers, however, can obscure patterns of sinful behavior that need serious attention.

In the sacrament of reconciliation, we accuse ourselves of sin and seek reconciliation with God and with the Church and promise to do all we can to sin no more. How often we sin has some bearing on our ability to be honest about our failings and to do better. The exact number of times that we got angry or drank too much or lied may not be that important, but the patterns of our sinful behaviors are. An occasional slip is one thing, and a more persistent pattern of wounding and destructive behavior is something else. Encouraging young people to think not only about what they have done wrong but also about the patterns of their behavior is important. Far from trivializing the sacrament of reconciliation, this attention to frequency will help them approach the sacrament with greater honesty and clarity.

BENEFITS AND PRACTICES

Going to confession can be emotionally painful, mainly because penitents have to confront personal faults and failures to live up to their calling as Christians. Acknowledging such failures is difficult, but it is also healthy. If we recognize our own failures, we are more likely to understand and forgive the faults of others, especially those with whom we interact regularly.

In addition to the pain of acknowledging our own sinfulness, there is the difficulty of having to admit it out loud to the priest. Protestants say it is sufficient to repent privately to God and generally to seek the forgiveness of God and the members of the Church community. The Catholic approach places the emphasis on the sinner being rehabilitated within the community, the community of saints. In order to be rehabilitated, we must admit that we have wronged the community and diminished its witness to Christ by acting contrary to the commandments and Church norms. The priest is the designated witness of the community who accepts the penitent's profession of guilt and also forgives in the name of the Church. The prayer of absolution is: "God the Father of mercies through the death and resurrection of His Son has reconciled the world to Himself and has sent the Holy Spirit among us for the forgiveness of sins. Through the ministry of the Church may God grant to you pardon and peace. And by His authority, I absolve you from all your sins, in the name of the Father, and of the Son, and of the Holy Spirit." So, reconciliation is a ministry of the Church, performed by the priest, with absolution granted to the penitent.

In order to encourage greater participation in the sacrament of reconciliation, parishes must address the obstacles that stand in the way of many Catholics. Four strategies can prove helpful in this regard:

- Set attainable goals for increasing participation.
- Alleviate confusion.
- Minimize embarrassment and maximize confidentiality.
- Increase the buzz about confession.

ATTAINABLE GOALS

Fifty years ago, many Catholics went to Holy Communion regularly and confession almost weekly, and therefore most Catholics who attended Mass regularly completed their Easter duty.[9] That is no longer the custom. However, a small group of Catholics—young and old—have returned to the custom of frequent confession, participating once every few weeks. This is laudatory, but it is highly unlikely the rest of American Catholics will follow their lead, considering most have not been to confession in years. In the present circumstances, it makes more practical sense for parishes to adopt a twofold goal to invigorate sacramental reconciliation. First, the parish will want to persuade people who are not participating in the sacrament to go to confession at least once a year, as the Church suggests. As a second goal, parishes could encourage those who do already participate in the sacrament yearly to increase participation to three times a year: once before Easter, once during the summer, and once during Advent in preparation for Christmas.

Strategy 1: Set modest and attainable goals for confession in the parish.

After setting these goals, a parish staff hoping to enrich parishioners' experience of sacramental forgiveness and reconciliation will have to address some very practical issues. For many Catholics, confusion and embarrassment undermine their willingness to go to confession. These are not insignificant obstacles, and unless they are addressed in a forthright manner, there is little hope that the sacrament of reconciliation will enjoy a participatory renaissance in the near future.

Beyond offering individual confessions, twice-yearly reconciliation services during Advent and Lent, and the celebration of first penance, there is very little buzz in most parishes about the sacrament of reconciliation. As a result, Catholics are not clear about the importance of the sacrament in terms of its spiritual benefits for individuals and for the Church.

ALLEVIATE CONFUSION

Confusion about the sacrament of reconciliation is a real obstacle to its reception. It is impossible for people to figure out what to do in this sacrament by watching others. Also, there are subtle differences in the experience from parish to parish. Catholics feel awkward about participating in the sacrament because they often do not know what they should expect or what they are supposed to do. The upshot is that rather than look foolish, some Catholics simply avoid the sacrament.

It would be truly sad if Catholics stayed away from the sacrament of reconciliation because they felt awkward or confused, especially when these obstacles are relatively easy for pastors and parish staffs to address. There are a number of approaches a parish might take in elevating the value and appeal of penance. For one thing, a parish could decide that it would spend the Lenten season focusing particularly on the sacrament of reconciliation. During those forty days, the pastor would speak directly about the sacrament and how the Church understands it. The staff could develop bulletin inserts that explain the history of the sacrament and how it has developed, as well as how it is understood and administered today. It would also be important pastorally to clearly recognize that Catholics are confused about the sacrament and often are unclear about what they should do when they go to confession.

A step-by-step explanation of what the penitent will experience in confession and what they should do needs to be provided generally to the whole parish. This should be as specific as the pastor deems appropriate. In general, if people are unfamiliar with something, they want to know how they are supposed to proceed. Making each step specific is better than providing many options. After a penitent becomes familiar with the contours of the sacrament of reconciliation, they are ready to think of options. Step-by-step directions will be most helpful when they are pointed and particular, include the fewest possible options, and are easily available to those interested in participating in the sacrament.

In reconciliation or confession, penitents go to a priest in confidence and accuse themselves of sins they have committed since the last time they went to confession. After penitents tell the priest how long it has been since their last confession and mention their sins, the priest usually gives them a few words of encouragement. The priest then assigns a penance, usually prayers the penitents are expected to say once they have left the confessional. After that, penitents express sorrow for their sins and a firm purpose of avoiding sin in the future, usually by reciting the act of contrition. After the act of contrition, the priest then says the prayer of absolution; authorized by the Church, the priest forgives their sins. Once the sins are forgiven, penitents never need mention them again. Their focus should be on avoiding these and other sins in the future. After leaving the confessional or confessional room, penitents say the prayers assigned by the priest, using the occasion to ask Jesus for strength and guidance in avoiding sin in the future.

Parishes might assume that most Catholics know this form fairly well, but many do not. Parishes might also assume that parishioners know the act of contrition. That, too, is often not the case. In earlier days, there was one generally accepted form for the act of contrition, and children were expected to memorize it. Catholics also went to confession frequently and often said the act of contrition daily. Consequently, there was little if any need to make the prayer available when confessions were being heard. Today, things are different. There is more than one form for the act of contrition, and confession is not a frequent experience for most Catholics. Also, while children might memorize the prayer before their first penance, because they seldom say it after that, it is soon forgotten. There surely are many Catholics who do know this prayer by heart, but even they might stumble over it in confession if they are feeling at all anxious. Some parishes now make sure that a card inscribed with one or more versions of the act of the contrition is available to penitents in the confessional. At the appropriate time, the penitent can read the act of contrition rather than recite it by heart. It can also make sense to have a confessional prayer book available in some designated place in the church for use after the penitent has confessed. From this booklet, the priest can ask the penitent to recite one or more of the prayers as penance.

Make sure that a copy of the act of contrition is available in the confessional, that there is a prayer book readily available which penitents can use to recite the penance, and that a simple, brief (on a card) description of the steps to be followed in the sacrament of reconciliation is widely distributed. This will serve to dissipate "performance anxiety" among those who might otherwise be reluctant to participate in the sacrament of reconciliation.

Strategy 2: Alleviate confusion.

DIMINISH EMBARRASSMENT

Although Catholics clearly understand that we are all sinners, it is difficult for most of us to admit our sins, and we feel acutely embarrassed about having to own up to them before others. When the sacramental setting for penance requires face-to-face confession, embarrassment can prove to be an insurmountable hurdle for many Catholics. There are penitents who are not at all bothered by face-to-face reconciliation, during which they sit in a room across from the priest. In fact, some Catholics prefer it. However, many other actual and would-be penitents would prefer to be anonymous, confessing their sins behind a screen and to a confessor who does not know them. In our judgment, embarrassment is a significant factor limiting the number of Catholics who frequently avail themselves of the grace available through the sacrament of reconciliation.

Small and dark confessionals that were used before Vatican II frightened some Catholics, and there were good pastoral reasons to provide a less intimidating venue. Fear is not an association most people have with confession these days, but embarrassment surely is. Once again, pastoral sensitivity suggests some accommodation should be made in this case that respects the desire for anonymity. All priests today are encouraged to get to know their parishioners personally. One simple manifestation of this personalism is the common practice of priests greeting and talking with parishioners outside the church after Mass, which is a good practice. However, closer association with parishioners can also make it more difficult for parishioners to confess their sins to a priest who will recognize their voice. With fewer priests and many smaller parishes, it takes real effort to provide Catholics with an opportunity for anonymous confession.

Priests candidly tell parishioners that they do not hold in their minds what people tell them in confession, and that whatever is confessed does not diminish the priest's esteem for penitents should he recognize them. But this is a hard sell to parishioners, and it has probably ever been thus. Those of us who went to confession as children fifty years ago can easily recall our relief when some visiting priest we did not know was hearing confessions on a Saturday afternoon. If there was a choice and we knew which priest was which, we always went to the one who would have difficulty identifying us. It was even better when we had the opportunity to confess to a priest who did not understand English well or who was known to be a pure listener. "Listening priests" neither chided you in confession nor made recommendations. They would simply listen to your sins, make no comments, and then give you a penance. The reputation of such confessors spread, and while we all felt a little guilty because this type of confession was so easy, we also felt lucky and blessedly relieved when we could confess to these priests.

Modern parishes facing "anonymity challenges" can take some straightforward measures to make penance easier on the penitents. Priests in the same geographical area can agree to trade places one or more times a month and publicize this fact in their parish bulletins. In this way, parishioners have the option of receiving the sacrament of reconciliation from a priest not stationed in their own parish. Many parishes sponsor reconciliation services at which many priests are invited to hear confessions. In such instances, the organizer should make sure that enough priests hear confessions in circumstances where the penitents will not be seen by the priest.

Strategy 3: Minimize embarrassment and maximize confidentiality.

CREATING A BUZZ

We have already suggested a number of ways for parishes to reinforce the importance of regular participation in the sacrament of reconciliation. The fourth strategy emphasizes the importance of special opportunities for reconciliation.

Making sure there is a priest or two to hear confessions immediately before Mass on Saturday evening or Sunday does increase the frequency with which people avail themselves of the sacrament. It used to be that people could easily make themselves available on a Saturday afternoon to go to the parish church and confess their sins. That is no longer the case at a time when both children and adults are madly in motion most Saturdays. Yes, they could arrange their schedules to get to church for confession, but they do not. On the other hand, they are willing to come to Sunday Mass ten minutes early to fit in a confession. Alert pastors should arrange to satisfy the desire to confess at this time if there are sufficient parishioners who would go before Mass but would not come for reconciliation during the normal period of time on Saturday afternoon.

Many parishes have a single pastor and no parochial vicars, and it would be difficult for the pastor to be available for confession immediately before Sunday Mass. However, it might be possible a few times a year to invite a guest priest to hear confessions before and after Mass. This might be done on some specially designated Sundays in Advent, Lent, and summer. The fact that a visiting priest will be available to hear confessions before and after Saturday evening and Sunday Masses should be well advertised in the parish bulletin and from the pulpit long before the priest arrives. If, for example, a visiting priest could come during Lent, the director of religious education for the parish might create an opportunity for most children in the religious education program to go to confession on Saturday afternoon. For children, it is always easier to go to confession if many other children are also going.

Some parishes have created a big buzz by sponsoring and advertising a special intense time interval during when many priests from outside the parish are available for confession. These twenty-four-hour grace initiatives or similar programs can be very effective in drawing people back to confession. *Strategy 4: Increase the buzz about confession.*

BUILDING A RELATIONSHIP WITH CHRIST

Christians are called to holiness and a loving relationship with God in Christ. Our relationship with Christ is grounded in our baptismal calling and fostered regularly through participation in the Eucharist, where we hear the Word of God, participate again in the sacrifice of Calvary, and receive Christ in Communion. This chapter acknowledges the realism of sin as well as the call of all Christians to be saints, to be holy. Our relationships cannot exist for long or progress if we are unwilling to admit when we hurt or offend the ones we love. Nor will they survive if our loved ones are unwilling to forgive us. Reconciliation, therefore, is a necessary component of any truthful, expanding relationship, and it is integral to our relationship with Christ. In the sacrament of penance, we experience and celebrate God's love and forgiveness revealed in the life, death, and resurrection of Jesus Christ. After being reconciled in confession, we are able once again to resume our lives in the world and to seek a deeper relationship with Christ in the Church. The next chapter examines how we understand God's action in our world. It also explores the personal steps the Church recommends we take to make sure that Christ remains ever at the center of our daily lives.

NOTES

1. Richard P. McBrien, *Catholicism* (New York: HarperCollins, 1994), 836.

2. See Gerard Fourez, *Sacraments and Passages: Celebration the Tensions of Modern Life* (Notre Dame, Ind.: Ave Maria Press, 1981), 97–115, for a discussion of the sacrament of reconciliation from the perspective of human development.

3. John Gray, *Men Are from Mars, Women Are from Venus* (New York: HarperCollins, 1992).

4. James T. Bretzke, *A Morally Complex World: Engaging Contemporary Moral Theology* (Collegeville, Minn.: Liturgical Press, 2004), 191.

5. Reason is also called understanding or intellect. Reason is to be understood as the process of analyzing how the various aspects of a situation or question interact. Because it is to be understood in a comprehensive way, reasoning includes memory, since memory is needed to incorporate relevant facts or principles for an adequate analysis of the issues.

6. See Holy See, *Catechism of the Catholic Church* (Vatican City: Libreria Editrice Vaticana, 2000 [1997]), 438 and 872.

7. See John Finnis, *Aquinas: Moral, Political, and Legal Theory* (New York: Oxford University Press, 1998), 20–22, 40–42.

8. See Holy See, *Catechism of the Catholic Church*, 455.

9. Easter duty is the requirement to receive Holy Communion at least once a year, during the Easter season. The Easter season extends from the first Sunday of Lent until Trinity Sunday, which is the first Sunday after Pentecost. In order to receive Communion, one must be free of mortal sin. Furthermore, according to Church law (canon 989), a Catholic "is obliged to confess faithfully his or her grave sins at least once a year." Assuming a person has committed one or more grave sins, he or she must confess these sins within a year. Because the sins must be confessed before receiving Communion and because another canon (988) recommends that the faithful confess venial sins, the pastoral assumption is that one will go to confession and receive Holy Communion during the Easter season. See the discussion of canons 920, 988, and 989 of Church law in *New Commentary on the Code of Canon Law*, ed. John P. Beal, James A. Corriden, and Thomas J. Green (New York: Paulist Press, 2000), 1114 and 1169–1172.

7

Divine Intervention and Prayer

Christians understand that God created us out of love and for love, and that God calls all of us to holiness. The general path to holiness consists in loving God with our whole heart and soul and mind and loving our neighbor as ourselves throughout our lives. God's invitation and grace to reach beyond ourselves to the transcendent always situates us with our fellow human beings in loving community. How we love God and how we love our neighbor, however, depends to a large extent on how we understand our position in the world. For Christians, the critical and saving event is the coming together of humanity and divinity in Jesus Christ. Jesus Christ is God's climactic and ultimate self-communication. He came to save us by revealing God's persistent and lasting love for us. Through His life, death on the cross, and resurrection, Jesus Christ reconciles the world to God. In the victory of love over death that is the resurrection, Jesus pledges eternal life to all those who follow Him. Handed on to us from the apostles by the Church, this message of salvation is our inheritance as Catholic Christians. As recipients of the faith, we are responsible for doing our part to nurture the message and carefully and faithfully pass it on.

God has invited us into an intimate relationship with the divine; prayer is both the language of that relationship and our regular pathway to holiness. In prayer, we are in conversation with the God who created us, who became one with us in Jesus Christ, and who is with us still. In prayer, we assent to our heritage of faith, hope, and love and come to terms with our actual situation before God. Prayer is profoundly important to Christian faith and to the Church. The previous three chapters focused on sacramental prayer. Chapters 4 and 5 addressed the central prayer of the Church—the

111

Eucharist. Chapter 6 explored the sacrament of reconciliation. This chapter looks at prayer in its other communal and private forms and the crucial role parishes play in cultivating, supporting, and encouraging a richer prayer life in the Church.

There is an unfortunate trend toward less frequent and less consistent prayer among Catholics. It is fueled at least in part by the increasing trust some Catholics have that science can provide all we need to know about ourselves and our world. By uncritically accepting the "scientific story," in which all events happen either by chance or conform to unbreakable laws of nature, and by clinging to it as the whole story, Catholics leave little room for God's providence. In doing so, they fundamentally question the need or usefulness of any private prayer. Parishes need to address this trend, and by using the strategic formula of effective narratives, norms, benefits, and practices, they can encourage richer habits of prayer.

NARRATIVES FOR WHY WE PRAY

Cherishing prayer and developing and sustaining habits of prayer are difficult for Christians in modern America. We are confronted daily with a knowledge explosion that seems to demystify human experience. We live at a frantic pace. We are immersed in a corporate, media, and entertainment culture whose radical individualist ethic undermines connections and community. Is it any wonder, then, that it is difficult for us to get around to praying? The rhythms of Catholic life that once encouraged and supported morning and night prayers, grace before and after meals, praying the Angelus, and daily recitation of the rosary are gone. They have simply disappeared in an avalanche of new demands and activities that make prayer seem at best a luxury we can seldom afford, and at worst a quaint custom we have simply outgrown.

What we as Catholic Christians know about ourselves and our God is our story. This story is foundational to why we pray. In every age, we tell this story again, but in order for the retelling to capture hearts and minds, it must attend adequately to the challenges of the times. We live at a point in history when people increasingly believe that scientific discoveries and knowledge are incompatible with faith and the concept of a creator-God. We also live at a time when the notion of committed love that moves individuals beyond themselves to something transcendent seems more myth than model. The story we tell in this generation to capture what we know about ourselves, and the little we know as finite creatures about the infinite God, will influence whether and how we pray. Consequently, Christians interested in prayer must find narratives that persuasively contend with these very real issues.

NARRATIVE 1: SCIENCE HAS LIMITS

Science simply cannot tell us all there is to know about human experience. Many people who consider themselves modern see no point in praying. They think everything is determined either by chance or by the laws of nature—the "scientific story." Believers in Christ who accept the "scientific story" as helpful see God's activity in this world as constrained. Exactly how constrained God chooses to be has to be figured out by His creatures, who have to determine how the world works. Perhaps the biggest stumbling block for modern Christians who view God in this distant way is evolution, which many view as an important component of the laws of nature.

Evolution is an explanation of how various genera and species came to be on earth. As a scientific explanation, evolution relies on empirically verifiable statements or on logically valid theoretical links between statements that are empirically verifiable. Four claims ground the modern theory of evolution. First, living things are determined by their DNA, which changes in small steps over time. Random, unpredictable changes occur very occasionally when the DNA is transmitted from one organism to its offspring. These changes may be advantageous or detrimental to survival. In the absence of a DNA change or mutation, the offspring is similar to the parent in the way it looks, functions, and acts. Second, those animals or life forms which are better adjusted to their environment produce more offspring, passing on to them DNA that works well in a given environment. Third, various life forms have developed over hundreds of millions of years. Unless long periods of time are involved, it is unlikely that, for example, animals such as apes or human beings could have evolved from aquatic life. Fourth, all events adhere to the laws of nature. Random changes or events occur because many "natural events" can turn out in a variety of different ways. That is, the laws of nature in many cases do not specify only one possible outcome.

The "scientific story" is that all events in creation can be adequately explained by four central assumptions: random changes in DNA, increased successful transmission of DNA more suitable to its environment, long periods of time, and universal validity of the laws of nature. These four fundamental claims, developed by modern science and assumed to be true, are able to explain how many of the animals we know developed over time. They also explain how other species that once existed were unable to successfully pass on their DNA to a large enough number of successors. Being able to explain such developments from these four fundamental claims is an admirable accomplishment, and most people rightly accord much trust to the basic methods of science. Although many things in evolution are not currently understood, it is likely that, as scientists continue to explore and develop the theory of evolution over time, they will successfully address many of these scientific gaps.

Despite providing explanations for many phenomena in the development of life on earth, there are of course many things, including empirical processes, science does not explain. At this point, for example, science does not claim to know how the first living cell came into existence. The first double helix of DNA simply remains unexplained. There are some tentative explanations for the beginning of life, but they are contested by various scientists. More fundamentally, in the scientific community, there is no universally accepted explanation for why the big bang or explosion of energy happened.[1] Scientists focus their efforts on the consequences of the big bang, not on the person or events that caused it.

When doing science, scientists are supposed to stick to verifiable claims or data. Therefore, they should not offer advice about how organisms ought to behave or whether human beings have genuine moral obligations. All true moral issues are outside the realm of science, as are human phenomena which cannot be empirically verified. As a result, there are many phenomena of great import to ordinary people that scientists do not currently explain. Nor, by adhering to their very demanding empirical method, will they be able to explain them in the future. That each human being has a free will and can freely choose whether or not to love another person, these things science neither affirms nor explains. And yet, despite the fact it is not possible to prove empirically now or ever that free will and love exist, Christians know they are real and have real consequences. Science does not really offer an explanation for why one person loves another person. Science does not explain whether a person should be commended for bravery. Science also relies on people telling the truth. But aside from pragmatic reasons, science offers no explanation for why they should. Science does not explain or acknowledge that a person who seriously and intentionally harms another person has done something wrong which makes him less of a person. It does not explain that a person who pours herself out in loving a spouse, parent, or child in great need of assistance is doing something admirable, whether or not her example is followed by others. Nor does science have a foundation for commending or condemning anyone for believing in God. Individual scientists may well be people of deep Christian faith, but science as science simply does not acknowledge revelation, love, valor, commitment, truth (outside of empirically verifiable truths), beauty, family loyalty, or kindness. An infinite God who can only be known by analogy and revelation is simply of no interest to science.[2] Finally, science can speak about global warming, but it has no scientific basis for encouraging this generation to spend money to diminish it. Similarly, it has no moral basis for promoting embryonic stem cell research. Science simply has no expertise in morals and, in its clearer moments, makes no claim to such expertise.

Perhaps fifty or a hundred years or more from now, scientists will be able to identify some chemical processes or changes in neurons in the brain associated with bravery, love, selflessness, and human evil. However, by reason of their scientific method, they will set aside the issue of whether these qualities are good. Aside from relying on practical considerations which need not apply to a particular individual, science will never be able to recognize human evil or claim that it is wrong and should be avoided. Similarly, they have no scientific basis for claiming that human goodness should be sought or that we should be kind to one another. Individual scientists who are personally convinced of the importance of love, kindness, or bravery, for example, must find their justification for these realities outside of science.

As central to our society and as significant and successful as science is, we must remind ourselves that much that is important in life cannot be explained by the "scientific story." Even if science eventually offers a partial explanation for realities currently outside the scope of science, it will be less than satisfactory for most people. Consider the reality of falling in love and suppose science has evolved so that it has an empirical "explanation" of falling in love. This explanation might track the important chemical changes in the brain involved in attraction and falling in love. These changes could be tracked and explained from the first day a person falls in love until, say, six months later, and the scientific data could be made available to interested people. But who, apart from scientists interested in this area, would look to such accounts as compelling ways to capture the essence of the experience? Who would want to rely on them for learning about love? When it comes to falling in love, art, novels, plays, poetry, movies, or songs are far more riveting than biological treatises. People want to be able to relate to what a person in love is thinking and feeling. Science will prove a poor guide for finding what they seek.

Science can tell us about the biological and chemical status of those in love, but science cannot tell people whether they actually love someone. Nor can it offer much of value about if or how they should love them. Similarly, science may identify biological and chemical components or reactions associated with bravery or self-sacrifice, but these are observations, not explanations. According to the Catholic philosophical tradition, grace builds on nature. Specifically, because human beings who experience themselves bodily also have spiritual longings and feelings, spiritual "events" in human beings will be accompanied by some physical or neurological movements. Similarly, there are likely to be physical changes associated with strong human feelings. But such associations tell us nothing about what we should do with these feelings or whether there are ways to manage them.

For committed Christians, what the "scientific story" puts forth in the theory of evolution is not so much wrong as in need of expansion. That is because Christians have a fuller conception of the place of human beings in the universe than does science. This appreciation is fueled to some extent by reason freed from the scientific constraint of only empirically verifiable explanations and in part by divine revelation contained in Scripture. As a result of these insights, Christians can accept contingency in nature. For Christians, contingent events should not be problematic, since God Himself makes His plan contingent on our decisions.

The "scientific story" offers a very limited view of reality and is of bounded application when considering the full breadth of human experience. Furthermore, when it comes to institutions and religion that involve human commitments, science has nothing to say. While they may not believe in God, scientists cannot base their convictions on science. The "scientific story" assumes God does not exist; it does not prove it.

Christians believe there is order in the universe and that order exists because of God's creative and sustaining acts. In other words, God acted to create in the beginning of time and has not ceased to support creation and help develop it. Order is evident in the movement of creation toward higher and higher levels of being that culminate in human beings who are part of the created order but also unique in it—they are the only creatures in nature who know that they know. Order is also evident in the way creation conforms to natural laws that are discoverable through human reason.

It is reasonable for scientists to assume that changes in DNA happen randomly over time. This means, of course, that for scientists as scientists, evolution has no direction. By the assumption of pure random variation, scientifically interpreted evolution does not result in escalating order over time or in an upward spiral in the creatures resulting from evolution. In fact, science has no way to decide whether one type of animal ranks over another type of animal. As far as evolutionary scientists are concerned, some organisms are more complex than others, but they do not have a higher significance or rank. This means that, although men and women have intelligence, in terms of the "scientific story" they are no more significant or important than any other animal. For scientists, human beings may be better able to survive than other animals, but that means nothing in terms of either their intrinsic value or significance. Intelligence may give human animals a favorable niche in the universe, but it implies nothing about their rank in the creative order. For evolutionary science, aside from indicating the temporal emergence of genus and species and noting how long they survive or survived in the soup of life, specific genera or species have no rank. Because science does not have to explain this type of order in the universe, it can assume a purely random process with no drift. Evolutionary theorists, however, should not go beyond their empirical methods to claim there can be no direction to random changes in DNA interacting with the environment. This is a philosophical claim which Christians challenge.[3] According to a Catholic understanding, mutations in DNA may well be largely random, but the random process of mutations has both a director and a direction. The director is God and the direction is upward, toward the appearance of man and woman. Christians believe men and women are the culmination of creation, who are made in the image and likeness of God. An approprately modified Christian evolutionary view requires stronger assumptions than those made in the scientific story.

Christians believe creation is revelatory of God. It displays order, beauty, complexity, and grandeur, and all these reflect and point to the God who made the universe. People sometimes interpret the laws of nature as an alternative to God's action or as somehow opposed to it. According to the Christian interpretation, however, the normal way in which God acts in the world is through the very laws of nature that God Himself set in place. This belief does raise difficult issues, since some things in nature bring bad consequences to human beings: disease, hurricanes, earthquakes, volcanoes, and much more. Nonetheless, God has also given human beings the capacity to make use of the laws of nature to protect themselves from the threatening aspects of nature, which are integral parts of God's creation.

God sustains and supports the created world primarily through the ways in which the world works. What scientists call the laws of nature are, according to a Christian understanding, God's modus operandi, or the normal way in which God shows care and concern for creation. As Christians, however, we believe God retains direct sovereignty over the world, and we believe that God can and does, on occasion, set aside one or more laws of nature to achieve a particular goal. In other words, we believe that God communicates Himself to us not only though natural laws but also through miracles. Simply put, when it comes to explaining human experience, *science has limits*.

NARRATIVE 2: PRAYER HELPS CULTIVATE LASTING LOVE

It is impossible to read the newspapers, watch TV, go to the movies, read a book, or see a Broadway play today without confronting the fragility of human relationships. Daily we read about escalating divorce rates, patterns of hooking up, abandoned children, the desperately poor around the world, and neglected older people in America. In a society that frequently champions the rights of the individual alone and the importance of unfettered independence, the idea that enduring love relationships between human beings are and should be the norm can be difficult to accept.

Christians believe, however, that we are made in God's image and likeness—the culmination of God's creation. God is Love and God made us for love. Pope Benedict XVI describes what this means in his first encyclical letter, *Deus Caritas Est*. The God of Scripture is, as Benedict points out, the ultimate source of being and the universal principle of creation. At the same time, God is "a lover with all the passion of a true love." In Jesus Christ, God's love for humanity takes on dramatic form and finds its culmination in His death on the Cross, where He gives Himself to save those He loves.

Human beings experience God's love in their creation. We were made in God's image and for love. Although we desire to love and be loved, from a young age we come to understand that loving others can be difficult. We see the world most clearly in terms of our own interests, and often we cannot get easily beyond them. Children love their parents, but still they disobey them simply because in their young body-spirit selves they are intent on doing what they want to do. And while we hope that in time childhood selfishness will gradually give way to a more generous spirit, there is no guarantee it will be replaced by an ability to love deeply and well. Unfortunately, we humans are prone to narcissism. Therefore, loving consistently and broadly throughout our lives is a struggle. The good news is that the great majority of people continue the struggle to love well.

The previous chapter explored the interaction between sentiment, intellect, and will. Because we have free will, we occupy a privileged place in creation. We are also affective creatures whose feelings, desires, and emotions express our lived relationships with others, including God.

Sentiment disorients and reorients us in ways that can shake the ground of finitude and provide glimpses of the divine. These affective aspects of our nature—wonderful as they are—are not always easy to identify or control. Our feelings and desires can lead us to true love, but they also can get mired in an overly romantic emotionalism that proves hollow in time. Only when tempered by reason, which in turn should be governed by will, can our emotional attractions become real love—the love that reflects God.[4] Reason makes it possible for us to know what is right in terms of those we love. Will, when it is not dominated by sentiment or otherwise emotionally overwhelmed, makes the choice to do what is truly loving.

Human love that reflects the love of God is complex and not easily achieved. It is forged in the exquisite and proper interplay of our sentiment, our reason, and our will. In trying to align their sentiment with reason and free will in order to love more authentically, Catholics have some distinct advantages. Through the Incarnation, Christians understand that God who is Love knows us, loves us, and has committed to be faithful to us for all eternity. Christians also can look to Mary, the Mother of Jesus, for lessons in how to love. Mary knew from the lips of the angel what God wanted for her and from her, and she was free to choose her path. Mary chose to love fully and courageously and with intense commitment. She did so when she agreed to conform her will with God's, leaving all else behind and accepting the risks, the opportunities, the joys, and the sorrows that would come from loving truly and saying yes to God. Another significant advantage for

Catholics is being members of the Church. Through the sacraments, we receive a share in Christ's life and love. Also, the community that is the Church teaches us to pay attention to our sentiments and to interpret them rightly. It points the way for our intellect to make right judgments; that is, it helps form our conscience. Through the graces of the sacraments, our wills are strengthened by being united to Christ's will.

An important skill adolescents and young adults must learn is how to respond rationally to sentiments of love and then to act accordingly. Even when young adults manage to temper emotional love with reason, they continue to struggle with a conflict between feelings, goals, and the centrality of love and how they should behave in the midst of it all. One of the things they find very difficult to manage is sexual attraction and desire. In a close relationship, we might describe someone as appealing because the person is physically attractive, kind, strong, gentle, sophisticated, genuine, deliberate, whimsical, or zany. These adjectives, however, may occlude a situation riddled with sexual feelings, which can be quite intense. Most people realize that yielding to sexual feelings without rational consideration can be hurtful to everyone involved. Knowing a situation is dangerous is one thing, and willfully managing the danger by getting some distance from it is quite another.

Whether a person is involved in a close personal relationship with sexual feelings, or a friendship where sexual tugs play only a tiny role, other sentiments besides sexual ones can also distort the relationship and impair love. Stature or standing is important from early on and can continue to be so at various times in any relationship. A mere perception—whether accurate or imagined—can lead people to feel slighted. And once slighted (or several times slighted), people retaliate—even in loving relationships where the parties truly want the best for each other.

These feelings and actions impair love; in some cases they nip it in the bud, and in other cases they wear away at it and grind it down until it becomes only superficial toleration. Love requires an ability to give oneself away—to take risks, to accept difficulties and disappointments, and to live with an orientation beyond the self. Christians look to Christ, who gave himself away to redeem us, as the very source of this kind of love. Christians know Christ wants us to love and He wants to help us love. He wants us to be able to love consistently for a lifetime. He is the source of lasting love that is communicated to us in the words and actions of prayer—in the Eucharist, in Scripture, in other sacraments, and in personal prayer. *Prayer helps cultivate lasting love.*

These narratives share some of what Christians believe. They help us to understand more fully the mystery of our God, whose loving gift of self created us, saved us in Jesus Christ, and continues to sustain us through the Holy Spirit. The God of creation invites us into an intimate sharing of the

divine in loving communion—to "raise our minds and hearts to God"—
and we do that in prayer.

HOW WE PRAY

Prayer is a pathway to greater intimacy with God that takes many forms and
strikes many different chords. Some of our prayers are prayers of adoration
that praise and glorify God. Others are prayers of thanksgiving that recognize and express our gratitude for all God has done for us and given to us.
Human beings are sinful creatures, and in prayer we ask God's forgiveness
for our sins. Also, in prayers of petition, we ask God for blessings for ourselves and others.

We pray in different circumstances and in many different ways, and we
have a choice about how we direct our prayers. Sometimes we pray with
others in communal prayer and sometimes by ourselves in private prayer.
In neither case, however, do Catholics pray alone. Always we come to God
united with the whole Church. Prayer is the dialogue that shapes our relationship with God and rightly should be rich and complex. Private prayer,
such as morning or evening prayer, offers praise, contrition, and thanksgiving. It shares our love, our losses, our limits, and our whole lives and should
be part of our regular contact with God. Our relationship with God is the
most intimate relationship we have, and its dynamic should at the very least
be similar to that of a friendship that deepens over decades in response to
countless conversations, both fleeting and in depth. Regular prayer, like regular conversation with a friend, leads to greater intimacy, stronger bonds,
and more heartfelt interaction over time. Many of us are less than consistent about how we pray and are most inclined to do so in times of need. We
should pray regularly, however, preferably each day, as the Church recommends.

Both in the official liturgy of the Church, the Mass, and in their private
prayers and devotions, Catholics pray as members of the Church, as part of
the community of saints. Prayer is directed to God; it is not primarily con-
templation on our situation in life. We ask God to bless us, and for special
favors. We thank God, we ask God for insight, and we tell God we are sorry.
That means that we begin our prayers by invoking God the Father, the Son,
or the Holy Spirit. It is appropriate and customary when we speak to someone on the telephone that we acknowledge them in some suitable way by
name or by an endearing phrase. It is no less important to acknowledge by
our address that we are speaking to God.

Prayer engages our minds, our hearts, and our bodies, and prayerful expression takes many forms and makes use of a variety of what might be
termed "spiritual tools." We have vocal prayers that adhere to specific for-

mulas and can be spoken or sung, and we have mental prayers that have no particular structure and use no spoken words at all. *Lectio divina* is a form of prayer that combines prayerful reading and reflection on sacred texts. While chief among these texts is sacred Scripture, selections from Christian classics or other types of spiritual reading are also employed. Liturgical dancers pray in choreographed movement. Some who pray engage their reason and imagination in meditation; some, using strong words, argue with God; still others prefer silence and contemplate God in awe, wonder, and gratitude.

Christian prayer is conversation with God that involves love, emotions, and reason.[5] It can be directed to any of the three persons of the triune God. However, no matter how it is directed, Christian prayer is always Trinitarian in that it seeks union with God the Father, God the Son, and God the Spirit. Prayer is also centered on Jesus Christ and occurs within the Church and by the Church. Christian prayer is empowered by the Holy Spirit and is oriented to our complete union with God at the end of time.[6]

God is a loving God, and our dialogue in prayer helps us love God more deeply. In prayer, we approach the God who is Love, share with Him our own loves, and ask God's blessings upon them. In the gospels, people come to Jesus and ask Him to cure those they love: a daughter, a son, a servant, a friend, a mother. We follow their example in asking God to shower grace and blessings on the people we love and to heal their hearts and cure their ills. In prayer, we acknowledge the ineffable mystery of God, fully admitting that God's ways are not our own.

There have been and will be times when our prayers seem not to be answered, and other times when we face dreadful loss, pain, or wounds of the heart, mind, and spirit. At these moments, we might stand before God in lamentation, as Jesus did when he cried out from the cross, "My God, my God, why have you forsaken me?" But finally and humbly, we follow Jesus' prayerful example in the Our Father and pray, "Thy will be done."

Devotion and prayer to Mary and the other saints are hallmarks of how Catholics pray that have frequently been misunderstood.[7] Mary is the first among the communion of saints. She is "full of grace," and her whole life is an exquisite prayer. She is also, after her Son, the preeminent teacher of how to pray. On earth, she was a person of prayer and she regularly spoke to her Son, as she does now. Both in her *Magnificat* prayer, "My soul glorifies the name of the Lord," as well as in her prayer with the disciples after the resurrection, she teaches us gratitude and humility in prayer. In the gospels, she is a model of how to interact with her Son. At the wedding feast of Cana, she presents Jesus with a need ("They have no wine") and then reveals her confidence in His love, compassion, and power by entrusting the matter to His good judgment. Because she is confident He will do the right thing, she goes to the steward of the feast and tells him to do whatever Jesus tells him to do. Mary also accompanies Jesus through His agony and crucifixion, the central event of our redemption. She is both physically present to Him and in prayer for Him to the Father. In speaking with Mary, we express our desire to learn how to have trust and confide in Jesus. By praying to her, we wish to imitate her attitudes of prayer.

Praying to other saints acknowledges with gratitude their contributions to building up the Church. The first contribution of the saints to the holiness of the Church was their life on earth, but that contribution perdures because it continues to impact Christians in subsequent generations. Christians praying to St. Augustine or St. Catherine of Siena, for example, acknowledge with gratitude the holiness of these saints' lives. But there is more to such prayer, namely, a special connection that links the needs of the individual praying or the object of their prayer with the unique attributes of the saint. Should we pray to St. Augustine, for instance, we might do so because we have some sense of a personal connection with him. We might have difficulty making up our mind, as Augustine did, or we might want to stop criticizing friends, an activity Augustine prohibited in his community. Alternatively, we might choose to pray to St. Monica, St. Augustine's mother, if we are praying for children who seem to have lost their way, as Monica prayed for Augustine during the years when he wandered far from God.

In prayer, Catholics are drawn to holy men and women who came before us in the faith. We celebrate the communion of saints and take great joy and comfort in the witness of their lives. When we pray to Mary and the other saints, we do not adore them. Adoration belongs only to God. However, by connecting with them as faith heroes and heroines, we are inspired and encouraged in our journey of faith, and through them we offer praise, thanksgiving, and gratitude to God.

There are seasonal rhythms in the Church calendar, and it is customary for our private prayers to reflect the annual liturgical cycle. Advent is a time of preparation and joyful expectancy as we await the birth of Christ, when God Himself became incarnate, born of the Virgin Mary. Lent is a forty-day period which highlights penitential themes as we prepare for the passion and death of our Lord, and in Eastertide we exult in the resurrection of Jesus Christ and the triumph over death. Christians are sensitive to these seasons and integrate their themes in their prayerful conversations with the Lord.

NORMS

Norms define what is accepted and expected in any culture, in other words, how things are done. For years, the sisters were primarily responsible for establishing and maintaining the norms for prayer in their own congregations, as well as for the broader Catholic community. This was especially true in the institutions they ran and in which they served. Today that responsibility lies first, of course, with families, as it did even in the days when the sisters held sway, and then almost entirely with local parish communities and communities associated with other Catholic institutions.

There is no better way for children to learn how to pray than from their mothers and fathers. Parents should take the lead in teaching their children how and when to pray. Children should also encounter their own parents saying prayers. Other members of the extended family, including godparents and good friends, can also make valuable contributions to this project. The Church relies on these familial networks to serve a primary role in forming the prayer habits of each generation.

In addition to attending Mass and receiving the sacraments, many Catholics pray regularly. Some take some time before or after Mass to pray privately while kneeling in a pew. Others choose to pray in front of the statue of the Virgin Mary or one of the other statues in the church, perhaps lighting a candle to focus and punctuate their prayer. Other Catholics are habitual in reciting parts of the liturgy of the hours, or they recite daily prayers at home. Many Catholics still regularly recite the rosary, and in many parishes, if you arrive early for daily Mass or stay a bit after Mass, you can observe a small group of parishioners participating in a communal recitation of the rosary.

Despite these obvious instances of prayer, there are signs that either a good number of Catholics these days are unaware of the norms of prayer or they rarely pray themselves. Perhaps the most piercing evidence of this occurs at public events, such as commencement ceremonies or a Christmas party at a Catholic institution, when a layperson is asked to lead the group in prayer. It is reasonable to assume that individuals asked to pray at such events are approached because they are committed Catholics. Furthermore, in most cases, the invitation is an honor that is accompanied by plenty of time to reflect and prepare. Despite personal commitment to the faith and significant preparation, it is not uncommon for the selected individuals to begin prayer as follows: "As we gather here this afternoon in anticipation of the feast of Christmas, it is important to remember that we are all children of God and that we should be grateful." To someone experienced in the norms of personal prayer, these beginning words are striking, because although well intentioned, they miss the mark.

The person who composed the beginning of the above prayer is probably a fine Catholic, but the prayer is simply not properly formulated. As indicated earlier, prayer is directed to God (unless one is praying to a saint, who is a friend of God and follower of Christ) and is not primarily a reflection of our situation in life. This example highlights the fact that Catholics are often at a loss about the form of prayer, which in turn suggests uncertainty about the norms of prayer. They have to learn by doing. In an appropriate form, Catholic parents should pray every day with their children, preferably at mealtime and before the children go to sleep. All Catholic adults should also pray every day, or almost every day, at least for a few minutes. While they can make use of many different prayer forms, all Christians—including Catholics—are expected to pray daily.

Leaders play an important role in the assimilation of norms in any culture. When they are clear and consistent about what is expected, cultural citizens respond. The same is true for leaders of the local Catholic community—the parish and the diocese or archdiocese. Unless the staffs at Catholic parishes are both prepared and willing to establish, explain, and model the norms of prayer, we will have significant difficulty passing on the rich tradition of Catholic prayer to subsequent generations of Catholics.

PRACTICES AND BENEFITS

Catholics today do not hear as many personal or quasi-private prayers as they once did. Fifty years ago, many Catholics would attend devotions on a Sunday afternoon or on a weekday evening, or they would participate in the parish mission or forty hours adoration of the Blessed Sacrament. At some of these devotions, the litany of the saints or other litanies and prayers would be recited. These devotions contained many types of prayers. Whatever the reason for unfamiliarity with prayer forms, it is important that Catholics understand that in prayer, they are primarily and directly addressing the Father, Son, or Holy Spirit.

Many evangelical Christians delight in frequent daily prayer. They rejoice in praying with others as they freely formulate their trust in God and approach Him for healing for themselves or others. Except when they are at Mass or devotions, many Catholics are reluctant to join together in praying anything other than the rosary or other traditional devotions. More decisively, many Catholics do not perceive prayer to be an important part of their daily activities. Catholics need not be fluent or comfortable with free-form prayer, but it is important for them to pray regularly using whatever form of prayer they find most appealing.

Culture focuses on the "usual way of proceeding," or what might be called "default" behavior. In terms of Catholic culture, "usual" or "default" behavior should include daily prayer. Parishes and parents can help cultivate a culture of prayer by adopting the following four strategies:

- Create a prayerful environment.
- Incorporate silent prayer during Mass.
- Establish prayer routines.
- Build routines around the liturgical cycle.

PRAYERFUL ENVIRONMENTS

Consider first the practice of private prayer at Saturday evening or Sunday Mass. It is not terribly difficult for most people to come to church a little bit early for Mass or stay a bit later when Mass is over. Both of these times can be used on a regular basis to pray privately. Parish staff can encourage parishioners to take advantage of these opportunities for private prayer by creating an environment of stillness and silence in the church that is conducive to prayer. At some point before Mass, the leader of song may wish to practice a hymn or give some other instructions to the congregation. But prior to this time, respectful silence in the church should be encouraged. Creating an atmosphere for prayer might be more difficult after Mass, when many parishioners catch up with friends and exchange greetings with the priest and other members of the parish staff. By moving to the back of the church and into the vestibule, however, parish staff signal they are respecting the prayerful "quiet" of the church and can still respond with the warmth that is a sign of true community to those leaving the church. Staff can encourage the practice of private prayer before and after Mass by clearly and gently explaining the opportunity in the bulletin and from the altar. If well done, the explanation will function more as an invitation than a reprimand and will likely increase the number of parishioners who make use of this time to pray.

Cultivating a prayerful Catholic culture must always include a process for ushering in the next generation of Catholics. The minutes before and after Mass provide wonderful teaching moments adults in the parish community can use to good effect. The practices of blessing themselves with holy water when they enter the church and bowing or genuflecting to the Blessed Sacrament before entering the pew are themselves small prayers that parents should model for children and also explain. Parents can also take the lead in spending some minutes in prayer themselves before they sit down in the pew. By providing the children with prayer books or helping them understand this time as an opportunity for talking to Jesus, parents will carve out the space and create a climate and disposition for prayer that can mature and develop over time.

Strategy 1: Create a prayerful environment.

SILENT PRAYER

The importance of personal prayer at Mass can also be highlighted by a simple communal practice which adds to the celebration of the Eucharist. The interval after the Lamb of God has been recited but before the priest holds up the Body and Blood of Christ and beckons the congregation with the words "Behold the Lamb of God" provides a special opportunity for the whole congregation. Depending on local custom with respect to kneeling or standing, this moment might be an appropriate time for silent prayer in a completely silent church. The celebrant might choose to remain at the altar in prayer for two or three minutes, while the congregation kneels and prays silently in preparation for the reception of Holy Communion. Or, instead of remaining standing at the altar, the priest, accompanied by the altar servers, could go around in front of the altar and kneel and pray. In this way, the priest leads the congregation in silent personal prayer. These few minutes of total silence can be a great incentive to personal prayer and also make those in attendance more alert to the great gift of the Body and Blood of Christ. Another benefit of a practice like this is that it teaches children the importance of prayer. Complete silence is so unusual in our society that when it happens, children understand immediately that something important is happening. When the community of faith pauses in silence before receiving the Eucharist, children will know it is the time when each Catholic kneels or stands immediately before God.

Strategy 2: Incorporate silent prayer during Mass.

PRAYER ROUTINES

Mealtime is a wonderful time for Catholic families to pray. The traditional grace or any of the many variations on grace now available in prayer books works well. It is also possible to use grace at meals as an opportunity to encourage spontaneous and personal prayer. At first the parents and older children can model how to proceed. Children are apt and eager students and will soon be delighted to offer their own prayers of thanksgiving. Some families find it helpful to say grace after meals. If children are edgy to get to other activities, the grace after meals can easily be said before the adults are finished dinner. The benefit to grace after meals is that it can mention particular things that are problem points for children during the next two or three hours, and the prayers can be tailored to each family. For example, a parent could include something like the following in a postprandial prayer. "Dear Lord, help us to do those things which will make us better persons. Keep the children at peace with one another during these next few hours. Help the children get their homework done and their room and clothes prepared for tomorrow. When it is time to go to bed, may the children not complain and may Mom and Dad be eager to spend time with them before they fall asleep. This we ask through Christ our Lord." The benefit of this approach is that the focus is on what happens in the next few hours. Also, this prayer can be repeated every night and the parents can recall the prayer when the child gets upset about something.

Parents who work outside the home usually develop a routine for going to and from work. It is easy for them to build daily prayer into this routine.

Suppose, for example, that a person drives to work. Either of necessity or choice, it is possible to park five or six blocks away from the workplace and then use the walking time to pray for family or co-workers or for the gift of love and patience in dealing with the many situations that arise in the workplace. The return walk to the car at the end of the workday could be spent in prayer that thanks God for the various gifts of the day or asks for grace to understand and attend to any difficulties and challenges that emerged at work. It's only a few minutes each day, but such prayer places work and effort in the context of God's providence and care.

Saturday usually involves chores, family events, and perhaps some exercise. If a walk is a regular part of the weekend routine, it is possible to use the first five minutes as time for prayer. On the days when children are part of the outing, they can join in and become partners in prayer. Just being with their parents on outings is a joy for children, and during these special times they respond naturally and easily to suggestions their parents make. If mothers and fathers are comfortable praying and include prayer as part of a variety of family activities, their children will take to it like ducks to water.

The pace of modern life from early childhood on is picking up. Most Americans, including parents and children from an early age, must manage a vast array of commitments that may include work, schools, sports, the arts, family and social commitments, civic voluntarism, and church. Schedules are complex and chaotic, and free time is seldom very free. We listen to the radio in our cars and iPods everywhere, watch television while we dine, check and send e-mail constantly, instant message, and text message. Our waking hours are spent in a whirlwind of activity and never-ending communication. While this feverish activity may well lead to great accomplishment, it can easily be an obstacle to our ability to appreciate life, to be imaginative, and to be still and listen—all qualities essential for lives well led and societies well-ordered. Regular and attentive prayer helps believers develop these capacities and habits that make life more meaningful and also lead to spiritual transformation. The keener the sense of wonder and imagination, the greater the ability to be still and truly listen. These are abilities that when developed make space for us to deepen our relationship with God. These same virtues and habits acquired in prayer are a rich part of Catholic culture. They enrich human life in all its various expressions and our children deserve to inherit them.

Strategy 3: Establish daily and weekly prayer routines.

LITURGICAL CYCLE

Adult Catholics can use the liturgical cycle of the Church as a special opportunity to emphasize personal prayer. During Lent, for example,

Christians are called to prayer, fasting, and almsgiving. The Church has established formal Lenten practices such as days of fast and abstinence, but these can and should be augmented by other practices or "cultural signals," woven into the nooks and crannies of daily life and regularly reminding us of the importance of the season. An example of one such "cultural signal" that would serve as an excellent prompt for both adults and children would focus around the common practice in this very mobile society of listening to the car radio, CD player, or iPod. During Lent, parents and children could agree they would forgo turning on the radio or other electronic devices when they are in the car and instead either say a decade or more of the rosary or some other prayer or think how they can be of particular service to family and community. Listening to music is a little thing, but because it is such a normal part of daily routine, interrupting it intentionally sends a powerful message.

The same practice could also be adapted as part of an Advent ritual. A short prayer such as the *Magnificat* could be memorized over the course of the four weeks of Advent, and saying it each day would underscore the preparatory theme of this pre-Christmas season. In the *Magnificat*, we hear Mary's words to her cousin Elizabeth, who is pregnant by God's grace with John the Baptist. Mary begins her prayer: "My soul proclaims the greatness of the Lord, my spirit rejoices in God my Savior, for He has looked with favor on his lowly servant" (Luke 1:46–48). Mary's prayer recalls the Incarnation but also reminds us that our spirit should rejoice in God our Savior because He has looked with favor on each of us.

These mini-rituals reinforce the importance of personal prayer in the liturgical year. At first, children might resist the interruption of their usual routine, but in short order they will get on board. Eventually they will even take special delight in reminding forgetful parents to turn off the music and start praying.

Strategy 4: Build some prayer routines around the liturgical cycle.

Our relationship with God deepens through conversation in prayer. But we pray, not as individuals, but as members of the community of faith, the Church. As members of the Church, we have a rich inheritance that is ours to know and faithfully pass on to the next generation of Catholics. Religious education is one of the most important ways we come to know our heritage, and it is to religious education we now turn.

NOTES

1. In Christian terms, they do not accept *creatio ex nihilo* (creation out of nothing), because their focus on empirical matter disallows such a claim. Similarly,

scientists have nothing to say for or against the new creation promised by Christ, which is to come at the end of time. It is outside their scope.

2. John F. Haught, *Is Nature Enough? Meaning and Truth in the Age of Science* (New York: Cambridge University Press, 2006), provides a compelling account of why the story of science, which he calls scientific naturalism, is both inconsistent and incomplete and, therefore, requires an additional theological layer in order to explain the subjectivity and the search for truth. For a discussion of the contradiction between the methods of science and the hopes of science, including its dismissal of the relevance of religion, see also Eric Cohen, "The Ends of Science," *First Things* 167 (2006): 27–33, and Owen Gingerich, *God's Universe* (Cambridge, Mass.: Harvard University Press, 2006).

3. See International Theological Commission, *Communion and Stewardship: Human Persons Created in the Image of God* (Vatican City: Holy See, 2004), especially 63–69.

4. Pope Benedict XVI, *Deus Caritas Est.*

5. Later in this section, we consider prayers to the saints, who can be described as certified friends of God. In our prayers to them, their names are mentioned first.

6. See Richard P. McBrien, *Catholicism* (New York: HarperCollins, 1994), 1067.

7. Many Protestants do not approve of the Catholic custom of praying to the Virgin Mary or other saints. The Protestant custom is to approach God directly, without the intermediary of a saint. Particularly in praying to Jesus, they say, no go-between is necessary. It is certainly correct to say that we do not need an intermediary in order to speak to Jesus or God the Father or God the Holy Spirit. Although it is not necessary to pray to a saint, many Catholics find it "natural" to pray to them, because the saints experienced many hopes and frustrations similar to their own.

8

Religious Education of Children and Adults

Religious education is an enculturation process. By fusing religious knowledge with religious practice, this process helps believers more fully understand and deeply experience their religious inheritance. From the mid-nineteenth century until the Second Vatican Council, the Catholic Church in the United States utilized a catechism as the primary pedagogic tool for transmitting religious cultural knowledge. In the wake of Vatican II, the American Church recognized inadequacies in this traditional approach and embarked on what became a decades-long search for a more satisfying and effective alternative. Unfortunately, the Church still has not found a concise, coherent, and agreed-upon approach for conveying Catholic cultural content. As a result, generations of Catholics have minimal knowledge of the faith that many only occasionally practice. Faced with this problem, the Church and local parishes struggle to effectively transmit the cultural content of Catholicism—its beliefs, values, attitudes and norms—in ways that make sense in our own time. This chapter addresses that dilemma.[1]

Traditionally, the Catholic Church emphasized the importance of handing on the faith from parent to child and from adult Catholic to young Catholics. Today, many Catholic parents attend to the first essential step in this process, by having their children baptized. Most of these parents go on from there to assure that their children participate in the sacrament of reconciliation, receive first Eucharist, and then are confirmed. This is the normal passage to Catholic teenage maturity. These are important steps in the Catholic enculturation process, but much more is needed. Only when beliefs are sufficiently internalized can they guide actions and play a role in shaping how decisions are made or what activities are pursued. It is important for young Catholics to grow in the faith and for the Catholic Church to continue to be a guiding force in the lives of all Catholics. For that to happen, religious education must successfully interweave knowledge with practice and be ongoing, compelling, coherent, and consistent in its approach.

All Catholic adults have a role to play in assuring the cultural vitality of Catholicism. To do that, they must know a fair amount about the Catholic heritage and how Catholic learning is applied to the issues confronting society and the Church today. Practicing the faith, especially participation in weekly Eucharist, is at the very heart of what it means to be a Catholic. As important as practice is, however, it alone does not satisfy the Christian commitment made in baptism. Just as Catholics keep informed about developments in secular society, adult Catholics should have some knowledge about important religious issues in society and developments in the Catholic Church. That does not necessarily imply taking courses in Catholicism and reading books or magazines. It does mean taking some steps to better understand the faith so that each individual Catholic can share it more effectively with others.

Responsibility for the religious education of the next generation belongs to all adult Catholics, whether or not they have children of their own. Some Catholic adults will assume that responsibility by playing an active role in passing on the faith through formal religious education programs.[2] Others will make their cultural contribution informally as exemplars whose lives serve as a witness to the power of their faith.

This chapter takes seriously both the religious education of children and the ongoing educational needs of adults. Its primary emphasis, however, is on appropriate approaches for educating and forming Catholic children in the faith. The education of children in the faith is not more important than the education of adults. Rather, it is a more obvious and effective launching pad for energizing educational efforts for all Catholics. Adults are primary players in the religious education of children. In order to meet the children's needs, adults have to be religiously knowledgeable. The Church has a responsibility to make sure they are. Although the majority of this chapter addresses the religious education of children, the last section deals directly with a variety of ways in which Catholic adults can keep themselves informed, alert, and observant. These approaches will enrich their own faith lives. They will also help adults to transmit Catholic culture more effectively.

The present educational context makes it necessary for today's Catholics to be better educated in the faith than Catholics fifty years ago. First of all, the general level of education in society has risen and this puts more pressure on Catholics to indicate how their faith fits into a knowledge society which reveres science. Not every Catholic has to be well educated in the Catholic faith, but there has to be a sufficient number of such Catholics to explain to others why faith and the practice of faith are not contrary to reason. That means that adult Catholics need more and better knowledge of their faith.

Realities within the Church also increase the need for better faith education among Catholics. The time-honored model of religious education in the Catholic Church relied on priests, brothers, and sisters. These men and women were well educated and carefully trained in the Catholic faith. The dramatic diminishment of their ranks has rendered this traditional educational model obsolete. Circumstances cry out for a new model. Whatever model emerges, however, will require a significant increase in well-educated lay Catholics who can take over from the religious men and women who preceded them.

Adult Catholics need more and better Catholic knowledge. But greater quantity and enhanced quality—as important as they are—will not be enough to create a vibrant Catholic faith and culture in the United States. The kind of religious education that enlivens faith is experiential as well as knowledge based and is rooted deeply in the practice of the faith.

We begin with a narrative that explores the intimate connection between knowledge and practice in the cultural development of Catholics. Using this narrative as a foundation, the chapter then moves on to examine particular practices which promote education in the Catholic faith at various levels. Finally, some tangible benefits that can accrue to those who engage in them are suggested.

NARRATIVE:
LEARNING THE FAITH WHILE PRACTICING THE FAITH

The only way to become a faith-filled and faithful Catholic is to *learn the faith while practicing it*. In that sense, religious education is akin to apprenticeship education and other kinds of experiential learning. Physicians learn to be doctors by practicing medicine as well as studying it. Aspiring actors and actresses develop their craft by practicing parts for the stage and screen at the same time they study "method" and work under the tutelage of directors. Sports figures practice on the field and play games at the same time they listen to coaches and pore over playbooks.

A good example of this experiential educational approach is the way small children learn to play musical instruments such as the piano. A young child may want to learn how to play the piano because the family has a piano and the child has always liked the way it sounds. However, for most children, liking the sound is usually related to the person making the sound, probably a parent, sibling, or other family member. Imitation is both the initial incentive and also the initial reward for most children who learn to play.

Prior to any formal lesson on the piano from a music instructor, children usually receive some informal help from, say, their piano-playing parents. First, parents usually teach children how to play some simple and enjoyable tunes they recognize. In addition, parents might give a little explanation while they are playing about something such as the treble and bass clef or perhaps the various scales. What's important about this process is the order of things. While parents and others might do a little explaining about the theory and mechanics of playing the piano, the explanation comes only after the child experiences playing—no matter how halting the playing might be. Without the actual experience of playing notes and hearing how they sound, music theory is less than compelling and means very little.

Proficiency with a musical instrument is primarily a process of learning while doing. The experiential component creates a framework that supports theoretical learning, which almost always lags behind. For example, a child will initially copy and practice playing a melody demonstrated by an adult. Only after playing it many times does it finally dawn on the would-be musician how the written notes on the music sheet relate to the melody being played. Over time, the budding pianist understands the basics of how to read music, mechanics, technique, and tempo. The further the child progresses in mastering the piano, the more the emphasis is on daily practice, doing scales and other finger and reading exercises, and interpreting different pieces. Explanation never really ceases, but the rigor of practicing scales and playing simplified works by famous composers becomes part of the regular routine of the serious piano player. Even concert pianists acknowledge the importance of regular, repetitive practice.

Just as playing the piano is a learn-by-doing process, so too is being a faithful and faith-filled Catholic. The most important part of being a Catholic is doing the faith. The practice of the faith (attending Mass, following the commandments, praying, caring for the needy, etc.) is followed by some age-appropriate explanation, which is succeeded by further practice and further explanation and on and on. A young person learns the faith primarily by experiencing the cycle of practice, followed by explanation or more theoretical learning.

Doing the faith is not just part of the learning process for Catholics; it is also the very heart of what it means to be a Catholic at any stage of knowledge or development. The measure of pianists is not their knowledge of theory, but how they play. So too, how Catholics live the faith, not their knowledge of it, is the measure of where they stand in the eyes of God and the Church. But without at least some explanation that is personally satisfying, Catholics are likely to cease practicing the faith over time. Therefore, knowledge and practice are both important. In short, the only way to become a faith-filled and faithful Catholic is to *learn the faith while practicing the faith.*

NORMS

Context is often as critical to successful education as content. In establishing a context that supports strong educational outcomes, parents are the most important teachers their children have. This remains true even if the parents themselves are not well educated. Parents with a very limited education and with little ability to speak English and perhaps with no ability to write English can be excellent teachers of their children, if they can establish a context conducive for learning. Well-educated parents, on the other hand, might be far less effective teachers if they fail to establish a positive learning environment. Parents who urge children to do their homework without providing a context conducive for making that possible fail to act responsibly, and in fact undermine the very outcomes they desire.

Parents create a context for learning by establishing a pattern for fulfilling the tasks set by teachers in their child's school. Willy-nilly, all parents establish a context of learning. Some contexts are conducive for learning, while others are detrimental.[3] To be conducive, a learning context must have three things: a pattern of activity that assures children complete all their homework assignments on most days, a system that reinforces positive behavior in school, and a system that reinforces academic performance. The word "conducive" indicates the learning context has a positive impact. It does not imply the parents create the best possible context for their child.

No matter how expert and patient teachers are, no matter how well run a school is, and no matter how smart or well educated parents are, if parents do not establish a context conducive for learning, most children will not perform well in school. Every teacher knows that some parents are more successful than others at establishing such contexts for learning. Teachers also know some children are very bright while others learn slowly. But it only takes a few weeks for a teacher to know whether a child regularly gets the homework done, how carefully the child does the homework, and whether the child pays attention in class. All these are directly influenced by parameters parents set in the home.

Parents play a significant role in the education of their children, and Catholic parents play an important role in helping their children learn about the Catholic faith. Parents have many tools and strategies they can use to establish a context conducive for learning which works for their children, but it is not an easy task. In many families, the one major hurdle to creating such an environment is the absence of adult supervision.[4] A learning environment without adult supervision can work, but in most cases a responsible authority who monitors the learning context in a consistent way is necessary. For ease of exposition, we assume the adult at home is a parent, though it could easily be a grandparent, a friend, a nanny, or a supervisor of an after-school program. If it is someone other than the parent, this individual must have the parents' trust and must communicate frequently with them about how things are going with respect to homework, behavior, and academic performance in school.

Attending to some practical components will ease the creation of a conducive learning environment. First, the parent has to communicate to the child the importance of making sure homework is done completely and neatly. By employing prevarications and circumventions and a variety of other creative techniques, most children can fool their parents about homework assignments in the short run. Eventually, however, the chickens come home to roost, usually in the form of a note from the teacher.

One traditional way parents highlight the priority of homework is to limit the array of activities children can enjoy before it is completed. Aside from a snack and outdoor recreation, the children would not have access to television, videos, iPods, Game Boys, or DVDs prior to completing the homework. Parents who take their role seriously understand the importance of their own example in shaping their children's values and behaviors. They are, therefore, willing to "walk the talk" and will sacrifice listening to music or watching the news themselves during homework time.

Ironically, the popularity of various electronic devices and gadgets makes the adult's task of creating a context conducive for learning easier rather than more difficult. The children really want to use their iPods or Game Boys. If the condition set by the parent is the successful completion of all homework assignments, many children will make sure they comply fairly quickly. Experience in after-school programs where electronic devises are usually not allowed demonstrates that the only thing more popular than these devices is doing homework with other children.[5] When doing homework together, children frequently consult and compete. They are forever asking one another, "How much of the assignments have you done so far?"

Another key to success is making sure all adults are on the same page about what is expected. If grandparents live with the family, parents can discuss school issues with them, both to get their advice and to share with them how their grandchild is doing in school. In general, it is easier for a child to get around one adult than two or more. When the adults all agree, wiggle room disappears. All this may sound idealistic, but many parents adhere to these general rules with impressive results. The guidelines help assure good secular learning and can be implemented in a variety of ways.

Catholic parents also establish the context for learning the Catholic faith. Learning the faith is an experiential process, and in order to know their faith, children must practice it. No amount of Catholic instruction alone can form practicing Catholics. Parents of Catholic children must provide them with a pattern of Catholic behavior and clear explanations for that behavior. Simply put, if Catholic parents want their children to be Catholics, they have to practice the faith themselves.

Most Catholic parents see the faith as important for their children for their whole lives, but they have difficulty making sure it is consistently practiced.[6] One important consideration in this process is to limit the number of their children's activities that relentlessly seek to occupy every available minute. Unless parents set limits, sports and other activities quickly become more important for children than anything else. Also, without limits, sports, dance, and other activities rule parental lives. The result is the burden of an overscheduled life for everyone.

Children understand that parents set the norms for behavior. And arguments and endless reminders aside, for the most part they adhere to parental norms that are seriously and consistently enforced. That is even true when the norms are only transitional. For example, young children know they will not always have to hold someone's hand when crossing the street. Nevertheless, they also clearly understand that while they are still young, they must continue to do so.

Parents can insist their children go to Mass each week, but if they seldom go themselves, they are teaching another lesson. Their children quickly understand the "Sunday obligation" is a child's norm, like holding hands when crossing the street. It does not carry over to adulthood. They also know their parents do not think practicing the Catholic faith beyond First Communion and Confirmation is important.

Empirical evidence indicates that children who do not attend Mass regularly when they are children are much less likely to attend regularly when they are adults. The teaching dilemma is fairly straightforward: parents cannot be adequate teachers of their children in the faith unless they practice the faith with their children. If the faith is to have a reasonable chance of taking root and growing in the child, the parents have to attend weekly Mass with the children and adhere, by and large, to the other norms of the Church. Some children will get religion when they are older, and some children will practice their religion even if their parents do not. But in order for parishes to prosper, parents have to attend Mass with their children and correct children when they break the commandments and praise them when they adhere to them.

With God's help, parents bring children into the world, and with God's help, they also create the appropriate contexts for their development. The most important thing for parents to do is to establish a context conducive for learning, for the general education of their children as well as for their Catholic education.

Parents also have to choose a level of their own Catholic knowledge appropriate to their circumstances. The level of knowledge has to take into consideration their own general knowledge background as well as what they aspire to do for the Church. If they feel they are being invited by the Holy Spirit to undertake an important mission for the Church that requires fairly extensive knowledge, they will find a way to secure that knowledge. If they realize their children pose many questions about the Catholic faith they cannot answer, they might wish to improve their knowledge of the Catholic faith.

PRACTICES AND BENEFITS

Developing strategies to improve and extend religious education is important, but before that can happen, it is important to understand two general points about effective ways to learn the faith:

- Learning the faith requires practicing the faith.
- A question and answer format helps people learn.

First, weekly Mass attendance is an essential component of effective religious education in the Catholic tradition. Not only is this the requirement of the Church for Catholics, but it is the best way to learn about the faith. Learning the Catholic faith is an experiential process that connects actions and explanation, and there is no substitute for participating in Mass with the parish each weekend. *Learning the faith requires practicing the faith.*

Second, the content presented in religious educational settings needs to be clear, concise, manageable, and broadly agreed upon. The formal teaching concerning the Catholic faith is contained in *The Catechism of the Catholic Church*. Using this book as a foundational document, the U.S. Conference of Catholic Bishops has developed norms for teaching the faith to children.[7] These norms are very sensible and carefully worked out. However, the norms have not helped us come up with effective forms of religious education that engage the entire family. The Church is facing a knowledge crisis among the faithful. It might now be time to revisit an old literary form employed for hundreds of years as a simple and straightforward pedagogic tool, the question and answer catechism. Of course, it would be important to reclaim and adapt it both wisely and well for our own time.

Traditional catechisms posed a series of questions in areas pertinent to the Catholic faith and followed each question with a brief answer. In the United States, the Baltimore Catechism was the most popular catechism, and for generations children were expected to commit the material to memory. There was also an expectation that teachers would drill students and provide age-appropriate explanations of the answers. This approach had distinct disadvantages that caused it to be abandoned in the post-Vatican II years. Four of them are worth noting. First, in using the catechism, more emphasis was placed on memorization than understanding. Second, since the answers were always the same, religious education became numbingly repetitious. It was like being stuck forever in a math class that dealt with nothing but multiplication tables. Third, the youngest children had little understanding of what they were saying when they dutifully memorized and repeated the catechism answers. And finally, since only short answers lent themselves to memorization, brevity trumped nuance in the catechism, suggesting that practically all things Catholic are black or white, with little place for the uncertain shades of gray.

Clearly there were problems with catechism-based religious education. Nevertheless, it also had an impressive advantage that is pertinent to our present situation. One of the catechism curses was that the basic questions and answers were the same for everyone. The blessing in this was that it provided and reinforced a universal Catholic language that children could understand better as they advanced through school. Even though the second graders might not have understood either the questions or the answers, as they matured and the explanations they received became more sophisticated, the children eventually could come to a richer appreciation of what these questions and answers were intended to convey.

Modern books in religious education do cover the full expanse of Catholic teaching as prescribed by the norms mentioned above.[8] Furthermore, the books are colorful and written in an engaging style. For pedagogical reasons, a book for a lower grade uses simpler language than one for the upper grades. This approach results potentially in greater understanding, but remembering the content is not as easy. To our way of thinking, that is in large part because the language varies and because certain statements are not singled out for memorization.

There are some complementary benefits when the language of faith instruction is consistent. The first is clarity and the ease of remembering the basic tenets of the faith. This characteristic applies whether or not it is associated with the question and answer approach. For example, it would surely be possible to have a modern text for religious education in which some formal statements are designated as important formulations of the faith that should be memorized. It would definitely be easier for children to remember the material if the same words were used whether in third grade or sixth grade to cover these concepts. Most modern religious education textbooks use a developmental approach that cultivates deeper understanding over the years. This approach certainly could accommodate and would benefit by using similar language at many levels.

Another modern reality is that religious education is taught by laypeople with uneven educational preparation. That is the case even if all of them have participated in the prescribed number of theology courses or units required by the diocese or archdiocese for teacher certification in religion. By virtue of their different backgrounds, each of these catechists has his or her own language or own way of presenting and explaining material. Absent an adapted catechism approach, two children in the same grade level but in different sections will find little commonality in what they are being taught. Even if the teachers in the two sections are communicating a single consistent message, the children might miss it because of the different examples and language being used. If, on the other hand, the two children are in different class sections and they both have to memorize the same sentence or two about a particular topic, they will be able, first of all, to converse about the topic. In addition, they could challenge one another to recite the sentence or two, and they could approach their parents to help them understand it. The way teachers explained the statement could vary without much confusion, because the explanation would be anchored in a statement familiar to all. *A question and answer format helps people learn.* We recommend reclaiming this method of the traditional catechism and using the same language as children advance in grade level.

Catholic religious education should always couple weekly Mass attendance with content-based learning. Clear, concise, and manageable content should also be reinforced by a common religious language. With those principles in mind, we can now focus on the three groups involved in Catholic education: Catholic children attending Catholic school, Catholic children attending all other schools, and adults.

CATHOLIC SCHOOLS

Our focus in this section is on the Catholic character of those Catholic elementary schools currently enjoying a solid financial foundation. It is true that many Catholic schools, especially those in urban settings, face large challenges. Nationally, the number of Catholic students attending Catholic schools has fallen slowly but fairly steadily over the past thirty years. Similarly, the number of Catholic schools operating has fallen approximately 30 percent over the same interval. There is no reason to believe that this trend will be reversed. We lament this reality. In practically all circumstances, Catholic schools close because they do not attract a sufficient number of students, whether Catholic or non-Catholic. Many factors play a role in parents choosing not to send a child to Catholic school, but certainly one important variable is the price.

From a comparative cost perspective, costs to the school or school system per student at Catholic schools are low. But costs to their parents are comparatively high. Annual costs at Catholic parochial schools (in urban areas, the cost is usually from $3,000 to $4,500 per student per year) compare favorably with the average cost of educating a comparable student at a public school (in urban areas, the cost is approximately $9,000 to $11,000 per student per year). Nonetheless, from the perspective of a tuition-paying parent, that is at least $3,000 more than they would pay at the local public school. Introducing education vouchers, as has happened in a few states, makes a large, positive difference in the financing of Catholic schools. In a voucher program, parents receive vouchers issued by the school district. The voucher states that a certain amount of money per year will be paid to whatever school, public or private, religious or nonsectarian, the student actually attends. The value of the voucher can vary from as high as the average cost per year to educate a student in the local public school district to less than half that cost. Whatever the level set, vouchers give a big boost to Catholic school attendance.

There are good economic and civic rationales for vouchers. The group most threatened by vouchers, however, is public school teachers; over the past few decades, teachers unions have pretty consistently lobbied heavily against vouchers. Given this strong opposition and despite the articulate endorsements by various education experts, the voucher movement has only slowly gained traction over the past thirty years. Therefore, for purposes of this discussion, we assume vouchers will not make big strides in the coming decade; we also acknowledge that over the next decade, a good number of Catholic schools will close their doors.

That said, there are many Catholic parochial schools that operate with sound finances, and some of these have a robust Catholic culture. Such schools may have other educational difficulties, but they are strong in presenting the faith. They do so through various activities related to academic areas and in various special activities which highlight aspects of Catholic belief and practice. We wish such schools well, but they do not need much advice. Not only are they doing well religiously, but they also seem to have a system which keeps the Catholic culture strong in their schools. Other Catholic schools are strong financially but are looking for ways to strengthen their Catholic culture. For the benefit of these schools, we describe practical activities that are somewhat novel and that can be integrated into their core educational activities. Because we are interested in strengthening a culture, which requires patterns of activities, we emphasize activities that can be repeated a number of times throughout the school year. These strategies can be summed up as follows:

- Encourage weekly visits to the parish church.
- Help parents create shared norms for children doing homework.
- Display student work in the parish church.
- Develop monthly student–teacher Mass days.

WEEKLY CHURCH VISITS

Most parochial schools are located next to or across the street from the parish church. The principal could encourage the students and the adults who pick up the children to make a visit in the church once or more a week after school. Since many parish churches are locked after the morning or midday Mass, it would be necessary to make arrangements to have the church open for about an hour around the time classes are dismissed. Such a practice should be recommended, not mandatory. Because it is voluntary, it introduces the concept that children have a very important role to play in developing their relationship with Christ. Especially as children get older and value friendships among their peers, the importance of spending time on developing a friendship with Christ will be attractive to some students.

Strategy 1 for Catholic schools: Encourage weekly visits to the parish church.

SHARED HOMEWORK NORMS

Parents are subject to intense cultural pressures from their children. Especially as they grow older and are increasingly influenced by the media, children want to watch television, go to the movies, listen to iPods, and play their video games. It is easier for parents to manage their children's environment if they know other parents are establishing similar regimens for their children. Principals can play a role in enabling like-minded parents to establish supportive networks that reinforce a common approach to such things as homework routines for their children.

At the beginning of the school year, the principal can meet with parents, discuss issues with them, and then develop three or four model homework plans, each with a particular name. These named programs would consist of timetables and practices that parents or relatives would impose on children to make sure their homework is done each day. There would be two central features of each plan. First, during the critical homework period or periods, no music, television, or other entertainment would be playing or available. Homework time would be reserved for homework only, not other activities. Children enjoy being with other children, and parents could arrange for children to do homework at some other child's house, provided they are under adult supervision and all the rules (in particular, no media) are agreed to beforehand and enforced. The second component would involve a religious practice. Each homework period would begin with a special prayer, asking the Holy Spirit for the gift of concentration and perseverance, and it would conclude with a prayer of thanksgiving for preparing well for class the next day.

In this approach, the clear benefit for parents is their being able to point to the network of other parents who have their children adhere to a similar schedule. There would also be tangible benefits for the children. For one thing, they would be well-prepared for class each day. At least initially, many children would not consider this a major benefit. However, a very real benefit they would clearly appreciate is the opportunity to do homework with a friend. Even if the latter benefit were only available twice a week, children would look forward to these shared homework sessions. Another benefit for children is the opportunity to expand their prayer repertoire beyond just the Our Father and Hail Mary. It is easy to select prayers for the children to say at the beginning and end of homework time based on their class level, and through repetition they will in time commit them to memory. A bonus is that parents would develop their own array of prayers and also become more comfortable in leading others in prayer.

Strategy 2 for Catholic schools: Help parents create shared norms for children doing homework.

DISPLAYS OF STUDENT WORK

Many Catholic schools suffer from a malady addressed earlier, namely, the failure of the children (as well as their parents) to attend Mass regularly on Sundays. One way to encourage children from Catholic schools (or from religious instruction, if they do not attend the parochial school) to regularly participate in the liturgy is to have students prepare short written essays or collages on a particular religious theme. Rather than post them in the school, the works would be posted in a vestibule of the church. The catch would be that they could only be posted by child and parent before or after Saturday evening or Sunday Mass. The works would remain posted for a few weeks and then would be removed. Children who attend Mass regularly throughout the year would have the satisfaction of hearing or seeing others commenting on their work. This practice could be explained to the regular parishioners as an outreach intended to draw children and parents to regular Mass attendance. Parishioners would then be encouraged to stop and view the essays on the way out of Mass and to make appreciative comments to the children who are invited to stand close to their essays or presentations.

Strategy 3 for Catholic schools: Display student work in the parish church.

STUDENT–TEACHER MASS DAYS

Yet another way to engage the children in regular Mass attendance is to work through their teachers in the Catholic school. Teachers could be asked to volunteer to participate in a program that has the teachers attend Sunday Mass in the parish church once a month with the children in their class. For teachers who live some distance from the Catholic school, the principal would likely have to provide them with some benefit to make up for the inconvenience of traveling to the Catholic school one Saturday or Sunday a month. Most children look up to their teachers and enjoy being with them. Sitting together with their teacher and with other children in their class will appeal to the children, especially if it is linked with something such as the dress-up Sunday described in a previous chapter. The direct benefit to the children is being with their teacher and their classmates. Although this activity is only once a month, it has the potential of encouraging some Catholic children currently not attending Mass at all to attend at least once a month.

Strategy 4 for Catholic schools: Develop monthly student–teacher Mass days.

CHILDREN IN THE RELIGIOUS EDUCATION PROGRAM

Religious education programs usually meet once a week for instruction lasting about an hour or an hour and a half. The traditional time when religious education (formerly called CCD) usually met was on a weekday afternoon during the week.[9] On this day, often a Wednesday, the children attending the Catholic school would be released early so that there would be classroom space available for the Catholic students coming from the public school. In a released time program, the public school students would be released early one day a week so that they could attend religious education classes. These classes began at a time that accommodated students from the public school. In recent years, many schools have switched the time of their programs from a weekday afternoon to a weekday evening. Other parishes have moved religious education to Saturday or Sunday, and it is linked to attendance at the Saturday afternoon or Sunday morning Mass.

In addition to the annually recurring task of attracting a sufficient number of catechists to teach the children once a week, religious education programs face three main challenges: intervals between meeting times are too long, too few students participate each year, and too few students attend Mass regularly.

The first challenge occurs because the instruction takes place only once a week, at best. During some periods around Thanksgiving, Christmas, and Easter, there may be a number of weeks between meetings. Even when students gather weekly, the intervening six days make it difficult for students to remember material from week to week. Consequently, time at the beginning of each class session must be spent reviewing what was covered in the previous week.

Most parents want their children to participate in religious education so that in the second or third grade they receive the sacraments of reconciliation and the Eucharist and then, some years later, the sacrament of Confirmation. The second challenge relates to the intermediate grades between First Communion and Confirmation. Some programs successfully secure the cooperation of the parents in promoting annual attendance at religious education. As a result, children attend religious education classes each week, whether or not the children are preparing for a sacrament. In many parishes, however, despite many different approaches, the children effectively skip religious education in the years after First Communion and prior to preparation for Confirmation. Some parish programs have addressed this issue forthrightly by requiring several years of religious education prior to receiving the sacraments. Most parishes, for example, require two years of preparatory classes for the child to receive the sacraments of reconciliation and the Eucharist. Similarly, most parishes require two preparatory years for receiving the sacrament of Confirmation. Some parishes now require three years of preparation for First Communion, which a child then normally receives in the third grade rather than the second grade.

The second challenge would not be so momentous if children were fulfilling their Sunday obligation each week with their parents. However, the third challenge has already been raised several times in a variety of contexts: many children do not attend Mass regularly. Yet this is the linchpin of religious education programs which have a lasting impact. If students go to Mass but not to religious education, this is lamentable. Nonetheless, parishes would far prefer this situation to a pattern in which children regularly come to religious education but fail to attend Saturday afternoon or Sunday Mass more than once a month.

In order to make sure that children in the religious education program attend weekly Mass, many programs have moved their instruction period to a time slot immediately following or preceding Saturday afternoon or Sunday Mass. In order to qualify to receive the sacraments of First Communion and Confirmation, children in these programs must attend both weekly religious instruction as well as Saturday afternoon or Sunday Mass. Many parishes also require the parents to attend with their children. Some of these programs are successful. At some parishes, however, the parents do not cooperate, but parishes are reluctant to deny the child the opportunity to receive reconciliation and First Communion.

Many more Catholic children receive their religious education through parish religious education programs than through Catholic schools. To be effective in transmitting Catholic culture, these programs need to address the three major challenges identified above and effectively weave together knowledge acquisition and practice of the faith. Parishes might be more successful in reaching these goals if they adopted some of the following strategies:

- Organize a weekly Mass with catechists.
- Launch whole-family catechesis.
- Run Catholic after-school academies (CASAs).
- Run Catholic early summer academies (CESAs).

MASS WITH CATECHISTS

For children to make the connections between content and practice, the catechists should be seen at the various parish Masses. Some parishes arrange the instruction so that children attend weekly Mass with the catechists, who, like the sisters of old, make sure the children are attentive and well behaved during the Mass. But even if this is not done on a weekly basis, it should be likely that a child who attends Masses at various times in the parish will occasionally encounter his or her catechist attending Mass and receiving Communion.

Strategy 1 for Religious ed: Organize a weekly Mass with catechists.

WHOLE-FAMILY CATECHESIS

A second strategy for parishes is to offer programs in whole-family catechesis: religious education designed not just for the children but for the entire family. The approach of family catechesis can take different forms, but the main goal is to get parents more active in reinforcing religious practices in the home. Typically, programs in family catechesis have parents participating in a number of education sessions. These programs are designed specifically for them and are oriented to practical ways for parents to reinforce religious habits in all their children, including adolescents and young adults. Various publishers of textbooks in religious education now have instructional books that incorporate learning activities for the entire family. Many dioceses have enthusiastically endorsed this approach. The new part of family catechesis is to offer parents ways to engage their children at home in learning and practicing the Catholic faith. An important way for parents to signal the family's commitment to their faith is for the parents to pray with their children each night and thereby teach them their prayers.

Nuns played an important role in the education of all young people in the parish. The activity of formal religious education is now being rendered by dedicated laypeople. But because the nuns had such stature and respect in the community, their impact on the children was great. Absent this impact, new ways are needed to strengthen the Catholic culture. Having parents play an enhanced educational and formative role is one way to shore up the Catholic culture.

Strategy 2 for Religious ed: Launch whole-family catechesis.

CATHOLIC AFTER-SCHOOL ACADEMIES

Yet another approach is to increase the frequency with which children interact with a Catholic culture. Instead of just once a week, religious contact could be more frequent. One example of this approach is a series of Catholic after-school academies, called CASAs.[10] These academies are designed for Catholic children attending public schools, and they are always offered in a parish setting. Basically, the programs are after-school programs with a Catholic component. They are offered every day of the school year for parents who need after-school care for their children. In addition to homework, snacks, and recreation, the children also say some prayers and receive some Catholic instruction. In suburban areas, the school buses drop the children off at the Catholic parish, and in urban areas, an adult walks the children from the public school to the parish site. The downside of the approach is that the parents have to pay for the after-school care. The advantage is that the children get some daily Catholic instruction in a Catholic environment. Depending on how extensive the religious education is, some pastors will allow this program to substitute for the regular religious education program. Others will view it as supplemental and will want children in the after-school program also to participate in the regular program of religious education.

Strategy 3 for Religious ed: Run Catholic after-school academies (CASAs).

CATHOLIC EARLY SUMMER ACADEMIES

A variation on the after-school program is what we call the Catholic early summer academy (CESA). This program is essentially a religious day camp, with some recreation added on. It runs all day for two or three weeks at the beginning of the summer. The entire day includes to religious learning and activities. The children can be dropped off early enough (7:30 a.m.) so that parents can get to work, and children can stay as late as about 6:00 p.m. The programmed part of a typical day includes about seven hours; the morning focuses on religious classes and the afternoon includes approximately two hours of religious activities, with the remaining time devoted to play and games. Over the course of two weeks, participating children will get about seventy hours of religious instruction. This is considerably more than a child gets during an entire year of participation in a traditional religious education program. If the CESA lasts three weeks, the daily schedule includes more play and perhaps some math and reading and less religious instruction. But the cumulative amount of religious instruction and activity varies from about seventy hours for a two-week program to about one hundred hours for a three-week program. Some parishes have this type of program and pastors allow it to substitute for the regular religious education program during the year, provided the parents and the children come to Saturday or Sunday Mass every week.

Strategy 4 for Religious ed: Run Catholic early summer academies (CESAs).

CONTINUING EDUCATION FOR CATHOLIC ADULTS

As important as youth ministry is, we skip over this activity to consider some aspects of Catholic adult education. Another important topic we pass over lightly is the education and formation of those coming to the Catholic faith as adults. For people interested in the Catholic faith but raised in another faith tradition or in no faith tradition, the Catholic Church has an excellent program called the Rite of Christian Initiation for Adults (RCIA). This program for converts to Catholicism is based on Scripture, prayer, the liturgy, and regular interaction with Catholics from the parish who serve as guides and mentors. Most parishes have such a program. There are also supplemental online RCIA computer resources. RCIA has been in existence for almost thirty years. It has been mandated by the bishops as the appropriate form of religious education for adults and older children for almost ten years. Like any program, it has a few drawbacks, such as the amount of time demanded of the lay volunteers who staff the program. But the program has evolved nicely over time and, God willing, will continue to do so.

Bypassing two very vital issues, we dwell on a third important issue: continuing education for Catholic adults. In the best of circumstances, Catholic adults have had years of religious education in the parish or some years of experience in Catholic elementary or high school or a Catholic college or university. Despite many years of exposure to Catholic practice and heritage, however, many adults remain confused on issues important to the Catholic faith. Are Catholics allowed to believe in evolution? Aside from acknowledging the leadership of the Pope, what is the main difference between Catholics and Protestants? What is the difference between a divorce and an annulment? Do Catholics believe that God will remain faithful to the promises He made to the Jews? Is it permissible to receive Holy Communion more than once a day? Is a Catholic couple allowed to have sexual relations once they are formally engaged? Can the Catholic Church morally approve a preemptive war?

A good number of these questions can be answered fairly easily by making good use of the index in the Catechism of the Catholic Church. Others can be answered by consulting books or online materials. Many adult Catholics, however, would like to keep themselves informed on important developments within the Catholic Church. While the Catholic community benefits from having Catholics informed about important issues, not all Catholics are interested in the same issues. And some Catholics will be content to practice their faith, share it with their children and others, and strive for holiness, without seeking extensive knowledge about the Catholic faith.

For those Catholics interested in staying informed and in learning more about how Catholic teachings are applied to modern issues, a variety of resources are available. Younger adults might enjoy consulting a variety of Catholic blogs, and there is now a great variety from which to choose.[11] Some sites (such as www.whispersintheloggia.blogspot.com, www.commonwealmagazine.com/blog/, and www.mirrorofjustice.com) post a few items every day, while others post less frequently. There are also online news services such as Catholic World News and Zenit. Some blogs have a more conservative slant, while others are more liberal. Picking one or two of these blogs and checking in on them once a day or a few times a week is a quick way to become better informed about some of the major topical issues facing the Catholic Church.

For those more inclined to print media, subscribing to a Catholic publication is an excellent way to stay informed. Our apologies in what follows for succumbing to the temptation to use vague terms such as liberal and conservative, but they convey at least a general flavor for a few of the specific publications we mention. *Commonweal* and *America* magazines are weekly publications that fall on the liberal side of the spectrum. *First Things* addresses many issues important to the Catholic Church on a monthly rather than weekly basis and does so from a perspective that conservative Catholics appreciate. Of course, the writers in these publications have viewpoints, which as long as they are consistent with Church teaching any reader is free to accept, reject, or modify. All other things being equal, Catholic parishes, Catholic schools, and other Catholic groups will promote a more distinguishable and inheritable Catholic culture to the extent that these groups promote political positions using principles in conformity with Catholic teaching. This is an important guideline for the way Catholics should draw upon the wealth of "Catholic views" available in the media. In these same publications, there are reviews of books of interest to Catholics. Reading a few reviews can help make it easier to select books that provide even more in-depth analysis of a particular issue or series of issues.

For those more inclined to formal study, many Catholic universities offer master's degree programs in religious studies. A good number of these programs are offered not only at the main campus but at satellite sites as well, making them more accessible to a broader number of people. Some of these programs are very good. However, as we noted above with respect to blogs and print media, interested consumers should consult with knowledgeable people before signing on to any of these programs. That way they will be able to determine whether the programs have significant Catholic content and a commitment to both Catholic teaching and practice.

Additional formal instruction on the Catholic faith is made available to teachers of religious education, or catechists as they are formally known. Catechists are expected to get training in a number of specific areas. Most of these programs do not grant formal academic credit. Nevertheless, they are usually well structured and taught by people who know Church teaching and understand religious educational needs.

CONTEXT COUNTS

Catholic religious education in all settings and with all groups should be experiential in nature and linked to practice. It will also be more effective in terms of making a lifelong impact if it takes place within a context conducive for enculturation. Catholics are called not only to know their faith but to live their faith as well. One of the ways we can do that is by providing loving service to our neighbor. The next chapter takes up the ways in which parishes can create a context for loving service that encourages parishioners of all ages and stages to regularly involve themselves in this practice.

NOTES

1. New ways parishes use to transmit the cultural heritage include *The Catechism of the Catholic Church* (Vatican City: Libreria Editrice Vaticana, 2000 [1997]), but most parishes do not currently make this document a principal component of their parish educational activities. Later in this chapter, we have more to say about the continuing relevance of the traditional catechism.

2. The technical term for a person trained to teach religion to children or adults is catechist. Catechists are the teachers of religious education who on a weekly basis during the school year review the teachings of the Catholic faith with students. Catechists play a vital role in sharing catechesis, and it is important that children see in them a mix of practice and content. In their weekly classes, the catechists review the basic teachings of the Church at a level appropriate to the group they are teaching.

3. Theoretically, environments may exist which are in between, that is, they have neither a positive nor negative impact on learning by children. In reality, most par-

ents constantly adjust the learning environment, either in response to pressures the parents have at work or because the child is not performing well in school. Therefore, the learning environment in many instances changes frequently and is unlikely ever to be at the single point at which it has no impact on child learning.

4. The routine for some families involves homework, under adult supervision, after dinner. This is a reasonable approach, though most parents prefer the children to get their homework done when they arrive home from school, with play and relaxation coming after homework.

5. In the experience of one of us who runs after-school programs (where no electronic devices may be used, except on days when school is let out at midday), the rule of gadgets keeps children interacting with one another while doing their homework as well as after it is completed.

6. Now, some parents only want their children to be initiated in the faith as part of their heritage and are not interested in making sure the faith is a vital part of how they will eventually live their adult lives. These parents will make sure the children are baptized, receive Holy Communion and possibly get confirmed, and do nothing beyond this point. To their way of thinking, faith is more a passage than something that is practiced for a lifetime. This parental approach is, of course, contrary to Church teaching, but it is a sad reality: some Catholic parents do not want their children to be practicing Catholics. They may be a small minority of Catholic parents, but they know what they are about.

7. See Holy See, *Catechism of the Catholic Church* (Vatican City: Libreria Editrice Vaticana, 1997), and United States Conference of Catholic Bishops, *National Directory for Catechesis* (Washington, D.C.: United States Conference of Catholic Bishops, 2005).

8. Most textbooks used in religious education have received the approval of a bishop or some group of bishops.

9. The initials "CCD" stand for Confraternity of Christian Doctrine.

10. A parish can launch such an after-school program on its own. Individual states have different requirements with respect to after-school programs, and some states require the programs to be licensed. For more information about these programs, see www.catholicexcellence.org.

11. "Blog" is derived from "web log." It is a site on the Internet where someone posts comments about some topic. The comments appear in reverse chronological order, with the most recent ones appearing first. As more information or perspectives are discussed, the person making the postings (the "blogger") adds comments and views. Most blogs concentrate on a certain area, such as politics, sports, or much more narrowly, wine, movies, or restaurants. Catholic blogs focus on issues related to Catholic faith and practice.

9

Loving Service in a Faith Community

The Church and all its members are called to be a witness to God's love in the world and to lovingly serve one another. The two greatest commandments are to love God completely and intensely and to love our neighbor as ourselves. While wrestling with what it means to love God completely and intensely, toxic ideological battles rage. Catholics on both sides of the ideological divide rant angrily against those with whom they disagree, assigning them the worst possible motives. And we do this within a Church called to love and unity.

The Catholic Church in the United States is in turmoil and transition. Fewer men and women are willing to commit to faithfully serving the Church as nuns and priests. Mass attendance is at an all-time low in many parts of the country. Catholics divorce at the same rate as non-Catholics, and Catholics do not have markedly different attitudes or behaviors from other Americans in terms of their use of artificial birth control, involvement in war, capital punishment, abortion, embryonic stem cell research, and same-sex marriage. At times, observers see a Catholic Church rife with division, discouragement, and dissent, whose members increasingly believe and act just like everyone else.

And yet, at other times, Catholics and non-Catholics alike admire the Church because of its unique message, consistent teaching, and heroic voice. No matter the cultural pressure, the Church has never ceased to teach the value of life from natural birth to natural death. Nor has the Church abandoned the poor and disenfranchised who suffer in our midst. While many in American society disagree with the Church's teachings in these matters, they acknowledge, and at times grudgingly admire, the moral force of an institution that does not waver in the face of strong opposing cultural headwinds. That said, on balance, the Catholic Church in the United States is seen by many today as more talk than action. The hierarchy is strong on preaching the faith and moral and doctrinal teaching, but Catholics—bishops, priests, and laypeople alike—are far from strong in how they practice that faith.

Catholics maintain that love of God and love of neighbor are inseparable. If we truly love God, we are compelled to respond lovingly in how we act. Catholics give witness to their faith and love of God by how we treat fellow human beings. We live at a time when the behavior of many Catholics has undermined the integrity of the Church's witness in the world. The Church can reclaim that integrity as a forceful witness only if Catholics strive to respond to God's love by living lives of faithful loving service.[1] For this reason, we believe it is important to extend both the range of loving services in which the Church is active and also to increase the proportion of Catholics who participate in these activities. Catholic parishes have a vital role to play in bringing about this cultural shift. By the deft use of narrative, norms, benefits, and practices, local parishes can help transform how Catholics live the faith they claim.

NARRATIVE: "SEE HOW THEY LOVE ONE ANOTHER"

The two greatest commandments enunciated by Jesus sum up individual demands and prohibitions. The followers of Christ are called to "love the Lord your God with all your heart and with all your soul and with all your mind and with all your strength," and "Love your neighbor as yourself" (Mark 12:30–31). In the commandment to love our neighbor, Jesus defined "neighbor" as anyone in need, not just fellow Israelites or foreigners living in Israel. For this reason, every follower of Christ is called to show love to all persons, particularly to those in greatest need.

In his encyclical letter *Deus Caritas Est*, Pope Benedict tells us that in proclaiming the word of God, celebrating the sacraments, and exercising the ministry of charity or loving service, "the Church expresses its deepest nature."[2] At Mass, these three activities come together, revealing the essence of the Church and what the Church and all its members must be in and for the world. Jesus Christ is encountered in the Eucharist, and in this sacramental moment, Christ's extravagant self-giving love is experienced. Because it is a profound and intimate experience of love in Christ, Eucharist impels and compels those who receive it to love and serve others.[3] Through the reception of the Body and Blood of Christ, we become one with Christ, who is one with the Father in love.

Loving service is closely connected with the Eucharist, and because human beings are far more likely to be persuaded by how people behave than by what they say, it is also a powerful component of effective evangelization. In one of his essays, the gifted early Church theologian Tertullian pointed out that nonbelievers would remark, "See how the Christians love one another." These nonbelievers found the commitment the Christians had to Christ and to each other both amazing and convincing. The early Christians did not love others in order to secure converts or to receive the approbation of others. They loved others because they loved Christ, listened to His words, and followed His example. Modern Christians are called to a similar self-emptying love. While such love may be observed and admired by others, that is not its purpose. The goal is to treat every person as someone cherished by God and therefore worthy of love and respect.

A Catholic, Christian conviction is that accepting the gift of Christ in the community of the Church enables us to love better, more consistently, and more selflessly. This happens because, through the sacraments, we become part of God the Father's eternal love for His Son in the Holy Spirit. Catholics have claimed for centuries that this divine love, shared with them through Word and sacrament, has results. Observers of early Christians noted that they behaved differently. The empirical impact of belief in Christ and membership in His Church should be as apparent today as it was to the early observers. When it is, people will be able to say about us, *"See how they love one another."*

NORMS

American society puts great stress on empirical, practical results, an emphasis shared by Catholics. People understand love when they see it. Because loving service, both inside and outside the family, is so "demonstrative" of our Christian faith, Catholics have to be deeply involved in it. Parishes must develop strong and clear norms that encourage, support, and sustain loving service in order for that to happen.

Traditionally, the Church teaching about loving service focused on our responsibility to perform the corporal and spiritual works of mercy. Corporal works concern the needs of the body and include feeding the hungry, giving drink to the thirsty, clothing the naked, sheltering the homeless, visiting the sick, ransoming the captive, and burying the dead. Spiritual works concern the needs of the soul and include instructing the ignorant, counseling the doubtful, admonishing the sinner, bearing wrongs patiently, forgiving offenses, comforting the afflicted, and praying for the living and the dead.

The corporal works of mercy are gratuitous acts, closely associated with social justice that are performed free of judgment about the person lovingly served. The spiritual works of mercy, which are also freely offered acts of loving service, differ somewhat from the corporal works of mercy. First, they are performed on behalf of those with emotional and spiritual needs rather than physical needs. Second, because of their nature, the spiritual works of mercy often require that those who perform them make judgments about the person being served. Unlike the corporal works of mercy, they can be either comforting or discomforting for the recipient. For instance, if a hungry person needs food, the Christian response should be to generously and compassionately attend to the need, giving comfort to the person who is suffering. In most cases, this loving service would be appreciated and graciously received. If, however, a married friend were having an affair, a truly loving response would require telling the friend they should end that inappropriate relationship and why. While taking this action would surely be an act of Christian compassion, it would hardly feel comforting for the errant friend, who might well respond with anger. In a slightly different situation, the friend may be involved in an amorous relationship he knows he should break off. In this case, his friend's encouragement and prayers may be enough to help him initiate and complete the painful process of terminating the relationship.

The Church no longer separates loving service into concerns for the body and concerns for the soul. Nevertheless, the lists of spiritual and corporal works of mercy are still quite useful as reminders of the full range of obligations we have as Christians. They also serve to remind us that loving service is challenging and complex, comprising as it does both the comfort and correction that we all need and also must be willing to provide to those we love in Christ.

An obligation to provide loving service is one of the cultural norms that supports and strengthens a dynamic Catholic culture. As part of their responsibility to cultivate Catholic culture, parishes must establish their own loving-service norms. In doing so, they will benefit by committing themselves to two things. First, the parish should provide at least one loving service to people in the local or broader community. Because Catholic culture is strengthened by exemplary activities that other parishioners feel impelled and compelled to imitate, at least one type of loving service provided by the parish should be highly visible. It should also engage a large number of parishioners. Any type of service is fine, as long as it includes one-on-one contact between parishioners and those being served. Second, the parish should provide opportunities for all able parishioners to take part in some loving service in the course of each year. These activities go beyond the admirable and necessary financial contributions parishioners make that support such programs. A strong culture of loving service has broad parishioner participation. In order to meet this second goal, many parishes will have to either expand current activities of loving service or add others.

Many people, including most parishioners, help members of their own families and their friends when they are in difficult circumstances. This assistance frequently involves important, often painstaking, long-lasting, and loving service which demonstrates Christian love of neighbor. Many people have made dramatic adjustments in their lives over long periods of time to care for aging parents or to help raise young children of relatives in difficult circumstances. This familial type of loving service is commendable and admirable. But Christians are impelled and compelled by their experience of God's love to do more than this. The cultural norm of loving service for Catholics and Christians is a commitment of time and energy on behalf of those in need beyond our circle of family and friends.

The loving service Catholics are called to give always involves three elements on behalf of those served: genuine love motivated by a commitment to Christ, direct contact or the offer of direct contact, and steadfast prayer. Loving service may be done in cooperation with a like-minded group of Christians, but it can also be provided in other settings which are not specifically Christian.

The clearest examples of loving service sponsored by Christian communities are activities such as soup kitchens, homeless shelters, adult education centers, pro-life initiatives involving educating or counseling young people and adults about the need to respect life in the womb, and family health clinics. In each of these cases, tangible goods (including prayers and information) or services are made available to the less fortunate, but the tangibles are provided by people who take a direct interest in the well-being and development of the people with whom they interact.

Practically all parishes have organizations that do good works. Many parishes in poorer areas have a soup kitchen which offers food to the poor, and at Thanksgiving many parishes either run special food drives for the poor or sponsor Thanksgiving dinners open to those who would otherwise be alone and in need. Whether through a St. Vincent de Paul Society or a group with another name, many parishes collect clothing and distribute it to the poor. In cities, some parishes have banded together and partnered with the city and state government to make housing available to the poor.

Each of these activities provides helpful service to those in need. Depending on the parish and the activity, the love of Christ, which speaks both hope and truth to the needy, might only appear fleetingly in these efforts. If parishioners have little or no opportunity to interact directly with those receiving the food, the clothes, or the service, their activity will be good and worthwhile, but it will be marginal loving service.

PRACTICES AND BENEFITS

Loving service frequently involves interaction with needy people who in many cases live on the margins of society. Exactly what parishes choose to do for service will depend on their circumstances. Some parishes located close to prisons might well choose to establish a program that serves the needs of the incarcerated and their families. Many parishes have hospitals located within their boundaries. After consulting with hospital administration, some parishes establish a service that not only brings Holy Communion to Catholics in the hospital but offers family assistance to all families with a loved one in the hospital. The parish itself or a group of local parishes could also choose to provide some trained parishioners to help families negotiate the normal difficulties encountered in dealing with health centers. These same parishioners could continue to offer support after hospital discharge, and they could pray for the whole family whose lives have changed because of the serious or threatening illness of a loved one. This latter service may be particularly fruitful now, because hospitalizations are so short that patients find themselves at home with limited support as they try to adjust to the new reality of impaired health.

Because it is important for most parishioners to be involved in loving service, parishes must offer a broad range of service programs and possibilities. To increase available options, some parishes might consider launching new forms of loving service that have broad appeal and are well adapted to aspects of modern American life. There is any number of such initiatives parishes could adopt, and what follows is a discussion of four such initiatives. In principle, these initiatives could be established in any parish and each of the four could accommodate the involvement of a large number of parishioners. Each would have to be tailored to an individual parish and endorsed and recommended by the parish. Participation in the programs would be strictly voluntary. Parishioners would decide for themselves whether this service opportunity was sufficiently compelling that they would participate in it on a regular basis.

Each of the programmatic strategies falls into a different general class of services. The first service focuses on financial support, the second on hospitality, the third on minimizing materialism, and the fourth on personal sacrifice. They can be summarized as follows:

- Tipping the balance.
- Hospitality counts.
- Presence, not presents.
- Upping the ante on fast and abstinence.

In each case, the particular service is described in some detail by highlighting its characteristics and explaining its potential appeal. Following each description is a list of other similar initiatives that might prove equally attractive but, because of particular circumstances, might be more fitting for a given parish.

TIPPING THE BALANCE

Tipping is an American cultural custom in which money is voluntarily given as a way of signaling appreciation for good service. On balance, tipping in the United States is understood as a quid pro quo. If service is excellent, a respectable tip is given. If service is poor, a small tip or no tip is in order. By tipping the balance on tipping, however, we can see it in a new light as a loving-service initiative.

Suppose a parish is located in a middle-class neighborhood near a goodly number of restaurants. Assume further that many people have a custom of eating out fairly regularly. In many restaurants, the employees—the waiters, those who clear and set up the table, those who prepare the food, as well as those who wash the dishes—are struggling financially. Many of the people who work in restaurants are immigrants or the children of immigrants who toil to make ends meet in their new adopted country.[4] Many of them are also saving money, despite their meager earnings, to send home to help their parents and other family members and sometimes to bring them to the United States. In these circumstances, a tip can make all the difference in the lives of people who work hard but often live on the margins. An extravagant tip can feel like a gift from God, and that is the point.

The first parish loving-service initiative is a program based on extravagant tipping in restaurants.[5] The motivation behind this initiative is primarily religious. God loves us extravagantly and without measure, and our response to that experience and encounter should be to love extravagantly as well. Parishioners experience the love of Christ in the Eucharistic meal, and because they do, they want to give witness to that love at other meals in other settings. Motivated by the love of Christ that they receive in the Eucharistic sacrifice, many parishioners could freely make a loving gesture by giving money away in restaurants in the form of a very generous tip.[6]

So, what counts as generous? Well, that depends on the perspective of the person leaving the tip. Throughout the United States, the norm for restaurant tips is approximately 15 percent. In some urban areas, such as New York, where the cost of living is higher, the norm is at least 20 percent. What is given depends largely on the level of service and the friendliness of the waiter. But what is being suggested here is an extravagant gesture: splurging out of Christian love. For this extravagance, the calculus changes. Doubling the normal amount would be a nice splurge. In an area where 15 percent is the norm, a 30 percent tip would certainly be generous. In an area where most people give 20 percent, a 40 percent tip would be most welcome and greeted with enthusiasm in the niches of the restaurant where the waitstaff gather and chat. In most cases this extravagance, while delightfully accepted, will not generate either a question or comment to the person picking up the tab. However, should someone ask about the method behind this apparent madness, it would make sense to briefly explain the parish initiative and how it serves to remind us of the divine extravagance inherent in the Eucharistic meal.

Because it requires the expenditure of funds, it might seem that this initiative would only be appropriate for more affluent parishes. But as the Scripture story about the widow's mite makes clear, generosity is not confined to the affluent. Those who struggle financially can and do find ways to splurge on others, even if it is only once or twice a year. Giving generous gratuities is an approach to loving service that is flexible enough to accommodate parishioners of various ages and socioeconomic backgrounds.

Any person could decide to double tip on their own, without the recommendation of the parish. But the parish endorsement of the practice does two things. First, parish support clarifies the reason for adopting the practice. Second, having this as a parish activity reminds the parishioners of their call to put the love of Christ into action in their lives in some regular, personal way.

An initiative that encourages extravagant tipping is one financial approach to loving service, but circumstances might well dictate that a parish does something else. A parish could institute an analogous program in a community where many poorer people are hired to clean individual homes once a week. One pays for such a service, but tipping is usually involved as well. Alternatively, there might be another activity, such as garden and lawn services, in which some regular interaction between the family and the group providing the activity takes place. Even though these services are paid for, tipping is often customary and is surely welcome. In situations like these, loving service involves taking advantage of the tipping feature within the free market system. In addition to parishes having the regular types of activity such as soup kitchens and outreach to the elderly and shut-ins, they can also provide other ways that are not terribly time consuming for a wide group of the parishioners to provide loving service during the course of a year. The types of interventions described here do not demand much additional time and are relatively easy to carry out. They communicate care and concern and also remind the faithful of a central tenet of Catholic belief.

Using the classification of Catholic, adaptive, and counteractive practices developed in chapter 3, very generous tipping would be an adaptive practice, since it puts the American custom of tipping to a Christian use.

Strategy 1: Extravagant tipping is a good form of loving service.

HOSPITALITY COUNTS

Hospitality is the cordial and generous reception and entertainment of guests—a practice of reaching out to others in convivial community. There are many people among us, including in our parishes and in our families, who are isolated, alone, or socially marginalized. They seldom have opportunities to be included in warm and welcoming social situations where they feel cared for and valued. Parishes can help parishioners to meet this social need by developing initiatives designed to extend hospitality to those who might otherwise feel alone and lonely.

Loving service in the form of hospitality requires time and financial resources to accomplish. As in the tipping initiative, this example has a direct connection to the life of Christ and the ideal life of the Church. In Luke's gospel, Jesus encourages His disciples to a different kind of hospitality: "When you give a luncheon or a dinner, do not invite your friends or your brothers or your relatives or rich neighbors, otherwise they may also invite you in return and that will be your repayment. But when you give a reception, invite the poor, the crippled, the lame, the blind, and you will be blessed, since they do not have the means to repay you; for you will be repaid at the resurrection of the righteous" (Luke 14:12–14). This is a message which has particular significance for Christians because it embraces the Eucharist, the most important meal to which we invite people. It is also a directive that some parishes might readily endorse in developing a hospitality initiative for parishioners.

This particular initiative encourages parishioners to extend their hospitality to those who might need or long for the companionship and conviviality of a shared meal. An individual, a family, or a small group of two or three parishioners could invite a homeless person, or someone who might be alone and lonely, or a family that has few financial resources, to join them for a meal at home or in a restaurant. The guest or guests could be members of the parish or anyone who would delight in a good meal or an occasional treat. Many people see homeless people on their way to or from work. Perhaps they give them some money and exchange a few words with them. If there has been some prior interaction over a period of weeks or months, the parishioner could say to the homeless or poor person, "My spouse and I would like to invite you to a nice dinner. She's a good cook and you might enjoy her food. Or, we would be happy to take you to a restaurant which you like. Whatever you prefer, we will do, and we will pick you up and make sure you get back to where you want to be." Alternately, the person could say that his family and another family would like to take the individual and two of his friends to dinner as a special treat. The homeless person might feel more comfortable having dinner with some of his friends present, since they can easily talk to their hosts about a variety of things. Yes, it all might be a bit awkward in the beginning, but loving people will quickly find ways to diminish the unease felt by the poor family or homeless person.

The purpose is simply to reach out to some people and offer them a convivial meal. Whatever particular form the meal takes, however, the hosts should not set aside their Catholic motivation and practices, especially since the homeless and those of modest means often readily acknowledge that God is the source of the good things that come their way. Thus, whether at home or in a restaurant, the couple should make sure to say grace before meals, thanking God both for the food they are about to receive as well as for bringing this group together to accomplish His will.

A hospitality initiative could take a number of forms and might be designed to reach out to people with needs other than poverty and loneliness. Convivial get-togethers could also be part of a parish's efforts to support married couples, particularly those couples in the first years of their married lives.

It is a painful reality that in the United States a great many Catholic marriages fail. Failed marriages bring great suffering to the couples directly involved. They also are deeply hurtful to the children involved, who are deprived of the model of lifelong committed marriage. Even when the Church acknowledges that marriages are irreparably damaged and, if important conditions are fulfilled, grants annulments, they do so with a sense of deep sadness for the psychological pain experienced by all affected in the divorce and annulment process. The tragedy of divorce is felt deeply by couples and their families, but it is not confined to them alone. Rather, this tragedy spills over into the whole Church community, wounding it as well.

A couple's fidelity to their marriage covenant is a witness to the whole Church and a reminder that the Church is called to be faithful to its covenant with God in Christ. Through the sacrament of matrimony, couples receive the strength to remain committed to one another until death parts them. Their belief in Christ and participation in the Church and the sacraments help sustain them as they faithfully live out their marriage vows. The whole of Jesus' life and message is "directed toward the loving service of others for the sake of creating and sustaining a community of love."[7] We are called by Jesus to love one another, and the sacrament of matrimony illuminates in profound ways the essence of what as Christians we are called to do. Divorce makes Jesus' message less credible.

Catholic couples, like all couples living in the United States today, need the support of a community as they try to faithfully live out their marriage vows. Their parish faith community should be at the top of the list of places these Catholic couples find support in their married lives.

National surveys show married couples are twice as likely to avoid divorce if they attend religious services regularly, a statistic which applies about equally across couples of different religious traditions. This certainly suggests that Catholic couples are more likely to have lasting marriages if they regularly attend Mass. Unfortunately, the reality is that many young married couples are not used to attending Mass. Many young parents feel they are so overburdened with things to do that Sunday Mass quickly gets eliminated from the to-do list.

Relatively newly married Catholic couples have definitely heard the information about regular Mass attendance decreasing the likelihood of divorce, since this is something covered in pre-Cana programs. Nonetheless, from their lack of attendance at Mass, we know many couples somehow are not convinced by the data, or naively think they can put off going to Mass to some magical later date and that the delay really will not matter. In this sense, such couples should be counted among the lame and blind when Jesus tells His disciples to "invite the poor, the crippled, the lame, the blind, and you will be blessed, since they do not have the means to repay you."

Parishes should do all they can to encourage couples who marry in the Church to stay involved in the parish after the wedding ceremony. They should also find ways to engage young couples and support them, particularly in the first years of their marriage and as they begin having children. Church-going patterns established by young couples in the early years of their marriage will become habits of a lifetime that can help sustain them and their families over time.

Outreach to young couples will be more effective if it is envisioned as a loving activity rather than a highly structured program with various steps and phases. The loving activity can be the same as the one mentioned above: inviting a couple or a pair of couples to dinner at someone's house for a conversation about what their local parish is trying to do. Two or three "host couples" might take it upon themselves to arrange for such invitational receptions or dinners two or three times a year. They could invite new couples each time they host a reception or dinner or host the same couples for all the events. Most young people want to meet new people in the area, and as long as the hosts are up front about their connection to the local parish community, the invitation will not be extended under any false pretenses. Aside from socializing and talking about parish activities and liturgy, there can be grace before meals and perhaps a more extended prayer at the end of the meal or toward the end of the evening. Alternatively, the hosts could make Sunday Mass part of the event. They could invite young couples to join them for Mass and breakfast afterward, either at a restaurant or in their home. The goal is to be hospitable and attentive to the newlyweds, offering assistance and also inviting them in some formal or informal way to become part of the worshipping parish community.

This type of initiative is designed to reach out to vulnerable individuals or counter the increasing fragility of married couples in our society. Consequently, these initiatives would be classified as counteractive practices.

Strategy 2: Extend hospitality and personalize loving service.

PRESENCE, NOT PRESENTS

Consumerism and materialism are serious problems in American society. Many parents in Catholic parishes want to find ways to resist these cultural trends. They struggle with how they might balance a healthy desire to appreciate the fruits of hard work with a more sinister drive to acquire. Local parishes can provide support to these families by developing initiatives that help them take the faithfully Christian stance that many of them very much want to take.

The third loving service initiative a parish might consider addresses this critical issue by focusing on Christmas presents for children. Parents take great satisfaction in finding presents that delight their children. Parishes also work hard to get and give presents to poor children that will bring them joy. The difficulty with these seemingly delightful practices arises around the sheer number of gifts children often receive, the opulence of some gifts, and the cultivated perception that only certain types of gifts are worth receiving. Even gifts provided by well-to-do parishes to children living in poor urban parishes can convey a message of materialism rather than generosity. In families, interesting and high-quality gifts from parents, grandparents, aunts and uncles can be so numerous that two things happen. First, children simply neglect many of the gifts because playtime is limited and a few of the many gifts are more appealing than others. Second and much more important, the stream of gifts teaches children an unhelpful, even destructive lesson for life, namely, that great joy comes through an abundance of material things. Most parents realize this is a terrible message to convey to children and one directly contrary to Jesus' words to His disciples. Jesus warns His followers, "Be on your guard against all kinds of greed; a man's life does not consist in the abundance of his possessions." Instead, Jesus warns us against storing up things for ourselves without being rich toward God (Luke 12:13–21).

As seen through the mass media, the dominant Christmas message to children is the more presents, the better. This is contrary to the good news of Jesus, but the secular Christmas message is potent, and many children learn it early to their peril. If they truly internalize this message, these young children could one day be adults who believe that the pursuit of money and things is more important than relationships and love. Parents are caught between the message of the dominant media and social pressures and a genuinely loving desire to splurge on their children.

One particular initiative a parish might adopt would be to invite parents to join a special Christmas program that both restricts the number of gifts given to children and also substitutes the types of gifts children receive. Participating parents would voluntarily agree to limit the number of physical gifts children receive at Christmastime. The parents would also communicate this information to relatives and friends, whom they would ask to support them in their efforts. For example, parents who sign up for this program might agree that each of their children would receive a limit of four (or some other agreed upon number) actual presents. In order to create a support group, the names of the participating families could be placed on some list in the parish so that children know which other families will be taking part in the program. When children receive their gifts on Christmas, the gifts might be numbered from one to four. Numbering the gifts reinforces among the children the gift limit. A child from family A can say to a child from participating family B, "What was your number two gift? Mine was a computer game." Children will always compare presents, but this can be used to good effect if it reinforces the limit. By numbering the gifts, the expectations of the children are kept within the limit, and the parents are reminded not to exceed the agreed-upon number of gifts.

The second part of the program relies on the fact that children prefer the presence of their parents to actual presents, and it encourages gifts that are not things but actual shared experiences for children and their parents. So, in addition to the particular number of agreed-upon presents, children will also receive two additional experiential gifts or "presence" presents. With substantial parental input, the children would get to decide on the first "presence" present. They could choose an activity they like which they want their parents (and possibly grandparents) to experience as well. This might be visiting an amusement park, going to some special restaurant, or going ice skating or to some other special place or event. The second "presence" present would be chosen by the parents and would be something appropriate for all the children in the family. The parents would select an activity they want their child or children to experience, and the family would all enjoy it together. Thus, there are two activities which are supposed to take place during the Christmas holidays, one selected by the children and one by the parents.

The parish could help participating parents by setting some general guidelines concerning the amount of time and money spent on the activity for each family. Families can do things together or they can do them separately. The message about these additional gifts should emphasize the "presence" part of the present. The fact that there are two activities should make things fun for the children. In addition, as all children love to do, they can compare their activities with those of their friends.

The rich detail in the description of this initiative, as in all the others, is intended to stir the imagination and to underscore the importance of particulars in shaping culture. It is not intended as a rigid blueprint to be followed painstakingly by parish communities. Parents are the ones who will run this program. They know what will work in their parish and what will not, and many are truly imaginative about how best to implement principles to create effective initiatives. Strengthening a culture involves important overall goals and serious attention to particulars or details. The details may vary, but details count. Specifying the number and types of presents in this particular initiative is important. Clarifying the overall goal, namely, that our presence to one another is the best present both now and later in life, is equally important.

Redesigning Christmas gifts to place a greater emphasis on family activities definitely involves loving service, but in this case it is of parents for their children and, in a sense, vice versa. Although this is not an outreach to people outside the parish, it does give witness to parents' willingness to confront a dominant culture of excessive gifts by creating a community that will adopt new cultural norms. The act of restricting gifts and redirecting some attention to family activities is a program that, over time, can form young people and instill in them more reasonable expectations with respect to material gifts and very positive expectations with respect to communal family activities.

This strategy is both a counteractive practice and an adaptive practice. It is counteractive because it challenges the consumerism generated at Christmastime. It is adaptive, since it modulates the types and number of presents children receive.

Earlier we referred to the practice of some parishes providing Christmas gifts to less affluent parishes. While these programs are well-intentioned attempts at loving service, they often undermine the very values they hope to embody. These initiatives do not take into consideration that most poor parents make sure their children receive some special gifts at Christmas. While the gifts poor children receive from their parents may not be as impressive as those received by children in upper-middle-income families, they are very reasonable gifts. Because gift-giving initiatives from more affluent parishes simply add to the number of presents the children receive, the "gifts from the suburbs" underscore the unfortunate message in our consumer culture that more is better. Also, no matter the approach of actual distribution of gifts to the children, the whole event quickly degenerates into a frenzied competition to get the "best gifts."

There are, however, better ways to provide loving service to less fortunate children that are not about competition or compensation. For instance, a more affluent parish could financially support a "presence" event at a poorer parish for parishioners and their children. Participants from both parishes would contribute something to the event, but the substantial donation from the wealthier parish would enable parents and children to be together in a festive parish setting. In our view, this would be far preferable than the wealthier parish sending more presents to less affluent children.

Many parents might prefer not to restrict their children's presents. For them, we offer an alternative which in a less direct way also challenges the culture that material gifts are the primary means for generating joy. As Christians celebrating Christmas, our primary joy comes from reliving the birth of Christ in the Eucharist. The best way to convey to children that this is the main source for our joy is to put it first in our celebrations. Parents could tell their children that the family will celebrate Christmas by doing the most important things first. In particular, before any presents are opened on Christmas Day, the family will attend Mass together and then have breakfast together. The children can be reassured that Santa's gifts will not run away; they will be there after Mass and after breakfast. This is not as radical as curtailing the number of gifts, but it also challenges the dominant culture which says that our primary joy comes from giving and receiving material gifts. Many families also encourage their children to save money during Advent; then, at some point before Christmas, the money is donated to some group which provides loving service to the poor. Putting these all together in a Christmas "package" for ourselves and our children emphasizes our Christian belief and combines it with practice.

Strategy 3: At Christmas, presence, rather than presents, is a good focus of loving service.

UPPING THE ANTE ON FAST AND ABSTINENCE

Food and drink are abundant in American society, and we have excellent food, including fresh vegetables, fruits, grains, seafood, and prime cuts of various types of meat. Certainly the wealthy have better food than others, but good food is available to many in our society, where obesity is a problem at all economic levels. In part because the offerings are many and our wills are weak, many of us eat too much. In particular, many among us consume too much junk food, soda, alcohol, sweets, and dessert. We want to eat and drink less, and yet we often find our greatest comfort in what we eat and what we drink, rather than in our faith and our loving relationships. Local parishes can help parishioners address the critical issue of overindulgence and help those who have little to eat by developing initiatives that reinvigorate the time-honored Catholic custom of fast and abstinence during Lent and Advent.

The fourth loving service we propose ups the ante on the practices of fasting and abstinence within the parish community. In this initiative, parishes recommend to their parishioners that Fridays during Advent and Lent would be vegetarian days and that on Fridays parishioners should go out of their way to give a generous amount of money to someone in financial need or to a group that provides loving service to the poor. Parishioners of a suitable age would be encouraged to refrain from eating meat or seafood, restricting themselves instead to vegetables, grains, or cheese and milk products. Parishioners would also be encouraged not only to adopt traditional fasting practices on all Wednesdays and Fridays during Advent and Lent, but to strengthen what fasting means. This would mean excluding sweets, desserts, alcohol, and soda on fast days. Abstaining would also be linked with the loving act of giving money to a poor person every Friday. There are many ways to give money to the poor, but nothing is better for children than for them to hand the person the money themselves or see their parents do so.

At present, the traditional practice of fasting means not eating between meals and eating less at meals. Abstinence is understood as not eating meat, including poultry, though abstinence does allow for eating seafood. In the Catholic tradition associated with Advent and Lent, fasting and abstinence are activities intended to shift our focus and attention. Instead of concentrating on satisfying our appetite for food and drink, we fix our attention on Christ and our utter dependence on His saving love. Advent is the four-week interval before the celebration of the birth of Christ, and Lent is the six-week interval leading up to the celebration of the passion, death, and resurrection of Christ. Both of these events are central in the history of salvation, and part of Church discipline is to prepare properly for them.

Part of the justification for fasting and abstinence is that they help drive home the true source of our happiness. Eating a wide variety of wonderful foods is delightful, but overdependence on food will never satisfy the hungry heart of any human being. Only Christ will satisfy our greatest longings. When we fast or abstain, we are admitting to ourselves that true happiness and contentment do not come from food or drink but from the experience of Christ's love. Consequently, when we fast, we can be and should be just as happy and friendly and caring with other people as we would be otherwise. And the reason is that we draw even greater strength during these periods from our relationship with Christ in the community of the Church as we experience it in our local parish. Recall that Christ admonishes His disciples: "When you fast, do not look somber as the hypocrites do, for they disfigure their faces to show men they are fasting. I tell you the truth, they have received their reward in full. But when you fast, put oil on your head and wash your face, so that it will not be obvious to men that you are fasting, but only to your Father, who is unseen; and your Father, who sees what is done in secret, will reward you" (Matt. 6:16–18). Jesus wants those who fast to fit into regular society and not ask for special recognition.

Fasting and abstinence are good things, and the Church's expectation for our participation in these practices is hardly onerous and actually minimal.[8] That does not mean, however, that a more robust practice of these customs would lack benefit, especially at a time when Americans enjoy such an overabundance of food in a world where so many go hungry. A more robust embrace of the practices of fast and abstinence would, of course, have value for the individuals directly involved, by more dramatically signaling what is truly important in the life of a Christian. It would also serve as a witness to the wider community that struggles with overeating and addiction about the source of true satisfaction. Our focus on these foods and beverages suggests that we place too much emphasis on this type of satisfaction and too little satisfaction on using these gifts to spread the Gospel. Advent and Lent are times for the entire parish community to focus on Christ and to imitate Christ, so united more deeply with Him in mind and heart, we may celebrate more genuinely the feasts of Christmas and Easter.

Like the hospitality strategy, the fasting and abstinence initiative is both counteractive and adaptive. The strategy is a counteractive practice because it is an alternative to habits of overindulgence in food and drink so often encouraged in secular culture that plague many Americans. As a more robust form of the Church's traditional recommendation concerning fasting and abstinence, it is an adaptive practice.

Strategy 4: Upping the ante on fasting and abstinence can be helpful loving service.

CHOOSING PARISHES

Traditionally, Catholics did not choose a parish to join. Instead, they belonged to and attended the parish within the geographic boundaries where they lived. For Catholics, "parish" meant the assigned local place where one attended Mass. Catholics, no longer geographically bound to a particular faith community, now choose their parishes. Many Catholics choose on the basis of convenience, music, good homilies, nice community, pretty church, Latin Mass, and so forth. Each item may legitimately play some role in making the final selection. However, there should be one or two pivotal variables. Previous chapters examined various forms of prayer in the parish church, and this chapter has examined ways in which all Catholics can provide some loving service during the year to others outside our families. All these discussions might suggest possible criteria for choosing a parish community as well as the importance of a more systematic consideration of how and why that choice should be made.

Catholics are expected to worship together weekly, pray daily, speak at appropriate times and in persuasive ways about Christ and the Church to others, and provide loving service to others. These should be the four factors that play a decisive role in determining where Catholics worship.

It takes a fair amount of time for parishioners to experience the impact of a parish on their prayer life, evangelizing efforts, and loving service. Most people are not going to invest significant time searching for a parish that is the best "fit" for them. The selection of a parish necessarily entails some arbitrary judgments. Individuals can only observe surface patterns, and then, based on limited information available, they have to decide to be a member of one parish rather than another. The very arbitrariness of the decision should inhibit Catholics from making any claims about the relative merits of parishes, even with respect to the needs and aspirations of the person making the decision. The best that can be said is that a particular parish appears to have liturgies, opportunities for loving service, and members—including priests, lay staff, and parishioners—which help the decision maker to be a more prayerful, moral, and loving Christian.

Realistically, even though people speak about choosing a parish, most people do not invest much time in exploring the array of religious services offered through a particular parish community. Therefore, in the absence of other information, the best choice is the local parish. In choosing the local parish, people trust that each parish has a sufficient array of activities to lead them to holiness and that they might make a positive contribution to the parish community. Should a person find too many grating realities in a parish he or she has attended for some years, it then can make sense to explore other options. Even in choosing a parish that we hope will lead us along the path to holiness, Catholics should avoid criticizing other parishes which we know at best through anecdote, hearsay, or occasional participation in their liturgies.

INTERSECTING ISSUES

In the previous chapters, the focus has been on issues at the parish level: justification for weekly attendance at the Eucharist (chapter 4), ways to draw people in to more regular participation of the Eucharist and reconciliation (chapters 5 and 6), approaches to prayer (chapter 7), more effective ways to strengthen the culture of Catholic and religious education (chapter 8), and ways to involve more parishioners in loving service (chapter 9).

In the third and final part of this book, we treat issues that have a significant impact on parishes but that also involve people and policies at the diocesan or archdiocesan level. Four issues strike us as especially important for their impact on how Catholic culture develops at the parish level in the coming decades: priests and their changing roles, lay ecclesial ministers, financial issues, and the public stance of bishops with respect to religious and moral issues.

NOTES

1. The focus in this chapter is on loving service of others, which emphasizes personal contact. Also very important is social justice, which is always a component of loving service. However, social justice has much broader goals, extending beyond the Church to the state. It is one focus of consideration in the final chapter, where we examine how the community of the Church witnesses to justice.

2. This chapter refers to "charity" by the somewhat clumsier term "loving service" because it avoids the association of financial donations to the poor and marginalized commonly associated with "charity."

3. Pope Benedict XVI, *Deus Caritas Est*, 25a.

4. Even when the workers are not immigrants or the children of immigrants, they are often in need of resources. We use immigrant status to motivate the practice, but it applies equally well when the workers are struggling artists or simply hardworking people trying to earn enough money to support their families.

5. One might want to restrict the practice to inexpensive restaurants, but on the other hand, many expensive restaurants pay low wages to most of their employees.

6. In most restaurants, tips are split among the employees according to some rule. So leaving a generous tip means assisting not merely one waiter with whom diners have had some interaction, but also with many of the other employees.

7. Richard P. McBrien, *Catholicism* (San Francisco: HarperCollins, 1994), 863.

8. During Lent, Catholics are expected to fast on Ash Wednesday and Good Friday, and they are expected to abstain from meat on all Fridays (seven of them) during Lent.

III

ISSUES FOR PARISHES AND DIOCESES

10

Priest Shortage and Pastors

The ministerial priesthood is an office in service of the people of God. Priests are called to follow Christ and imitate His particular service of religious leadership. They do so by providing leadership to the worshipping, praying, and loving community of the faithful. While priests share the general priesthood with the laity, the unique responsibility and role conferred in the sacrament of Holy Orders belongs to them alone.[1] The threefold role of the priest is to offer the Eucharist and the other sacraments, to lead the local community of the faithful, and to help the Church spread Christ's message. The Church needs priests—good and gifted men who are willing to commit themselves to this life and this work.[2] And yet, we find ourselves in the midst of an intensifying priest shortage that has dramatic effects on parish life.

Parishes need priests. They are also the primary place where young Catholic men first encounter priests and begin to understand what priesthood means in and for the Church. Parishes do not control the flow of priests through the seminary, but they are places that cultivate priestly vocations. It is important to better understand how parishes can be more successful in fostering and encouraging priestly vocations.

A CULTURAL CRISIS ALREADY UNDER WAY

All Christians are called to follow Christ and to form the priesthood of the laity. In his first letter, St. Peter says: "As you come to him, the living Stone—rejected by men but chosen by God and precious to him—you also, like living stones, are being built into a spiritual house to be a holy priesthood, offering spiritual sacrifices acceptable to God through Jesus Christ" (1 Peter

2:4–5). Peter also makes clear that we "are a chosen people, a royal priesthood, a holy nation, a people belonging to God, that you may declare the
praises of him who called you out of darkness into his wonderful light.
Once you were not a people, but now you are the people of God; once you
had not received mercy, but now you have received mercy" (1 Peter 2:9–10).
The Second Vatican Council highlighted the calling of all the faithful to the
royal priesthood in *Lumen Gentium* (see paragraphs 9–10, 1964).

Laypeople can and do perform services which have an enormous impact
on the well-being of the Church. Some laypeople are even more faithful to
Christ's calling than some priests. And at times, the thankless task of prod-
ding timid priests, bishops, or cardinals to act for the benefit of the Church
has fallen to them. As important as laypeople are, however, they are no substitute for priests, and if it is to prosper, the Church needs both laypeople
and ministerial priests, each exercising their distinctive roles.

The Catholic Church in the United States is no longer anticipating a
priest shortage; it already has one. In response, the Church has adopted
three different approaches to addressing it—*reconfiguring parishes, importing
clergy,* and *approving lay administrators*—and all, while justifiable as short-
term responses, have problematic long-term implications.

Reconfiguring parishes is an approach to addressing the priest shortage that
parishioners at best find inconvenient and at worst wrenching. Some recon-
figurations combine a group of parishes under the leadership of a single pastor. While this is the least disruptive reconfiguration model, it still limits
priestly availability and local access to daily Mass and the sacraments. More
painful restructuring approaches include the suppression of parishes and the
sale of Church properties. No matter how it is handled, closing parishes up-
roots parishioners and leaves them feeling powerless and estranged.

Importing clergy is another less than ideal strategy for addressing the critical shortage of priests. Although many foreign-born priests are beloved, cultural differences and language difficulties can create problems for those
who serve in local parishes. This approach is also problematic because it al-
leviates a shortage in the United States by exacerbating a more critical shortage in Third World countries. It is unfair to the priests' countries of origin,
where the ratio of Catholics to priests is considerably higher than it currently is in the United States.[3] Foreign-born priests are often quite pleased
to serve the Catholic Church in the United States. But this is a strategy of
robbing Peter to pay Paul.

Approving lay administrators and some deacons to administer parishes is an
approach that makes excellent use of talented laypeople in service to the
Church.[4] Unfortunately, it also necessarily eviscerates the full sacramental
experience that defines Catholicism. This approach represents a significant
cultural loss for parishioners, who will likely find it increasingly unsatisfactory over time.

Eucharistic liturgy or Mass, according to the documents of Vatican II, "is the outstanding means whereby the faithful can express in their lives, and manifest to others, the mystery of Christ and the real nature of the true Church."[5] Only a priest can say the Eucharistic prayer and change the bread and wine into the Body and Blood of Christ. At a Communion service presided over by a layperson or deacon, this central part of the Mass cannot take place. The Sunday service in parishes with an appointed lay administrator is not the Mass. Rather, it is a celebration of the Word of God, accompanied by the distribution of Holy Communion.[6] Parish administrators are well trained and motivated, and they make a very important contribution to parish life at this time. However, they cannot make the Eucharistic liturgy "the source and summit of the entire Christian life."[7] Parishioners may be willing to accept this liturgical limitation as a short-term necessity. In the long-term, it will undoubtedly prove unsatisfactory.

All these strategies for addressing the priest shortage are imperfect and cause cultural disruptions that wound the Church. Any truly viable long-term solution for this problem will have to maintain the Eucharist at the core of each worshipping community, be sensitive to the needs of the Church universal, and respect parish commitments and loyalties. In other words, the Church needs to generate more vocations to the priesthood in the United States. This can only happen with the support of local parishes.

THE NARRATIVE

If the Catholic Church is to flourish in the United States, we need to inspire young men to give their lives to a priestly vocation and encourage their families to support and sustain them in that choice. In order to do that, we need a compelling narrative that makes four things very clear:

- The Church greatly needs outstanding priests.
- Priesthood is an exciting opportunity for exceptionally talented individuals.
- Priests will be appropriately supported in the work they do.
- Life spent in service to the Church as a ministerial priest is richly rewarding.

If the church in the United States does not believe these things, does not make sure they are true, or fails to share this good news with its members in the United States and elsewhere, we will not help the Holy Spirit and most likely the Church will not attract enough good men to meet her ministerial needs.

NARRATIVE 1: THE NEED IS GREAT

The Catholic Church in the United States needs priests if we are to continue as a sacramental Church composed of parish communities of an appropriate size. The Catholic approach forms its parish communities with an eye to enabling parishioners to develop a sense of belonging and loyalty that both nurtures their spiritual and moral growth and empowers them to action on behalf of the Kingdom of God. The special service and role of the ministerial priest is essential to this reality. The priest expresses the sacramental reality of the Church by celebrating the Eucharist, forgiving and anointing in the name of the Church, welcoming new Christians through baptism, anointing the sick, being the Church's official witness at the sacrament of matrimony, and celebrating the nuptial Mass. In addition, the ministerial priest leads and directs the local congregation in prayer and good works. He also provides religious education to people at various levels of maturity, and in and through all of these activities mediates the saving work of the High Priest, Jesus Christ.

Ministerial priesthood is an essential and unique apostolic vocation that is central to the Church. Whether young men actually decide to seek ordination depends on a calling by the Holy Spirit and their reaction to it. However, the Church has a responsibility to establish a context that is conducive to the effective operation of the Spirit. Parishioners play an important role here. Unless they embrace the need for priests fully, they simply will not have the necessary number of priests to serve the Church. The priest crisis will also deepen, and parish life as we know it will of necessity change in ways parishioners find ultimately unsatisfying. In the situation in which we find ourselves, *the need for priests is great.*

NARRATIVE 2: AN EXCITING OPPORTUNITY

The Catholic Church in the United States finds itself in difficult times that cry out for a courageous and talented cadre of priests. In a situation of uncertainty and without a clear strategy about how to proceed, priests, and particularly pastors, have the opportunity to try new ways to reinvigorate Catholic culture and practice at the local level. The Church is still adjusting to new components of modern culture in America and elsewhere, and it must do so without the large numbers of nuns who historically played such an important role in creating and sustaining local parish culture. Absent the strong religious presence of the sisters, the parish has to develop new models. This is a pioneering moment in the history of the American Church, as new models are being forged for sustaining and passing on Catholic knowledge and culture and tradition to future generations of Catholics.

Laypeople have always helped parishes function. For most of American Catholic history, they did so in supporting roles. That was especially true with the nuns. The nuns were technically laypeople, although they were not normally perceived as such by non-nuns. The laypeople who were not nuns provided the nuns with material assistance and staunchly supported them in the way they taught and trained Catholic children. Now laypeople, not the sisters, are the people primarily responsible for providing invaluable assistance to pastors in organizing groups, instructing children and adults, and promoting Catholic culture at the local level.

In fulfilling this role, laypeople will create new models that offer exciting collaborative opportunities for today's priests. These models will also provide for various levels of committed service. Some laypeople will make full-time commitments to serve the Church as the sisters did. Others will make sustained but less intense commitments, and some will make more episodic contributions to help the local parish. Pastors will have the opportunity in these changed circumstances to work creatively with all of these laypeople in developing dynamic ways to effectively transmit Catholic culture.

The U.S. Catholic Church continues to struggle with scandals that rattle its very foundations and present unparalleled motivating challenges for all of its priests. The scandals have blemished the Church in general, and the episcopacy and the priesthood in particular. In order to once again speak with authority to Catholics and to effectively evangelize, the Catholic Church in the United States has to become and be perceived as more holy. This requires outstanding priests who are models of holiness both personally and in their leadership.

As holiness "experts," priests need to demonstrate extraordinary commitment in three areas: Scripture, the Eucharist, and obedience. In this context, a priest committed to Scripture is not primarily one who has great knowledge about scriptural origins and historical context, but rather, a priest who finds daily nourishment in both the Old and New Testaments. Similarly, priests celebrate the Eucharist every day. A priest particularly committed to the Eucharist talks to Christ and shares his hopes and expectations. Because our salvation came about through the obedience of Christ, even to death on the cross, the priest whose expertise is holiness must be obedient to the will of God and to the Church through his bishop.

It is difficult for priests to become holiness experts, and it is almost impossible for them to do it alone. Only by availing themselves of the benefits of spiritual reading and spiritual direction are they likely to have much success.[8]

Priests have a responsibility to help fix what ails the Church. (If only more of them had taken this responsibility seriously, ways to discipline and regulate the priests who sexually abused children might have been crafted.) That does not mean, however, that they are called to be her cranky critics. While criticism has always had its place in the Church, constant criticism and even anger are culturally corrosive and do not attract many to join priestly ranks. Young men will surely not give up marriage and a career to serve primarily as institutional critics. Being part of a chorus of cranky confreres is hardly an appealing life choice.

Nothing in life is perfect, and the Church is no exception. The faults we will always have with us! However, it is human nature to be attracted by the positive, not the negative, and that is surely the case for those who might consider priesthood. Husbands and wives see failings in their spouses, but letting these faults overwhelm the goodness they love and admire in their spouse is a recipe for marital disaster. So, too, priests must never let the failings of the Church overwhelm the beauty of its tradition and mission that attracted them to priestly service in the first place. Even more important, priests have to work in collaboration with the Holy Spirit to attract young men to their ranks. They are more likely to succeed at this if they are positive about the Church and the contributions a priest will likely make as the Church in the United States undergoes substantial change. *Priesthood today is an exciting opportunity.*

NARRATIVE 3: A SUPPORTIVE ENVIRONMENT

Young men who pursue priesthood are embarking on a vocational choice that requires fidelity, witness, flexibility, and resourcefulness. The local church provides them expert training, both in the seminary and beyond, that will hone their skills and effectively prepare them for the many demands they will face. Priests are being asked to fulfill their responsibilities in a context likely to involve significant change in parish structure and practice over the next three or four decades. Priestly candidates will need special assistance, and they should be assured they will receive it in two particular ways. First, priests should have access to a spiritual director who will be responsible to guide them in the ways to holiness and who will help them maintain their vocational commitments. In seminaries, a movement has been under way for about ten years that provides greater training for the spiritual trainers of future priests. Programs at some Catholic seminaries and universities now provide more expert information and training to seminarians' spiritual directors. Professionals in the academy, in medicine, in business, and in other professions have mentors who inform, support, and encourage them as they grow and develop in their life's work. So, too, priests are encouraged to have regular contact with a spiritual director or mentor after they are ordained who will help them progress and mature in their priestly vocation.

As the parameters of being a pastor will change substantially in the next decades, pastors will need training in order to more effectively channel their time and energies. Special efforts must be made to develop an adequate number of these programs to meet the needs of local pastors. *Priests need support to serve.*

NARRATIVE 4: A REWARDING VOCATION

According to studies, priests are more satisfied with their vocational choice and life's work than doctors, lawyers, and academics. They are also happier than Protestant ministers. And although conventional wisdom might suggest that imposed celibacy is problematic, most priests are very happy despite the fact that they do not enjoy marital relationships and the wonderful graces of family life.[9]

Priesthood in the Roman Catholic Church is a richly rewarding vocational choice, and most priests are happy being priests. As Andrew Greeley points out, "Priests are clearly happy and satisfied men [who] report on the average that the priesthood has been better than they expected it would be, that they are very satisfied with their lives as priests, that they would choose to be a priest again, and they are not likely to leave the priesthood."[10] Unfortunately, priests are often reluctant to actively recruit others to the priesthood or to tout the joys they find in the vocation they have chosen. The priesthood is a rewarding vocation. That statement is not spin, but rather the considered opinion of most individuals who serve as priests. If priests would only be willing to tell their own stories and let the chips fall where they may, more young men might see *priestly life is rich and rewarding.*

NORMS

Future pastors will be operating in a context that continues to change. In these new circumstances, pastoral ministry will take different forms and will have to be more carefully planned. It will also require effective collaboration with laypeople. Pastors will spend more time on Eucharistic and sacramental functions than was traditional, and they will not be able to work as closely as they once did with parishioners. Pastors and parochial vicars will always have some contact with parishioners, but because in many cases they will be offering Mass at a number of locations, they will not have as much time for informal interaction as when all their activities were concentrated in a single location. Consequently, pastors will have to rely on the expertise of laypeople, particularly their pastoral teams, to carry out many of the other functions of the parish.

Priests need pastoral training specifically suited for the circumstances they will encounter in parishes. Priests already receive extensive training in seminaries. Much of the training is theological, although there are practical units of instruction as well. Furthermore, the theology faculty understands that future priests want to know how to appropriately apply their theological knowledge in a parish setting, and they teach accordingly. Seminaries are attentive to preparing seminarians to become good preachers, to celebrate the sacraments correctly and effectively, and also to attend to the administrative duties in a parish. This type of preparation, which combines theology with advice about how to handle regular issues in parishes, is important. Without it, young men will not feel confident about their ability to preach the Gospel and serve the needs of the faithful.

Circumstances require that relatively recently ordained men be appointed as pastors in ever more complex situations. In order to be adequately prepared, they need more specific instruction and advice. No longer will it be sufficient for a priest to be appointed pastor of a parish and then, before arriving, be given a socioeconomic profile of the parish as well as a brief sketch of its recent history. After taking the pulse of the parish, no priest will be able to simply introduce changes he deems appropriate. Laypeople are playing a more decisive role in the ordinary running of the parish, and new pastors will have to be attentive to the laypeople's analysis of what needs to be done. Also, because future urban parishes are likely to have been crafted together from previously independent parishes, the challenges will be greater. In fairness, a new appointee assigned to a parish in challenging circumstances should be given some idea of what the diocese expects. General directives such as "Do your best!" or "Try to balance the budget!" simply don't cut it and are unfair to a pastor who, given such vague directives, could never know whether the diocese thinks his performance measures up.

Dioceses have always provided some general advice to seminarians about different types of parishes. In addition, many new pastors usually participate in seminars over a period of weeks or months which make them aware of their new responsibilities. Finally, some Catholic universities offer degrees, and some groups run workshops on how to be a more effective pastor. A goodly number of these seminars focus on management issues. Despite all these helpful programs, more will need to be done. Programs will have to attend to specific issues that pastors will confront in their newly assigned parishes. These programs should provide pastors with requisite pastoral skills to balance the many different objectives—religious as well as financial—they are expected to achieve in their new parish.[11] Seminaries already prepare seminarians to serve in parishes with one or more prominent ethnic groups. Future preparation will have to accommodate not only the greater number of Hispanics in parishes but also the various degrees to which Hispanics have been acculturated into American society.

The role of the pastor in the next twenty years is likely to be both more constrained and more challenging. Pastors will be collaborating with lay staffs who are more directly involved in providing religious and social services in the parish. The pastor also will be constrained in the activities he has time to perform and in the degree of oversight and scrutiny he receives by people in the diocesan pastoral center. For this reason, it is important for diocesan leadership to identify different types of parishes and outline the strategies and tactics a good pastor pursues in each type. If dioceses want their priests to perform well, the priests have to know what constitutes good performance. Organizations normally portray good performance by indicating the steps the manager is expected to take under various conditions. Diocesan authorities should develop a general approach, gather a group of successful and experienced pastors, and then invite in a Catholic university or independent group to develop a training program for pastors.[12]

The ratio of lay Catholics to priests is increasing in the United States, and many Catholics exist on the fringe of the worshipping community and do not attend Mass regularly.[13] Priests will have to increase their efforts to reach out to Catholics who have drifted away from the regular practice of their faith. In the coming decades, priestly services will be more ministerial, evangelical, and hortatory than in the past. The danger here is that priests will become dulled by the constant repetition of liturgical events. In order to maintain their spontaneity, priests will have to make sure they set time aside every day for prayer and conversation with Christ.

Central diocesan authority is now exercising more budgetary oversight over parishes. This shift is a response to two major scandals in the Church in the past few decades: sexual abuse and financial mismanagement. It means pastors will likely have less freedom to run parishes as they see fit.

Greater financial oversight is necessary because of the large settlements to victims of sexual abuse by priests and to their families. These settlements often represent several times the annual budget of the diocesan office. A number of financial scandals involving priests or laypeople at the local and diocesan level has also received media attention in the past several years. They, too, necessitated greater diocesan oversight.[14] In large dioceses until about ten years ago, many pastors of parishes that were covering their expenses had a free hand in running the parish. Their only constraint was the need to secure permission for parish capital expenditures in excess of an amount set by the diocese.[15] Otherwise, as long as they made generous contributions to various diocesan and national appeals, the pastor was at liberty to decide how money was spent in his parish. Such freedom and lack of oversight are no longer tenable. In the light of revelations concerning malfeasance by some clergy and staff, the faithful are calling for greater financial transparency and expecting the Church to adhere to accepted procedures for making sure money is collected and disbursed honestly. Diocesan financial officers now expect all parish budgets to be submitted for review and all end-of-fiscal-year statements must be submitted to the diocesan authorities. Many parishes now hire auditors to provide an end-of-year audit of their books, which is then made available to parishioners. Because of highly publicized financial scandals, pastors now must reassure the faithful that prudent procedures are in place and outside groups carefully review parish finances.

PRACTICES AND BENEFITS

The Catholic Church in the United States is a large organization that functions in many ways like any other organization. And as in any well-functioning organization, incentives and rewards such as increased responsibility and authority should play a role both in motivating clergy to perform more effectively and in acknowledging particularly good performance by priests.[16]

In what follows, four major changes in practice and a fifth change that is minor in some respects but significant in others are recommended. These modifications can have a positive impact on priesthood and also make it more appealing to a greater number of young men. They can be summarized as follows:

- Reward success with more responsibility.
- Develop ministerial internships.
- Highlight satisfactions.
- Enhance compensation.
- Increase visibility.

TRUST AND RESPONSIBILITY

The current pastoral and management structure is too flat to motivate priests for forty or more years of ministry. The normal sign of appreciation for a successful pastor is to assign him to a larger, wealthier parish. In a previous era when churches were often full, this may have been a reasonable strategy, but it is a poor strategy when talented, experienced pastors are needed to revitalize important parishes fallen on hard times. A still relatively young pastor who successfully rejuvenates a flagging parish today should not be rewarded with a comfortable assignment in a well-to-do parish. Rather, he should be entrusted with another big challenge appropriate for his talents. This assignment should also be accompanied by some responsibility and possibly a title that acknowledge his previous success.

Presently, there is insufficient variety in intermediate steps that signal significant accomplishment to both the pastor and the faithful. Priests are not paid more for doing a good job, but they should know when they do and receive appropriate recognition from the bishop. By introducing some intermediate distinctions and activities, a bishop can promote certain things in the diocese and show his appreciation for priests who have extended themselves and performed well. Each bishop has to identify the positions and responsibilities which fit the circumstances of his particular diocese and its priests. But in order to clarify what is intended, some possible activities and responsibilities are outlined below.

Dioceses have vicariates that are headed by vicars and also smaller units, called deaneries, headed by deans. Deans are almost never bishops, and in many cases vicars are priests.[17] Some dioceses form clusters of parishes whose pastors meet together regularly, with one pastor serving as the convener of the cluster. One benefit in this arrangement is that pastors get to share ideas and exchange information. The difficulty is that vicars, deans, and cluster conveners usually have no authority in their group. As a result, not much gets done, and whatever the title given to the convener of the group, the pastors know it barely qualifies as even honorific.

As an aid to pastors and to help the diocese, bishops should consider asking a number of successful pastors to assume greater responsibility over some particular issue or activity in a vicariate. The bishop would tap experienced and trusted priests who know how to interact well with other pastors. These individuals would be expected to achieve some particular goal in a particular area within a specified period of time. It might be as simple as coordinating Mass schedules in a certain region. With the limited number of priests, this would facilitate ready access to daily and Sunday Mass for parishioners. Another possible responsibility might involve coordinating youth services for a particular area. The bishop could give the pastor a title such as senior pastor or senior coordinator, and the bishop would also provide a written account of the responsibilities the senior pastor takes on. This "job description" would then be provided to those pastors expected to work with the senior pastor.

Bishops might also involve some trusted pastors in evaluating other pastors. In business, everyone, no matter how senior, gets evaluated. Even the annual performance of the chief executive officer is reviewed by the board of directors. Unfortunately, pastors rarely receive the benefit of annual evaluation. Most are reviewed when they are being considered for reappointment as pastor, but these reviews usually occur only once and are seldom performance reviews. Rather, they are coordination reviews; if the review is positive and the pastor wants to stay, he is usually reappointed for another five years or so. This approach is not helpful to the pastor.

Most pastors conduct formal employee evaluations every year.[18] Just as employee evaluations make good sense, so also do evaluations of pastors. Ideally someone should review a pastor's accomplishments and lapses each year. There are two surmountable difficulties with carrying out such an annual evaluation. First, the pastor does not directly report to anyone other than the bishop, who usually has too many other responsibilities to be even dimly aware of what a particular pastor accomplished in a given year. That means that the person who really should evaluate the pastor is not in a position to do so. Second, in order to be fairly evaluated, the pastor has to be given clear, verifiable goals, if not by the bishop, then by the director of priest personnel, the vicar, or some other person in authority. An evaluation does not provide much useful information to the pastor if he was never given a list of goals or objectives. Some of these goals might apply to all parishes with a similar profile. Others would be particular to his situation. A first step toward generating helpful evaluations is setting realistic goals for pastors. Adhering to the standard approach of economists to problem solving, which assumes that a difficult task has magically been accomplished, let us assume that clear goals have previously been communicated to the pastor. Now we focus on who conducts the evaluation.

One approach would involve developing a group of "senior pastors" who would serve as an evaluation team. In this scenario, a bishop would select some experienced pastors to evaluate other pastors. These men would be priests the bishop admires for their accomplishments and for their sensitivity to problems faced by other pastors. They would form a pastoral pool expected to evaluate other pastors and provide them with feedback. In order to make the evaluation less threatening and more helpful, individual pastors could request a particular reviewer for their annual or biannual reviews. All these reviews would follow an agreed-upon procedure. For example, any senior pastor would certainly consult with parish staff as well as some parishioners involved in the parish. The evaluating pastor would be able to get a good sense of how hard the pastor is working, how effective his efforts are, where and how he functions particularly well, and areas where the pastor could improve performance.

If, however, there is no such arrangement in the diocese or if this can only be done every two years, some second-best alternatives are appropriate. Two such possibilities come to mind. In the first, the pastor could gather a small group of parishioners—three or four people—who have had experience reviewing job performance and ask them to fulfill that role. The pastor would write up a report, indicating both the goals set for him by the diocese as well as his personal goals for the past year, the steps he took to achieve these sundry goals, the difficulties he encountered, and the successes and failures he had. The first year or two would be tough sledding, because laypeople have never had to review a pastor's performance. The comparative component which is part of any good evaluation would also be difficult for them to manage effectively at first. The particular benefit parishioners bring to this process is their familiarity with the parish. The disadvantage is that pastors might not be able to share with them all relevant information.

The second alternative approach would entail forming a group of four pastors who trust one another and are reasonably familiar with the operations in each other's parishes. This group would do a formal review of two parishes each year. They would also conduct a casual review of the other two parishes. Most confidential information could be shared among pastors, and consequently all involved could be quite candid with each other. There is a serious drawback to this approach, however. Not unlike most group cultures, priest culture is more about support and loyalty than criticism and correction. Because the four priests will know and trust each other, they are likely to be too "chummy" to be critical. It will take time for priests to get comfortable evaluating each other. But this kind of evaluative program, conducted by a few experienced pastors, will likely provide helpful feedback and a good reality test to all.

Strategy 1: Reward success with responsibility.

ATTRACTING CANDIDATES FOR PRIESTHOOD

The Church needs to attract more young men to the priesthood. A broadly conceived program that asks all young Catholics to volunteer their services to the Church for a period of time would help accomplish this goal. The Church of Jesus Christ of Latter Day Saints has a particularly fruitful missionary program designed to engage young people in the work of their church that suggests possibilities. Mormon missionaries pay their own way, contributing about $400 per month for the time of their missionary sojourn. The money for this missionary activity comes from savings these young people put away from their youth and also from donations made by family members and friends. These young people are impressive in their enthusiasm. It is truly extraordinary how many willingly embrace this commitment.

A variation on the Mormon model could make sense for Catholics. The Catholic Church in the United States could establish a program that encourages all young Catholic men between twenty and thirty years of age to commit a year to living in a small community of like-minded Catholic volunteers. The Church would provide accommodations, perhaps a former rectory or convent. The young people, helped by stipends for services provided to the local Catholic parish, would cover their other expenses. The year would be one of service and spiritual growth. The community would be assigned a priest as a chaplain, who would say a special Mass for them once a week and provide them with spiritual counseling.[19]

The motivation for such a program is twofold. First, it would provide direct assistance at a moderate cost to parishes. Although the parish would provide a salary that covers living expenses, the rectory or parish school would get assistants or teachers for the year.[20] Second, young people could experience the needs of the parish and the life of a priest close up. Having these small communities associate closely with local priests in the context of providing spiritual ministry to the faithful could encourage a number of young men to consider the priesthood as a possible vocational choice. There would be no expectation in such programs that a Catholic volunteer would enter the seminary at the end of the Catholic volunteer year. On the other hand, the young men involved would develop close working relationships with priests and might consider priesthood for themselves at some future date. Participation would also make it far more likely the young men would speak positively about priesthood to others. A similar program could be established for young women, who would also live together and volunteer for a year or more. This experience would cultivate their willingness to consider religious life or parish ministry as a vocation.

This program will make young men and women more aware of the sacerdotal needs of the Church. Other variations could easily be adapted and adopted. The length of commitment could be shortened. The place where the young men stay might rather be at the home of parishioners who volunteer to house and feed them. The time of their lives when the service is undertaken might be between high school and college. Vital to all programs would be significant work for the parish, regular contact with at least one priest, and some enhanced religious practices, such as Mass attendance one extra day per week. It makes sense for the program—however it is conceived—to start out small. To have a big impact, however, the program would eventually have to be a big program. The Catholic Church in the United States has pressing needs and many dedicated priests who give their lives trying to meet them. A volunteer program similar to the one outlined here awakens young Catholics both to the needs and the priests.

Strategy 2: Develop ministerial internships.

POPULAR PERCEPTIONS

Priesthood is popularly perceived as a way of life that is lonely and isolating, a perception that hardly entices young men to sign on. In fact, priests are part of a lifelong fraternal community with strong and positive bonds. It is important to find ways to highlight the satisfactions that nurture a priestly vocation.

Young men understand that being a priest means dedicating your life to service in the Church. With the inspiration and guidance of the Holy Spirit, they can make and keep this commitment. On the other hand, they need to be prudent and make sure they are taking reasonable measures to protect and promote their vocation. It is also true that young men have to be more attracted to the priesthood than put off by certain of its aspects. Predictably, many people will be apprehensive about becoming a priest. They simply do not know whether they can forgo marriage and promise obedience to the bishop. Even those who can get past these two hurdles must respond to the even more fundamental question of whether they can find satisfaction in the priesthood. The following recommendations address the basic issue of satisfaction.

To be effective servants of the Church, priests have to be satisfied in their vocation. To be effective in promoting the vocation of priesthood in the minds and hearts of young men, priests have to be perceived as being fulfilled in their vocation. This means they have to have a positive priestly culture. One component of a healthy priest culture is "job satisfaction" that is heartfelt and apparent.

A culture is constituted by visible, accustomed ways of acting. Priests are regularly seen celebrating the Eucharist and other sacraments. They should also be seen on occasion working together, enjoying one another's company, and praying together. The working together, relaxing together, and praying together capture the central dedication priests have to the welfare of the Catholic Church and also demonstrate the personal relationship with Christ that is at the center of their lives.

An effective priest culture is inheritable, that is, it can be handed on to the next generation. In order to be handed on, it must be visible to a broad group of the faithful, including single young men and women, married couples with young children, and older men and women. Priestly vocation comes out of the faith community and must be encouraged and nurtured by it. If the community does not believe priests like being priests, they will certainly not encourage the young men they know and love to consider it.

Priests are dedicated to Christ and His Church. This personal commitment should be clear to the faithful in the way a priest extends himself to develop his relationship with Christ. Some occasions where parishioners see priests in private prayer together, praying for the Church, for their parishioners, and the needs of the world will help make this clear. This type of shared prayer is a witness to the community of faith. It also helps priests remain humble and dedicated to the service of the faithful as well as respectful and responsible in how they interact with their fellow priests.

The faithful can also benefit from seeing priests enjoying each other's company in social settings. Priests are supposed to have a modest lifestyle. Therefore, it would not be appropriate for priests to eat out every night in a restaurant. On the other hand, it would be helpful if parishioners occasionally saw priests from different parishes having a common meal together and enjoying themselves. Whether this is at a restaurant or in the dining room of a large rectory in which a good flow of parishioners come and go, the faithful want to be reassured that priestly life is convivial.

Strategy 3: Highlight priestly satisfaction.

COMPENSATION

If priesthood in the United States is going to demand much more of young men in future decades than it did in the past, greater financial compensation can help make the challenge more attractive. Diocesan priests have traditionally been provided with room, board, retirement benefits, and a modest salary. In most American dioceses, the compensation package has enabled priests to live at about the median income level in American society.[21] Until recently, the compensation package did not stand in the way of attracting the approximate number of priests necessary to provide the most important priestly services to the diocese. Even without any special adjustment, total compensation for diocesan priests should increase as the median level of American income increases. Certainly over the past decade, in some dioceses that has not been the case. Such dioceses will require additional funds to get to what we consider normal parity.

Although young men choose diocesan priesthood primarily because they want to serve the Church in a special way, salary and benefits play some role in their decision.[22] For example, if the diocese offered no or very poor health benefits to priests, it would be an obstacle for young men who might consider a vocation to the priesthood. Similarly, if diocesan priests did not expect to earn enough money to provide some support to elderly parents, they might be deterred from priestly life. In dioceses where priests' retirement benefits are clearly inadequate, a priestly vocation can also seem less than appealing. Priests do not expect to lead a comfortable life. They also realize that, due to the priest shortage, many of them will be working in parishes until they are seventy-five or older. However, they expect, God willing, to be able to retire at some point. The priest retirement plan should be realistically funded to make retirement a goal to be welcomed, not a predicament to be avoided.

In general, at the margin of their decision to become a priest, financial compensation makes a difference. The real issue is how much of a role it actually plays in the lives of most diocesan priests. Pastors will have to shoulder greater responsibilities for more years in the coming decades. They will also have to demonstrate greater resourcefulness in new situations. Perhaps they also should be partially compensated by having more opportunities for relaxation. Indeed, they might be encouraged to get away regularly so they can maintain a healthy perspective on the parish. A generous supplement over and above what priests traditionally received would make this option a possibility.

How much of a role finances will play in priestly vocation decisions is unknown. All that can be said here is that they can play a role. The only viable strategy for making adjustments is to allow differences, as is currently the case. If some dioceses actually offer better compensation packages than others, bishops can analyze that data and make adjustments in their own packages when warranted. Bishops will certainly consult with experienced priests in the diocese about what these should be. In the end, however, it is the responsibility of the bishop to make sure the financial package is reasonable. If there are complaints, the ordinary, not the priests he consulted in the process, has to shoulder them.

With respect to money and financial resources for priests, a caveat is in order. Some priests place far too much emphasis on securing enough money to buy a vacation house, a nice car, an entertainment system, and so on. They take advantage of ambiguities about how money in special collections can be disposed of and generate substantially more income than many of their confreres. Some priests are tempted by money and sometimes abuse their position of authority. When other priests have good reason to suspect this of happening, they should speak up and speak out. The American Church does not need any more scandals.

Strategy 4: Enhance priestly compensation.

INCREASING VISIBILITY

All of the previous recommendations depend to some extent on priests being visible. Visibility is important for any group or firm that provides service. In corporate America, service firms insist that employees wear uniforms that help people who need assistance identify them. Hotel workers, food service workers, police and firefighters, people working on trains, buses, and airlines, people working in department stores, health care workers—most of these workers wear uniforms or white coats or have something identifiable that indicates their position. In all these cases, the uniforms and badges make simple statements to others: "I am here to serve you. Tell me what you need."

This development in the broad, dominant secular culture has real value for priests. Being a priest means being ready and willing to provide loving service to others. Greater visibility for priests would help make that possible. Wearing clerical attire in most situations when they interact with the faithful and when they are in public is a reasonable way for priests to be more visible. Clearly there are many times when it is appropriate for priests to forgo clerical attire. It also should never be donned for the sake of drawing attention to priesthood as privilege. Rather, it should be worn to help priests achieve a number of positive goals. Wearing clerical attire is a constant reminder to priests themselves that they are called to serve. It reminds Catholics that priests are very available to the faithful, who are always welcome to approach the priests with requests or questions. Clerical attire can remind priests of their own commitments and indicate a willingness among priests to be visible and accountable for what they do and how they behave.

Finally, wearing clerical attire is a visible reminder to young Catholic lay-men of the priestly vocation they might consider, and it is an indicator of a willingness on the part of priests to entertain questions about priestly life.

Strategy 5: Increase the visibility of priests.

ADDITIONAL CHANGES

In this chapter, we have recommended five practices. In reality, many more are needed, though not all at once. The structure of how and where priests live, the way they provide religious leadership to their parishes, their mode of interacting with the bishop and diocesan authorities, and how priests prepare themselves for future assignments have changed or are in the process of changing. Any one of these realities should prompt a modification in the narrative, norms, and practices for priests.

Consider just one change. According to recent data, about 40 percent of young parish priests ordained five to nine years live alone in rectories. This number will only increase in the coming decade.[23] Priestly life has been built around rectories with three or four priest residents, even though this has not been the norm in most parishes for several years. Living alone is not good for a priest's health or security. Living alone also makes priests more vulnerable to temptations with respect to chastity. Many pastors and bish-ops understand this and realize that new practices are needed. In urban ar-eas, it may be possible for three or four pastors to live together in a single rectory. Where parishes are geographically dispersed, other practices will have to develop. For their virtue and sanity, however, wherever priests live, they must gather together in some appropriate format at least once or twice a week. This is a problem with many possible solutions, but at least one so-lution has to be proposed by the bishop and then tried.

Diocesan authorities should consult about these various changes and note peculiarities to their own situation. Perhaps with some general direc-tives, they could ask the seminary leadership to develop a plan to address any single new reality. In the real world of priests, much is changing all at once. In a more extended treatment, we would recommend several more practices, linked to the basic narratives we have provided. Because both life and this book are relatively short, however, we merely alert the reader to an area requiring far more detailed attention.

THE PARISH LEADERSHIP TEAM

Ideally every parish would have a pastor to lead the community of faith. But any good parish relies also on significant lay leadership. In fact, over the past fifty years, lay leaders have been emerging in parishes. Some of these leaders are volunteers and take the leadership in running various activities or events. Others are full-time employees who make it their vocation to serve a particular parish and the diocese. It is to this collective group of lay leaders that we turn our attention in the next chapter.

NOTES

1. This distinction is highlighted in *Lumen Gentium*: "Though they differ from one another in essence and not only in degree, the common priesthood of the faithful and the ministerial or hierarchical priesthood are nonetheless interrelated: each of them in its own special way is a participation in the one priesthood of Christ. The ministerial priest, by the sacred power he enjoys, teaches and rules the priestly people; acting in the person of Christ, he makes present the Eucharistic sacrifice, and offers it to God in the name of all the people. But the faithful, in virtue of their royal priesthood, join in the offering of the Eucharist. They likewise exercise that priesthood in receiving the sacraments, in prayer and thanksgiving, in the witness of a holy life, and by self-denial and active charity" (para. 10).

2. There is much discussion in the Church today about the impact that ordaining married men or women would have on the shortage of priests. We have chosen not to examine these issues in our discussion, nor to address their potential impact on vocations. The Church's position on these issues is clear, and local parishes have no authority to change those positions. For both reasons, it makes little sense to spend time on the issues. Our focus is on the role of parishioners and parish staff in renewing parish culture.

3. See Philip Jenkins, *The Next Christendom: The Coming of Global Christianity* (New York: Oxford University Press, 2002), 213–214.

4. At the current time, approximately 17 percent of parishes in the United States are run by a lay or deacon administrator without a resident priest. The lay administrators have theological training, but since they are laypeople, they are not ordained. Therefore, they cannot celebrate the Eucharist, hear confessions, confer the sacrament of the anointing of the sick, or, unless they are deacons, perform weddings.

5. *Constitution on the Sacred Liturgy*, n. 2.

6. In 1988, the Holy See issued the *Directory for Sunday Celebrations in the Absence of a Priest* and encouraged bishops to establish procedures in their dioceses in conformity with this document.

7. *Constitution on the Sacred Liturgy*, n. 11.

8. Regular reading is very helpful to keep a priest active and committed to Scripture, Eucharist, and obedience. Many priests find much wisdom in authors such as Ronald Rollheiser, Stephen Rossetti, John Shea, and George Aschenbrenner, S.J.

9. Many people believe that celibacy is the major cause of the downturn in priestly vocations. For a number of reasons, we believe this position is not compelling. Celibacy has always been a difficulty for many young men who might otherwise be inclined to become priests. To claim this is the main cause for the downturn, one would have to argue that celibacy is a greater hurdle now than it was fifty

years ago. It is true that many young people do not want to forgo marriage. However, many more young people are not getting married, many more of those who do marry are getting married later in life, and many married couples are having fewer children. It would appear, then, that celibacy, though still a requirement that dissuades some young men from becoming priests, is not as telling or forceful a hurdle as fifty years ago.

10. Andrew M. Greeley, *Priests: A Calling in Crisis* (Chicago: University of Chicago Press, 2004), 58.

11. Dean R. Hoge and Jacqueline E. Wenger, *Evolving Visions of the Priesthood: Changes from Vatican II to the Turn of the New Century* (Collegeville, Minn.: Liturgical Press, 2003), document the desire many priests have for greater practical training in the seminary. Their emphasis is on liturgy, homiletics, and marriage issues (pp. 136–137) rather than topics relating to effective strategies for managing different types of parishes.

12. Data from a survey of priests and business managers in parishes show that priests rated leadership qualities more important than managerial skills. The same survey, conducted by Prof. Charles Zech, also showed there were some areas, such as conducting reviews of staff performance, for which both pastors and parish administrators considered themselves unprepared. See *Cara Report* 11, no. 4 (2006): 11. In general, pastors seem to be ambivalent about leadership and administrative skills. They seem to know they are important and feel they have the skills, but they would rather spend their time doing more pastoral things. They seem to resent having to be administrators.

13. Some commentators explain that the increasing ratio of lay Catholics to priests is not as ominous a problem as the numbers suggest. They note that deacons now perform a number of duties previously carried out by priests, and that the number of Catholics attending Mass regularly is far lower than it was fifty years ago. Deacons do indeed perform valuable ministerial services and should be included in some appropriate way in the statistical ratios when doing policy analysis. On the other hand, the fact that a smaller percentage of Catholics attend Mass regularly now should be an indication that more priests are needed in the ministry of evangelization.

14. A reasonable question is whether modern priests are less trustworthy and, therefore, more likely to have their hand in the till than previous generations of priests or whether this generation is similar to earlier generations of priests, with the difference that embezzlement of funds by priests in earlier times was less frequently detected. We know of little literature on this subject. Our opinion is that sociological changes have resulted in priests more frequently yielding to the temptation of embezzlement. Fifty years ago, three or four priests lived together in a rectory. A pastor could do as he pleased, but two or three priests were always looking over his shoulder. Now many pastors live alone, due to a lack of priests. The temptation to take the money is the same, but because there is less likelihood of being observed, yielding to the temptation is easier and probably more frequent.

15. Savvy pastors often found ways to bypass this constraint.

16. Personnel policies for laypeople should include policies which reward managers and employees for valuable service and which outline a system for promoting staff to higher responsibility and compensation when they have performed well for some time at a given level.

17. If the vicar happens to be a bishop, this reinforces our point that there are too few positions of authority for priests who have been pastors for many years.

18. If done well, these include a review of clear and verifiable goals, a written evaluation, opportunity for review, reaction and possibly correction by the person being reviewed, and finally a discussion of the evaluation. Effective evaluation also necessitates that pastors include amended written accounts of evaluations and the ensuing discussions in individuals' personnel files. This process is time consuming, but it is an important component of collaborative pastoral ministry.

19. The groundwork has been laid for this rather ambitious program. There is already a vital network of service programs sponsored by various religious orders. Among them are the Jesuit Volunteer Corps, the Mercy Volunteer Corps, and the Capuchin Franciscan Volunteer Corps. A slightly different program is the Alliance for Catholic Education (ACE), run by the University of Notre Dame. All of these are excellent programs that benefit both the participants and the Catholic communities in which they live.

20. If cost is judged to be a significant factor and there is strong sentiment for trying such a program, the diocese can make the implementation of this type of program conditional upon raising sufficient funds.

21. For example, if a diocesan priest comes from a well-to-do family and can draw upon the family's financial resources, he can afford a higher level of living and expenditures. The percentage of diocesan priests in such financially abundant circumstances is traditionally quite small. Our estimate is that less than 10 percent of diocesan priests can draw upon substantial family resources.

22. In the matter of lifestyle, there are essential differences between diocesan priests and priests belonging to an order or congregation. Order priests (these are priests belonging to religious orders such as the Jesuits, Franciscans, Benedictines, Dominicans, or a host of other orders and congregations) make a vow of poverty, which means they own all things in common. Clothing, computers, and cars are owned by the order, though sometimes used exclusively by an individual. If a priest earns money through teaching at a Catholic high school or college, the check is made out to the individual but deposited in an account controlled by the religious congregation. Diocesan priests do not make a vow of poverty. They own their own car and, in some cases, a modest vacation or retirement home. Order priests do not pay income taxes, provided they work for an approved Catholic not-for-profit organization and provided their paychecks are under the control of the order. Diocesan priests do pay income taxes, federal as well as state and local.

23. See Dean R. Hoge, *Experiences of Priests Ordained Five to Nine Years* (Washington, D.C.: National Catholic Educational Association, 2006), 83. The actual number is 42 percent and it refers to diocesan priests ordained five to nine years.

11

Lay Leaders in the Parish

It is the age of the laity, and laypeople now play a major role in shaping Catholic culture in the United States. These lay leaders follow in the footsteps of religious sisters and accept responsibility for the Church's work in all Catholic institutions. And just like their predecessors, they, together with the priests and bishops, will be accountable for the vitality of the Catholic culture they leave behind.

Religious sisters did much of their amazing work at a time when civic and private secular institutions provided strong support for morality and ethical standards. That is no longer the case, and this represents a big change in the competitive environment in which the Church and her ministers must operate. It also poses a significant challenge for them. How are they to shape an effective Catholic culture in an age dominated by dogged individualism, relativism, and skepticism about authority and institutions? Meeting this challenge requires that the Church's various institutions, most importantly its parishes, become stronger. In strengthening them, we cannot re-create the cultural heyday of religious sisters in the Church. Nor should we want to. We can, however, appreciate and imitate approaches that served them well.

This chapter begins by situating today's lay ecclesial ministers within the ambit of Catholic culture. It defines how culture relates to local parishes and lays out what lay ecclesial ministers must do as cultural actors to make an inspiring impact on parish culture. The chapter also describes two types of standards or norms that can invigorate the work of lay ecclesial ministers: first, diocesan norms for training and developing lay ecclesial ministers, and second, professional expectations and performance standards determined within local parishes. Finally, the chapter provides an array of practices that animate these norms and positively impact parish culture.

197

Chapter 3 preemptively identified three particularly potent threats to Catholic culture: an escalating marriage crisis, greater availability of and ease of access to pornography, and increasing evidence that individuals lack a sufficiently developed moral compass or capacity. These may not be the most important topics in Catholic morality. They do, however, represent a direct challenge to the possibility of shaping a Catholic counterculture that is vibrant enough to resist the powerful tide of American social forces. And because of the threat they pose, they must be resisted in a robust and compelling fashion. This chapter addresses how to shape such a culture.

NARRATIVE:
LAY ECCLESIAL MINISTERS SHAPE CATHOLIC CULTURE

Institutions play a key role in shaping culture, and every institution is bound to a culture. "Institution" emphasizes the more formal structure of an entity, such as a corporation or a firm, that people usually identify with tangible realities such as buildings, the products produced, or the people in charge. "Culture," which comprises content, symbols, and actors, is the medium in which institutional identity grows and mission flows. In the case of a single parish, the institution refers mainly to the place—the church, rectory, and other parish buildings—but also the people, the pastor, his professional lay staff, and other important figures in a parish. Parish culture emphasizes the content and symbols, without, however, losing sight of the actors. As we noted when speaking about the nuns, some actors play a greater role in defining and changing a culture, and we refer to them as cultural catalysts. The complementary set of actors are cultural citizens who sustain the culture, day in and day out, by drawing on the content and making regular use of its symbols. Strengthening Catholic culture in the parish means shoring up the content, symbols, and actors. Doing that might entail either making more effective use of the content and symbols or modifying them to adjust to circumstances. With respect to people, it means identifying more cultural catalysts, and possibly even new ones, as well as securing the regular cooperation of the cultural citizens.

Lay ecclesial ministers take responsibility for sustaining, adjusting, and promoting the Catholic culture in today's parishes. They are characterized by their commitment to and responsibility for advancing liturgy, evangelization, and loving service in the parish.

Pastors are responsible for authorizing and developing an ensemble of lay ministers to assist in the work of liturgy, evangelization, and loving service. Some of these lay assistants are full-time, many are part-time; some are paid while others are volunteers. By virtue of their training in religious matters, their educational functions, and their commitment to the work of the

Church, some are designated lay ecclesial ministers. This group usually includes the principal of the Catholic school and teachers of religion in the school, catechists, pastoral associates, directors of religious education, and ministers of music. In some settings it can include the director of the sports or CYO program, parish nurses, and those who care for the religious needs of the elderly. This chapter focuses on the full- or part-time employees of a parish whose jobs directly or indirectly involve liturgy, evangelization, or loving service. These individuals at the parish level are the ones collectively referred to in this chapter as lay ecclesial ministers.[1] In addition to this professional group, the parish often employs a secretary and a maintenance person and relies on a large number of volunteers who regularly serve as extraordinary ministers of the Eucharist, lectors, altar servers, and ushers. Parishes also rely on volunteers involved with yearlong projects and others who contribute their efforts for specific events. Although secretaries, maintenance people, and the great army of volunteers are important to how well parishes function, our focus is primarily on the professional group of lay ministers.

For the most part, parish lay professionals are Catholics, though not necessarily parishioners in the parish where they work. It is quite possible for any competent secretary, maintenance person, or receptionist to find the parish situation appropriate and congenial. Their working at the parish is a job rather than a ministry and does not include a religious commitment to the particular parish. In what follows we assume all lay staff members—Catholic or not—support advancing the parish's Catholic mission.

Lay ecclesial ministers serve in parish settings, but the diocese often intersects with the parishes in ways that affect their employment. They are prepared and trained for parish ministry under the direction of the bishop and adhere to guidelines he has approved. They are expected not only to be committed Catholics but also either to prepare themselves by attaining an advanced degree in theology or ministry or by participating in various instructional sessions. Because the period of preparation for ministry is lengthy, most people enter such programs with the intention of being active in ministry for some period of time in a specific area or region.[2] Although lay ecclesial ministers prepare themselves to serve in a diocese and when hired are subject to diocesan policy and practice, most are not hired by the diocese. Rather they are hired in individual parishes by pastors who alone have the power to hire and, when warranted, fire them. Prior to being hired, lay ecclesial ministers often have no idea where they might serve. Similarly, once employed in a parish, long-term employment is not guaranteed. Over time, with the arrival of a new pastor or due to a parish closing, their services may no longer be desired or needed. At that point, they may find themselves back searching in the diocesan market for a suitable position.

An even more basic intersection point between the local parish and the diocese is the appointment of the pastor by the bishop. Once installed, the pastor is the leader of the parish. As leader, he chooses his staff based on the needs he perceives for the parish. In many cases, a new pastor will perceive different needs from the previous pastor. It is often precisely because of the advantages accruing from new perspectives that pastors are regularly changed. New pastors bring new views, experience, and skills from previous assignments. They also introduce a change in style. Invariably, some in the parish will like the new style while others find it disruptive or off-putting. Whatever the circumstances, a change of pastor offers parishioners a growth opportunity. They can develop a greater capacity to absorb change, adjust, and through it all maintain their commitment to Christ within a particular worshipping community. A change of pastor can also bring an end to service for some lay ecclesial ministers.

In subsequent sections, we will address the occasionally precarious position of lay ecclesial ministers in parishes who serve at the pleasure of a pastor who may not have hired them. At this point, however, we wish to reaffirm the central role they play in promoting and strengthening the Catholic community in the parish they serve. *Lay ecclesial ministers shape Catholic culture.*

DIOCESAN NORMS

Two types of norms shape the experience and effectiveness of lay ecclesial ministers. The first are diocesan norms for training and developing lay ecclesial ministers. The second define professional expectations and how the lay staff minister in the parish.

In order to be effective on the front lines of Catholic culture in parishes, lay ecclesial ministers must be knowledgeable and nimble. Educational and training programs that attend to cultural changes and emerging ministerial needs are therefore most helpful to them. Nuns were masterful at this kind of education and formation. The sisters had a pattern of adjusting their training to fit the needs of the hospitals or schools where they served. They also made adjustments in response to the broader changes in society. Earlier we cited a pertinent example. Up until the 1950s, sisters had very little theology in either their training as novices or afterward. Once sufficient feedback indicated there was a need for theological education, the training of the sisters was modified to include it. Most dioceses and archdioceses have programs for training and updating their lay ecclesial ministers, and much of it pertains to Church teaching and practices. Since most of those who teach these courses are themselves active practitioners in the field, their courses are geared to addressing the difficult practical issues catechists, directors of religious education, pastoral associates, and others actually confront. This approach makes it likely that diocesan-based training for lay ecclesial ministers has real utility for the work they do.

Religious sisters worked long and hard over a lifetime in service of the Church. They did not, however, need to worry about job security. That is not the case for lay ecclesial ministers. Like any for-profit organization that hires employees at market wages, most dioceses and archdioceses have personnel policies. These policies address issues relating to salary, experience, benefits, and procedures for making appeals about personnel decisions. What they do not address is any diocesan commitment with respect to long-term employment. Pastors, relying on analysis, personal style, and priorities, decide which personnel work best in their situation. That means lay ecclesial ministers sometimes lose their positions, and when they do, they are in a tough place. If dioceses want to have excellent lay ecclesial ministers, they have to address this problem. Giving those lay ecclesial ministers let go by a pastor some priority in securing other positions in other parishes is one way to go. Reasonable criteria for establishing priority would be years of experience and breadth of responsibility. By virtue of acquiring some expertise in theology as well as particular professional competence, lay ecclesial ministers demonstrate a commitment to the diocese. In return, the diocese should display an appropriate level of commitment to them. All things considered, a diocese will do better if it has a balanced number of experienced lay ecclesial ministers. This means a small percentage should have approximately twenty years or more of experience, and a larger percentage should have rather fewer years of experience.

Articulating personnel policies that keep lay ecclesial ministers working within the diocese is good for the diocese. Such policies will have an impact on the pastors who are asked to give priority in hiring to those lay ecclesial ministers with broad experience. Although this may be a constraint on any particular pastor, it will work for the benefit of the diocese or archdiocese as a whole.

PROFESSIONAL NORMS

Pastors hire lay ecclesial ministers and are responsible for establishing the standards for their employment, including compensation in conformity with diocesan guidelines. In order to be effective shapers of parish culture, the candidates should be able to demonstrate a number of commitments and competencies. They should be virtuous individuals with a deep and abiding faith that animates their lives and their vocational commitments. They should also have a hope-filled outlook that helps them persevere, and a love of God and neighbor that inspires their ministerial service.

It is also very important for lay ecclesial ministers to understand they do not act as private individuals. They are perceived to be and they are representatives of the Church, in particular of the diocese and the parish. In accepting their role, they accept the responsibility to live and do their work in ways that authentically and faithfully represent and reflect the Church's teaching. In other words, lay ecclesial ministers must bear witness to the faith.

Lay ecclesial ministers must also be knowledgeable. It is often said that culture is caught, more than taught. While that is true to some extent, it is also somewhat misleading. There is a great deal of content in any culture, and cultural fluency requires mastering that content. In order for a culture to survive, it needs knowledgeable experts who can pass on this rich content to the next generation. Catholic culture is a thick culture with rich content. Lay ecclesial ministers must master this content so they can be the "knowledge experts" within the parishes they serve.

Lay ecclesial ministers must be accountable for the work they do. These individuals make a commitment to serve the Church and the local community and to do so faithfully and effectively. Ministry is a vocation, but it is also a profession that requires demonstrated competence and a willingness to be accountable. Performance review is an essential component of collaborative ministry, and pastors have an obligation to make sure lay ecclesial ministers are constructively evaluated every year.

Lay ecclesial ministers do not take vows of poverty, and they have a right to expect reasonable compensation. Low salaries are an affront to justice. They also set a tone that can poison professional performance. Underpaid staff can rightly feel they are doing the parish a favor. This attitude fuels resentment, weak performance, and a lack of accountability. If parishes want their lay ecclesial ministers to be experienced, trained, and innovative professionals, they must have a salary and compensation structure linked to a review procedure which rewards these attributes.

Depending on their financial circumstances, parishes also have to be willing to hire people full-time for some positions. Because benefits packages can be costly, many smaller parishes prefer hiring people part-time (less than twenty hours per week). This makes it possible to avoid costly health benefits, which are legally required in many states for full-time empoyees. If there are many qualified senior people in an area who only want to work part-time, this approach can make good sense. By and large, however, a good full-time person provides greater stability and reliability than two part-time lay ministers.

All Christians are called to holiness. Ministers, however, have both a particular commitment to holiness and a responsibility to help the community they serve grow in holiness. Holiness is based on the recognition of who we are in relationship to God and Jesus Christ, and it is this awareness that leads us to love God and our neighbor and to live lives of virtue. Lay ecclesial ministers must never lose track of who is at the center of their work, and they must strive to deepen their relationship with God through Jesus Christ. It is a simple fact that the men, women, and children they serve in parishes look to lay ecclesial ministers as guides and exemplars of holiness in the same way they look to religious sisters and priests. Admittedly they do not live in community, most of them are married, and they do not take vows of poverty, chastity, or obedience. Nonetheless, they are in our day those individuals Max Weber identified as religious virtuosi.[3] And it is primarily because of this perceived "virtuosity" that parishioners are willing to listen to, learn from, and cooperate with the staff in a parish setting.

Most parish staffs today appropriately consider themselves members of a team. Although each minister has individual responsibility for a particular area, they work together to create an overall impact on parish culture. As is the case in an elementary school, a high school, or a college, the impact of the institution is much greater if all the people in the institution clearly and consistently promote a single culture. Even one or two dissidents can substantially diminish the work of the majority if they undermine various aspects of the culture. Suppose in a parish setting the staff has agreed to promote personal, daily prayer by children at the elementary school level. If one of the staff—either a catechist or another lay ecclesial minister—deems this emphasis to be misplaced and tells students they need not concern themselves with it, there can be a substantial overall impact. Other students will learn about it and word will spread. Eventually a rebellious kind of shadow culture can develop that undermines the various practices other ministers recommend to make sure their students pray daily.

The lay staff has to hammer out among themselves the points they are going to emphasize in common. If it is unlikely they can agree on one approach, they should try a different tack. It is far better for the staff to agree on a less aggressive approach that has universal support than to try to implement a high-stakes program that has one or two strident opponents.

Catholic culture operates within the ambit of broader American culture, which is strong and vibrant. Because it is so pervasive and strong, American culture easily overwhelms gentle, delicately modulated cultures within it. So, for Catholic culture to thrive and not simply be washed away under the powerful wave of the broader culture, it must be clear, vibrant, and resilient. To be resilient, a culture needs repetition and reinforcement. That means, then, that local parish culture relies ultimately on the strength of Catholic family culture. A central focus of parish activities, therefore, must be families and helping to support them in instilling Catholic content and norms. For the culture to be strong, both parents and parishes should be emphasizing approximately the same religious and moral things to young people.

American society today suffers from a crisis of moral capacity. This does not mean that young people and adults are not aware that such things as lying, stealing, killing, and rude behavior are wrong and should be avoided. Rather, it means they have gaps in their understanding as well as little appreciation of the degrees of wrongness in various acts. Some things are seriously wrong and others only moderately so. Unfortunately, many in our society seem unable to perceive the difference. Simply put, many Americans—Catholics included—do not have a very good moral compass. To even begin to address this crisis in our culture will require a new generation of religious educators who care as deeply as the nuns and who are willing to work every bit as hard as they did in shaping moral character.

The reasons for this diminished moral capacity are certainly complex. However, one contributing factor is that children do not receive a moral education that makes sense to them and makes a lasting impact. Children actively participating in a Catholic parish receive instruction on moral issues either in their religious education classes or at their Catholic school. They also occasionally hear about moral issues at Mass and at other parish events. But many young people go to Mass only occasionally, and their parents seldom address moral issues at home.[4] Also, many clergy and lay ministers shy away from being particular and establishing boundary lines that distinguish permitted actions from prohibited activity. As a result, many young people do not have a clear idea about what is right and wrong and which actions are seriously wrong. Catechists do their best against strong odds to morally educate children, but it simply is not enough. If we hope to make any headway against looming moral bankruptcy in our society, we have to do more. Parishes must mount comprehensive programs for young Catholics to develop their moral capacity for a lifetime. And they must involve the entire parish staff in the effort.

PRACTICES AND BENEFITS

The previous section listed a group of professional norms and a group of service norms. In order to have an impact, norms must be animated by practices that can beneficially impact the entire community. We recommend the following five pastoral practices as ways to animate professional norms.

- Thoroughly vet candidates before hiring.
- Hire fewer staff, but hire them full-time.
- Collect data from parents about moral norms for children.
- Words and actions of lay ministers should promote Catholic marriage.
- Ecclesial lay ministers should enthusiastically promote an authentic Catholic view of human sexuality.

CANDIDATES

Lay ecclesial ministers are expected to be virtuous people who can lead the community. Determining someone's virtue is important, but it is not always easy. At the very least it is possible for the pastor of any parish to make sure the staff has no serious impediments to ministry in their background that will be detrimental to the parish community. In the aftermath of the sexual abuse scandal in the United States, all dioceses now have norms for people who work with children in parishes. All parish personnel working regularly with children must have a background check regardless of whether they are paid or volunteer, whether they are priests, religious, or lay. In addition, all must participate in initial and ongoing education programs. These programs deal with how to spot sexual abuse and the steps that must be taken when individuals are suspected of violating diocesan norms. Along with securing the background checks mandated by the diocese, individual pastors should check references thoroughly. Far too often employers are willing to write positive references as a way to deal with ineffective or difficult employees. Unless would-be employers do some careful "digging around," these undetected problems will become theirs.

Professional Practice 1: Thoroughly vet candidates before hiring.

FULL-TIME STAFF

Excellent lay ecclesial ministers want a reasonable compensation package for the work they do. No one is in ministry to get rich, but parish staffs do expect a fair wage. Many parishes try to expand the number of lay ecclesial ministers they hire so they can provide more service. This approach can have a negative impact on the compensation packages they offer. It might make more sense for a parish to pare down positions and be more strategic about programs and initiatives they undertake. That will make it possible to pay fewer staff members more competitive salaries. This approach makes sure that the parish does not seek to balance the books on the backs of its lay ecclesial staff. If parishioners want more services than the staff can provide, better stewardship will have to make up the difference.

Professional Practice 2: Hire fewer staff, but hire them full-time.

CHILDREN'S MORAL NORMS

The service norms we suggest focus particular attention on families and developing moral capacity. Ideally, parish programs should support the Catholic culture parents instill. In order to develop such programs, the parish staff must first know what things families value, and that requires getting some data. An inventory of those parents worshipping in the parish that looks particularly at their religious and moral emphases would be a useful first step. Using a questionnaire or meeting with individual groups of families, the staff can get vital information about the religious and moral points parents emphasize. They can also find out what practices parents use to reinforce these points.

As a result of this survey, it might well become clear that a given parish faces particular challenges regarding Catholic culture and practice. The pastor may want the staff to confront these challenges in a comprehensive way. In order to be "comprehensive," any approach the staff takes will have to articulate and reinforce moral norms already important to families. Lay ministers can also supplement the parental points. However, the type of tight, integrated culture that we described earlier will not materialize unless there is considerable overlap between what the parish and the parents emphasize.

Parishes have to start with the possible, not the ideal. As the years go by and the culture is strengthened, the staff can do more. As long as they keep communicating with the parents, they can introduce additional emphases. At first, parents might be only passive in their support of these initiatives, but over time, these new emphases can take root and eventually flourish.

Professional Practice 3: Collect data from parents about moral norms for children.

SHAPING CATHOLIC CULTURE

We now address the three threats to American and Catholic culture we identified earlier in the book: an escalating marriage crisis, greater availability and easy access to pornography, and increasing evidence that individuals lack a sufficiently developed moral compass or capacity. Lay ecclesial ministers cannot and will not be effective as shapers of Catholic culture unless they are willing to be moral guides, to be seen as moral guides, and to work with parents in giving both guidance and support. As moral guides, they will need to communicate what the Church teaches and work with all parishioners in developing their moral capacity.

In order to describe a practical approach for moral guidance, we consider some particular cultural realities in a parish that poses a challenge for the staff. In what follows, we first describe two problems (marriage irregularities and pornography) and what general approach a parish might take to address them. We then make particular recommendations about how the parish staff should proceed to both clarify and reinforce a different behavior, especially for younger Catholics, that reflects Catholic cultural mores. In other words, our focus is on how the lay staff can clearly convey to parishioners what constitutes morally unacceptable activities as well as highly desirable activities in selected areas of American culture.

ANIMATING MARRIAGE NORMS

In the section on practices in chapter 9, two proposals were introduced for couples. One was an initiative for couples in which they gathered young married parishioners for dinner and talked about life and times particularly as they related to parish life. This initiative sought to get them more regularly involved in attending Sunday Eucharist and other activities of the parish. Our interest here is also on couples, but it is concerned with what being a Catholic couple means for how the couple behaves. These are delicate issues for lay ecclesial ministers to engage. They have to maintain a tactful balance between stating clearly what is expected of Catholics and offering a sufficiently inviting path that people might choose to go down.

We begin with a situation that focuses on families: divorced or unmarried couples living together. In one sense, most currently divorced couples or unmarried couples living together understand they are not acting in accordance with Catholic cultural norms. But for some reason, they have not done anything to change their situation. Some think dealing with the situation means an end to their relationship—and they could be correct. These couples are reluctant to even inquire about what they would need to do to set things right. Other couples basically understand things can be worked out, but because they do not believe that it makes a big difference, they put it off. Even though they cannot receive Holy Communion, they are not motivated to address the issue. From the parish point of view, these couples need pastoral guidance. In both cases there are reasonable steps the couples can take at the very least to clarify their situation in the eyes of the Church. After that, the pastoral challenge gets more daunting. If the situation can be remedied without severing the relationship, some couples will be willing to take the necessary steps. That is particularly true if they understand why the Church is so insistent. When the only way out of the dilemma for couples is to end a long-standing relationship, however, many, if not most, will be unwilling to proceed. This last situation is very painful for couples and difficult for lay ecclesial ministers, who must approach it with the greatest sensitivity and compassion.

Clarifying these situations is important for the couples involved, but it also has an impact on other people in the parish. It is a particularly excellent way to teach and reinforce norms for a group of young unmarried parishioners who are not living with a boyfriend or girlfriend but are looking forward to marriage at some point in the future. The important thing about this group is that they are on the threshold of making important decisions about how best to prepare for marriage. They need to be very clear about the Church's moral teaching about marriage and what motivates it. They also need to know that it matters to the Church and the Catholic community that they abide by these norms. If the staff communicates this information clearly and effectively to them, they will be in a far better position to make the wise choices that will support and sustain a lifelong commitment.

We are not recommending specific plans to reinforce the importance of making and adhering to one's marital vows "until death do us part." Many parishes already have initiatives that do this. We are instead emphasizing two important realities. First, in order to create a situation in which Catholic couples have the desire and skills to make and keep their marital vows, parishes generally have to do substantially more than they are doing now. After all, the statistics on cohabitation and divorce for Catholic couples are distressingly high and similar to the rest of the American population. Second, it is a fact that divorce among Catholics and the practice of unmarried Catholics living together wounds the Church.

Catholics understand that the sacraments provide sufficient grace to sustain and support couples in their marriages. It is not always easy for lay ministers, let alone the community, to keep this in mind. That is particularly true in the case of couples who face real difficulties because the Church does not sanction their relationships. Nevertheless, lay ecclesial ministers have a responsibility in these situations. By their words and actions, lay ministers should be making communal strength available to couples. The goal is to increase the number of marriages that embody a Catholic understanding. Lay ministers have to try hard, but they cannot compel results. Individual couples may choose not to respond to the graces of marriage, or faith communities may not provide the human and social supports grace relies on to have its impact. As leaders of the faith community, however, lay ministers have to lead the effort in providing the proper human and social support.

The larger context also counts. All Catholics are called to love their neighbor as themselves. The first site for love is the family. It is appropriate for lay ministers to help young people understand how they can prepare themselves to love another person for a lifetime and to provide support and direction to couples who are validly married as well as those who should marry. But it is also important to relate this love to a much broader love which embraces all of God's creatures. Loving, however, must always be specific. We are correctly skeptical of people who claim to love the poor in other nations but do not love their own spouses. Similarly, we are turned off by people who ooze love and care for a spouse but are never motivated to extend this love to others, either in the same community or country, or in other countries. Cultural integration of big concepts such as love requires attention in arenas large and small.

The staff of a parish cannot change an entire secular culture. But by finding effective ways to remind parishioners about the norms of Catholic moral teaching, they can have a cultural impact. Consider an analogy from the nonreligious world. In secular society, people are told not to eat too much, not to take drugs, not to smoke, not to drink too much, not to be too sedentary. They are encouraged to exercise a few times a week, eat healthy foods, be trim, and drink wine, but in modest amounts. Both the negative and positive approaches are good, helpful, and to be applauded. But secular society almost never says no to sex. For secular society, sex is fun, and the only possible negative consequence is a sexually transmitted disease.

Secular society does not have high goals for marriage and love in marriage. Similarly, secular society is completely unrealistic with respect to sex. It assumes that all teenagers will engage in "responsible sex," if that concept is not an oxymoron outside of marriage. For most young Catholics in our parishes, the only group which presents high ideals of love and marriage, coupled with realistic moral guidance about abstaining from sexual relations outside of marriage, is the Catholic Church. This is a reality in our society. Priests and lay ministers should accept this reality and draw the appropriate consequences, prudently but realistically, and without abandoning the central message of lasting love.

Many lay ecclesial ministers might find this approach less than appealing. Richard Gula, S.S., points out that when it comes to giving moral guidance, particularly in terms of sexual morality, lay ministers have a hard time.[5] While they understand they must be clear about Church teaching, they also want to be compassionate in how they deal with people. If lay leaders lack compassion, their judgment could push people away from the Church rather than reconciling them to it. But if, in their desire to be compassionate, lay leaders fail to represent Church teaching faithfully, they will not help individuals expand their moral understanding. They will also cause confusion about what the Church actually teaches.

Professional Practice 4: Words and actions of lay ministers should promote Catholic marriage.

CATHOLIC PUSHBACK TO PORNOGRAPHY

Pornography is not a new phenomenon in society by any means. What is new is the extent of its availability and the ease with which it can be accessed. In the previous century, this industry's wares were available almost solely through the mail or in adult entertainment enclaves located in and around airports and other less than savory parts of local communities. Now, pornography pours into our homes—often unbidden—on cable television channels and through the Internet. Pornography is, of course, a pervasive problem in

American society, but one that is low on many people's worry list. Unless pornography involves children in its content or is accessed by them, secular society generally considers it benign or at most a nuisance. Because most people believe it does no harm to others, American society tolerates pornography and the courts protect it under the right of free expression. The Catholic Church has a radically different perspective. Catholic moral teaching sees it as a pernicious influence that distorts human sexuality and turns human beings into objects to be used for personal gratification.

Finding ways to deal with this growing problem is a critical issue for the Catholic community and for parishes. After all, while pornography is a national and international reality, it is most frequently accessed locally. Lay ecclesial ministers can make a difference here, and they should seize the opportunity. But in doing so, they must be careful not to expose young people to the issue before they should even be aware of it. Helpful articles made available to parents, an occasional talk in the parish for young adults, occasional data in the parish bulletin—all these are avenues which can be used to communicate the Catholic approach to those in their teens or older. The focus here is not so much on particular programs but rather on approach. In order to make any real impact, the staff will need to act repeatedly in a variety of ways that reinforce Catholic cultural norms.

Individuals develop moral clarity as a result of knowing what is recommended, what is permitted, and what is forbidden. Any good strategy for developing greater moral clarity about an issue has to address all three categories of behavior. That means the staff will need to clarify what exactly the Church teaches about human sexuality and the place of eroticism in healthy human sexual relationships. They will also have to be quite clear that pornography is beyond the pale and explain why.

A good place to begin is with the positive. God designed human beings as wonderfully complex creatures, made in the image and likeness of their Creator. We have an intellect, by which we understand other people and figure them out and also understand how the world works. Because there are many things we can do in this world and because God calls each one in a different way to do important things, we have a will by which we choose what to do. We also have the power to love other people and we hope for love in return. God also made us embodied. We understand by using our brain, we make selections by examining different alternatives, and we love people by words, gestures, and actions.

Human beings are physically attracted to one another. Physical attraction can be the start of love, it can assist love, it can propagate love, and it can induce great acts of valor. Unfortunately, sexual attraction can also undermine love or ruin love if it is not disciplined and managed. And thousands of generations of human experience, recorded in literature and the oral tradition, offer abundant evidence that it is not easy to manage physical attraction. As far as we can tell, all human beings have to struggle so that the physical attraction they experience is guided by their intellect and will.

The human body is good and, in the right context, sex is good. It is only when we misuse the body or sex that we have problems. God made us as bodily spirits, but He also embedded within us the realization that we have to develop in our ability to control our impulses. Not everything we want is good for us; not everything we yearn to have right now should be indulged. Our parents repeat this to us a hundred times and eventually we learn that they are correct. Just as children learn to control the movement of their bodies through sports, gymnastics, and dancing, which are also fun, so it takes years for a person to understand how to use his or her body in interaction with other men or women. Learning what must be managed and how to manage it becomes especially challenging after the hormonal changes of adolescence occur.

On the negative side, the challenge is to avoid reducing another human being to a single dimension, the sexual one. Consider a nonsexual example of reduction one of us had at a university some years ago. On a lark, one of the undergraduates, a very nice and popular young man, entered a hot dog eating contest. Not only did he win, but his photo was on the front page of the local newspaper. From that day forward for several years, many people would interact with him only by speaking about this event and his ability to consume hot dogs. He was patient with people, but after a few months it became both boring and trying for him. He did not want to criticize people, but somehow he had been reduced to a hot dog eating machine. For many of his acquaintances, he was nothing more than a fun person to speak with because he had been publicized for winning a funny contest.

In a similar but more serious way, it is wrong to reduce other human beings to nothing but primary or secondary sexual characteristics. To do so is a demeaning reduction that is corrosive of full human relationship. It is also wrong to sexually entice or treat another person like a sexual animal to be aroused, regardless of whether there is any intent to have sexual contact. This kind of behavior distorts and diminishes the full complexity of human beings who have feelings, aspirations, convictions, and commitments.

Through sexual intimacy, human beings express love and bring children into the world. But the law of God, experience, natural law, and the tradition of the Church teach us that sexual intimacy belongs within a lifelong commitment, made between a man and woman, which includes accepting children lovingly from God. In this context, sexual intercourse is good and fitting. But, outside of marriage, neither sexual acts nor sexual images should be used for recreation and personal pleasure. Indulging in this kind of recreation is seductive, but dangerous. It makes it much more difficult for us to relate to another man or woman in a full way, and it also makes it more difficult for us to manage our sexual impulses.

Young people must be given appealing and persuasive materials that explain and extol a Catholic understanding of human sexuality, including its boundaries and limits. Young people are inquisitive, but curiosity is not a sufficient justification for their dipping into the pornographic trough. And they have to be told this by parents, lay staffs, priests, and other respected authority figures in their lives. After all, it is possible to waste a whole life trying to satisfy curiosity. We live in an age that for commercial reasons sexualizes human beings even when they are still young. The fashion industry, television, art, and film offer a myriad of not-so-subtle suggestions that the role of women is to tantalize. It is a bitter irony that the feminist movement that once heartily resisted such offensive and undignified messages about women now seems to embrace them as signs of independence, freedom, and "making it" in what was once a man's world. Catholic parents, Catholic institutions, and the staffs of Catholic parishes have a moral obligation to give other messages to young people. They need to make it perfectly clear that pornography is offensive to human dignity, dangerous to healthy sexual development, and simply off-limits for people who are serious about psychological health and holiness. They also need to make it clear to young women that provocative dress is not benign and can undermine their own desires to be appreciated fully for all their God-given gifts and capacities and their full humanity.

Pornography is distinct from but related to the broader media industry. Television, movies, music, and print media revel in using sex to attract people's attention, interest, and money. In order to keep their moral balance, Catholics must be adept at navigating the media. Lay ecclesial ministers can help them by pointing out that the choices Catholics make about what media to consume should be based on expectations about content. The media are convinced that people will continue to choose sex and violence as their preferred themes, week after week and month after month. Young people should be encouraged to avoid films, music, and television programs that use sex as a hook. In his first letter to the Christian community in Corinth, St. Paul asks whether the Christians have forgotten what happened to them as a result of baptism: "Or do you not know that your body is a temple of the Holy Spirit who is in you, whom you have from God, and that you are not your own? For you have been bought with a price: therefore glorify God in your body" (1 Cor. 6:19–20). Yes, we Christians should stay healthy, trim, and fit. But Christians should also avoid sexually exploitative media. They not only pose a problem for individuals here in this country but also fuel the hype that will attract countless more viewers around the world.

Some Catholics defend going to movies with heavy sex or violence with comments such as "It's just entertainment" or "I never think of it afterwards" or "That's what life is like and we should not hide from it." In fact, such movies and their more graphic images are never just entertainment.

People do remember the films they see. Just think of how readily we join a conversation when the topic is a particular film we, too, have seen. Images stay with us. Lay ministers should remind parishioners that movie choices and all media choices they make should reflect a Christian calling.

Professional Practice 5: Ecclesial lay ministers should forcefully promote a Catholic view of sexuality.

PROVIDING MORAL GUIDANCE

Discipline is an essential component of moral character, and institutions that give moral guidance and develop character must have disciplinary systems. Without them, they cannot effectively communicate cultural norms and taboos. That was certainly the case in Catholic schools when the nuns were running them, and it is true today under the leadership of lay ecclesial ministers. How authorities discipline young people shapes their moral character. If it is done well, consistently, and fairly, children learn what is right and wrong and begin to appreciate the nuance that is part of developing moral capacity and a good conscience.

Practical strategies are essential for creating good moral capacity in children. The strategic approach we suggest is designed to help young Catholics understand what kinds of behaviors are seriously wrong. It also creates an opportunity for lay ecclesial ministers to interact with young people as moral authorities and helps young people develop a moral compass. The Church benefits in the process and so does society at large. The approach has four particular strategies:

- Call children to task for their bad behavior.
- Expect children to memorize some moral norms.
- Create lists of "dos" and "don'ts."
- Allow students to make up for mistakes.

BAD BEHAVIOR

The principal usually is the ultimate disciplinary authority in schools, and individual teachers are the ones primarily responsible for discipline in their classrooms. Most classroom issues pertain to maintaining order and quiet at designated times. However, issues with respect to lying, stealing, and cheating—significant moral issues—also arise in Catholic school classrooms. Teachers are expected to address such issues in a full, forthright manner. Students involved in these types of behaviors are usually referred to the principal, who gives them an appropriate sanction. The Catholic school is one sphere of parish life in which lay personnel have a well-organized and effective disciplinary system operating. In most parishes, however, the vast majority of Catholic children attend public school. While these schools certainly have disciplinary systems, they are not focused on forming conscience in the same way Catholic schools are. Catholic students in public schools need Catholic moral guidance. We owe it to the many children in our religious education programs, as well as those who only show up at Sunday Mass, to assist parents and catechists in the formation of childrens' consciences. A unified parish staff can make a substantial impact in this regard.

Lay staff can assist parents and catechists and play a vital role in forming consciences by adhering to four principles. First, the approach should be a team effort. Second, one staff member should be the primary disciplinary authority—or primary authority as we term it—in charge of a disciplinary team. The team will be composed of all members of the parish staff, both full-time and part-time, both paid and volunteer. It is important to remember that when children seriously misbehave, they either know they are doing something wrong or strongly suspect it and want to see whether they can get away with it. The children expect adults to correct them. If an adult sees children doing something wrong and does nothing, the children get the message and typically continue the same behavior. Only now they are less sure there is something wrong with what they are doing. Some intervention by any adult about inappropriate public behavior is usually good as long as it is a measured reprimand. More serious issues should be referred to the primary authority. Third, the team should also have a moral guide, someone different from the primary authority, who is responsible for presenting to students both general moral principles as well as specific examples of serious and lesser wrongs. Fourth, the staff should model the difference between more serious and less serious behavioral disruptions in their own reaction to incidents. If a child does something seriously wrong, the primary authority should intervene directly with the student; if appropriate, the parents should be called in and a reasonable sanction should be imposed.

As indicated, one staff member should be perceived as the primary authority. This person is both responsible for articulating policies and, in referred cases, implementing the policy. Children expect adults to monitor their activities; when they are out of line, they expect to be told so by adults. The primary authority makes sure this happens consistently. Children should know they can appeal disciplinary sanctions to this person, who also attends to doubtful cases referred by the staff. When a teacher or another staff member is unsure about what to do in individual cases, they should just send the young people to the primary authority. If that person is not around, an appointment should be made for a reasonable later time.

This helps assure clarity and consistency, which are important for helping children develop their moral capacity. Also having time for children to consider what they will say to a person in authority about some event that occurred can be very educational and formative. If staff members disagree with an approach taken by the primary authority, they should not undermine the decision but take it up later and in private. Dissatisfaction with an approach taken is material to be discussed with the disciplinary team or, if necessary, with the pastor.[6]

Strategy 1: Call children to task for their bad behavior.

MEMORIZING MORAL NORMS

The second aspect of moral development focuses on education and reinforcement. The moral guide has the responsibility of articulating and consistently repeating important moral principles with appropriate applications. The moral principles should not vary much in their formulation from the lower grades through high school. That way they become engraved in the young Catholics' developing minds. However, the applications of the principles to particular circumstances should definitely vary according to age.

What the moral principles should be is up to the parish staff. They should be of such a length that they can be memorized and clear enough so they can be applied. One very good set of principles would be the Ten Commandments. All children above the third grade, for example, would be expected to have the Ten Commandments memorized. Children could be informed that they should be able to state any or all of the Ten Commandments to a staff person, parent, or catechists when asked. If the Ten Commandments are the basic building blocks, the moral guide can put short pieces in the parish bulletin or publicize them in other ways so that children understand what constitutes serious and lesser wrongs against one of the commandments.

Strategy 2: Expect children to memorize some moral norms.

DO AND DON'T LISTS

A supplemental approach provides a more detailed list of actions, stating them both as prohibitions and positive actions, whenever possible. The advantage of listing the prohibitions is that they clearly define the boundaries. The list for children in the younger grades would be short, but the list could be increased as the children mature. For example, the list for children in the younger grades might include: no lying—always tell the truth; no stealing—respect other people's property; no hating—be kind to everyone; no bad language—speak well of and to others; no fighting—settle your differences fairly; no disrespecting parents or teachers—always be polite and obedient to parents and teachers; and no missing Mass on Saturday or Sunday—go to Mass each week and on Holy Days. For children in the older grades, the list can be supplemented with other rules: no drugs, no cheating, no sexual touching, no hitting or physical violence, no suggestive dressing, always complete homework, give money to and pray for poor people. For high school, the list can be extended even further and made more explicit in terms of things teenagers must confront: no sex outside of marriage, no abortion, no war, no euthanasia, no pornography, no masturbation, no slander, and no artificial birth control. On the positive ledger: frequently offer to help a parent or teacher; work once a week with the poor, the ill, or the elderly; ask questions when you do not understand something. Whatever the specific items included on the list may be, the staff should know the list well and occasionally ask students to recite it.

Strategy 3: Create lists of "dos" and "don'ts."

MAKING AMENDS

A fourth way to promote moral discipline among the young is to impose small sanctions for misbehavior that allow students to "redeem themselves." Children in particular like to be offered the opportunity to make up for mistakes by doing something positive for the parish. Having an opportunity to help a staff member is a good approach. That way the children understand they have been forgiven and that they are not being shunned or excluded in any way. The staff should also not shy away from potentially difficult circumstances, such as teenage dances. Things will undoubtedly happen at these events and the staff will have to deal with them. But how the staff does that will be an important component in their moral development efforts, and it will be a further help to young people who are forming their own consciences.

Strategy 4: Allow students to make up for mistakes.

OUTCOMES

The staff should gather data to determine whether their approach is effective. Most important is whether, over time, young people gain greater knowledge about what is right and wrong. One can use an established questionnaire, or the parish can compose its own.

In his various writings and talks, Pope Benedict has urged the West to draw on its Christian tradition to gain strength for the present. The Holy Father wants the Catholic Church at its various levels to preach the Gospel in ways that animate Christians in their current situation. Clearly the parish staff has an integral role to play in this important work. They are the people who will bring Catholic tradition to bear in the lives of many Catholics. They will be the men and women who shape the Catholic culture. Christianity has powerful resources in its tradition. We must be willing to call upon them in effective ways as we reach out to children, teenagers, and adults.

FAITH AND FINANCES

Parishes are faith communities, but they are also organizations that have financial realities. Without financial wherewithal, parishes will not long exist, nor will staffs be hired, or services be provided. In order to have a strong culture, parishes must manage their finances in order to effectively accomplish their religious mission. The next chapter focuses on finances and parish culture.

NOTES

1. For ease of reference, we use the term "lay ecclesial ministers" to embrace a broader group of parish lay workers than those designated by bishops. The document published by the U.S. Conference of Catholic Bishops, *Co-Workers in the Vineyard of the Lord* (Washington, D.C.: 2005), provides a guide for bishops to policies concerning lay ecclesial ministers. The document characterizes lay ecclesial ministers as people who, to fulfill their jobs, need religious preparation and formation as well as authorization from the bishop, and who exercise leadership in specific areas at the parish level and also collaborate closely with priests, deacons, and the bishop in carrying out their ministry (p. 10).

2. In large metropolitan areas, the local region may include a number of dioceses. In most cases, however, there is but a single diocese embracing the region.

3. According to Max Weber, all religions have a small group of individuals who aspire to or demonstrate a religious intensity or capacity for witness that is recognized and legitimated by other adherents. See "Social Psychology of the World Religions" in *From Max Weber: Essays in Sociology*, eds., H. H. Gerth and C. Wright Mills (New York: Oxford University Press, 1958), 287–288. See also Patricia Wittberg, *From Piety to Professionalism—and Back? Transformation of Organized Religious Virtuosity* (Lanham, MD: Rowman & Littlefield, 2006), 4–12.

4. Parents address behavioral issues almost daily with their children, but many parents do not highlight the moral significance of behavior.

5. Richard M. Gula, *Ethics in Pastoral Ministry* (New York: Paulist Press, 1996), 57–58.

6. For any issue pertaining to sexual abuse, a staff member should always adhere to diocesan policy. Any suspect infraction should be reported to the proper civil authority.

12

Finances and Growth

In order to provide helpful services, parishes need adequate resources. Practically all these resources come, in fact, from the community that a parish serves. Some parishes are situated in well-to-do communities, while others are in poorer communities. Nonetheless, with some exceptions, the parishes are expected to generate enough revenue to cover their annual expenses. Beyond balancing the budget, parishioners are asked to contribute to diocesan projects, national and international episcopal projects, and the Holy See. Whether parishes continue as individual units depends in large part on their ability to balance the expense of services offered with the revenues they receive. After describing what is expected of parishes, this chapter focuses on the culture of giving and the importance to the Church for as many parishes as possible to have some funds available for growth.

NARRATIVE

The Church on earth is engaged in the three activities of liturgy, evangelization, and loving service. In most U.S. parishes, these activities are traditionally carried out with a priest and a modest lay staff. St. Paul did not wish to be a burden in fledgling Christian communities, and, as much as possible, he avoided imposing himself on them. Speaking in the plural, Paul reminds the Christian community at Thessalonica that "[we did not] eat anyone's bread without paying for it, but with labor and hardship we kept working night and day so that we would not be a burden to any of you" (2 Thes. 3:8). Keeping the staff small and expenses down is a good way for the modern Church to imitate St. Paul.

St. Paul worked at a time when Christians, who were few in number, met for their Sunday celebrations in the homes of well-to-do Christians. As the Church spread, more resources were needed to build churches, provide assistance to widows and the poor, and support missionary activities.

In the United States, bishops decided to establish a parochial school in as many parishes as possible. The responsibility of raising funds to cover the cost of these schools was given to the local pastor. A sizable fraction of parishioners' children, but by no means all, were educated in parish schools. Congregations of nuns were an essential component of this educational enterprise, and they provided both instruction and leadership in the schools. Religious orders needed funds to train their sisters, and these funds came not from the parish but from individual donors (themselves parishioners in some church) who supported the work of particular congregations.

Religious education programs have always been a fixture in local parishes. These programs provide faith instruction for Catholics attending public or non-Catholic private schools. In recent decades, as more and more Catholic children opted out of Catholic schools, parishes devoted more effort, personnel, and resources to these religious education programs.

In general, the Catholic Church in the United States has adhered to three principles with respect to generating support for parishes: first, balanced budgets for most parishes; second, a balanced budget for each diocese with diocesan revenue stemming from parish levies, diocesan-wide collections, and aggressive fund-raising from wealthier donors living in the diocese; and third, support for poorer parishes for a limited period of time. We also identify and heartily recommend implementing a fourth principle: developing funds that can be used for growth, outreach, and investment in physical plant. This last principle is pertinent to fulfilling our responsibilities as Catholics in our modern situation.

The first principle is that parishes should be self-supporting and not rely on diocesan subsidies to cover their annual expenses. This application of the subsidiarity principle puts responsibility for raising and spending funds with the smallest unit that most directly influences both expenses and revenues collected—the local parish. It is appropriate that decisions relevant to administration and organization of the parish be made there. Finances have a big impact on the parish, which must coordinate expenses and revenues so as not to run a loss over the long run. A diocese is willing to make loans to individual parishes, but the general expectation is that the loan will be repaid in the ensuing years. The parish is expected to gauge which services should be provided and at what expense. It then must reconcile this judgment concerning services and the costs of providing them with the reality of what financial resources can be raised from parishioners. If donations turn out to be insufficient to cover the expenses, the expenses have to be reduced.

Included in the expenses of every parish are the *cathedraticum* and Peter's Pence. The cathedraticum is a moderate type of tax collected annually for the support of diocesan needs that is taken out of general parish funds and transmitted directly to the diocese by the parish. The diocese determines the dollar amount of the cathedraticum for each parish but takes into consideration normal annual revenues from the parish when making the calculation.

Peter's Pence is an annual appeal for funds to support the worldwide activities of the Holy See. Once a year in the United States, parishioners are urged to be generous in contributing to a second Sunday collection dedicated to Peter's Pence. The total amount, which is collected in specially designated envelopes, is sometimes supplemented by general parish funds. It is then forwarded to the U.S. Bishops Conference for processing and transferal to the Holy See.

To summarize, the basic expectation is that parishes operate with a balanced budget after accounting for their own direct expenses and the cathedraticum. Pastors have to justify any deviations from this norm to the diocese, and the diocese must approve them.

Aside from some fairly small financial accounts, most parishes have no independent wealth. The parish usually includes a contingency fund in its annual budget. In addition, it may have some modest assets in some bank accounts and perhaps also some endowments for special purposes. The endowments generate funds each year, which can be used only for the purposes designated when the endowment was established. Many of these endowments provide scholarship money for students studying at the parochial school, prize money for outstanding student performance, or money to support special awards or parish events. The annual funds generated by these endowments, however, are relatively small, usually far less than 10 percent of the annual revenues generated by a parish.

Most dioceses have larger foundations that support seminarians, and some have foundations supporting inner-city parochial schools or other particular activities. With the exception of such funds, most dioceses rely on the *cathedraticum* or other regular diocesan collections or fund-raisers to cover their annual expenses.

The second principle takes into account that some activities important for the maintenance and spread of the faith extend beyond the parish. These activities occur within the diocese or within a broader political or geographical unit. To cover the expenses incurred by these operations, revenues are generated in two ways. For the ordinary expenses of the diocese, each parish is expected to pay the *cathedraticum*. For additional special diocesan projects, collections are taken up in the parishes, and parishioners are expected to contribute according to their means. There are similar collections undertaken on behalf of the assembly of all bishops in the United States, the U.S. Conference of Catholic Bishops.

In addition to and distinct from appeals made in parishes, the diocese itself or the national group of bishops organizes fund-raising activities. Those
raising funds for these units reach out to specific nonparish groups or potential donors and ask for significant contributions to fund special projects.
Similarly, church organizations with a national or international scope, such
as religious orders of women or men, must generate funds through the services they provide to the faithful or do their own fund-raising.

The third principle recognizes that some parishes are in special circumstances. Parishes in this category are not capable of raising enough money to
cover their basic costs. In this situation, parishes would usually be expected
to reduce their expenses to bring expenses and revenues into equilibrium.
The parishes in this third category warrant an exception (which implies
diocesan support) for a variety of possible reasons. The most frequent reason for a compelling exception is the strategic location of a parish or a tem-
porary decline in the ability of the parish to generate sufficient revenues.

A poor parish might have an impressive church building that is expensive
to keep up. Were the parish community beginning anew, they would build
a more affordable structure that was less expensive to maintain. But the
structure is there and usually has an impressive history embedded in its
stones. The diocesan hope is that, over time, more Catholics, perhaps some
with greater financial means, will gradually become associated with the
parish. At that point, the parish would once again be able and expected to
cover its expenses. For an indeterminate amount of time, however, it may
make good sense to support the parish from general diocesan funds rather
than suppressing it and selling the property. A slightly different argument
may prompt the diocese to cover the expenses of poor parishes. In this case,
even though no financial turnaround is expected in the short or intermediate run, the diocese has the means to support poor people and chooses to
give them encouragement by providing assistance to the parish.

The fourth principle is observed by some ecclesiastical units, but not by
most. We recommend that it be more widely implemented, even in parishes
with very modest resources. This principle asserts that every church unit
should have some funds available for growth, outreach, and investment in
physical plant. This means that most parishes, dioceses, and national
groups of bishops should allocate some funds annually to activities which
promote evangelization and the spread of the Gospel. Reasonable people
may disagree about the correct appropriation in the annual budget for a category including growth, outreach, and investment in physical plant. To us,
a reasonable average annual amount would be approximately 4 or 5 percent of projected annual revenues.

Ministerial needs involving financial outlays have greatly increased in the
United States in the past thirty years. There are more Catholics, and Catholics
also have an expanded sense of what the Church should be doing. Also, as we

have noted many times before, the Catholic Church in the United States is still adjusting to the tectonic changes brought about by the steep decline in the number of religious sisters and the similar, although not as dramatic, decline in the number of active priests. For all these reasons, parishes have had to hire more lay assistants. When most nonpresbyteral ministry was performed by sisters, expenses were limited. The sisters lived simply, and the parish usually only covered the expenses of running the convent plus food needs for the sisters and other incidental expenses. The sisters received no health or retirement benefits, which, unfairly, were deemed the responsibility of the religious congregation. This arrangement minimized expenses to the local parish and transferred considerable expense to the sponsoring religious congregation.

The increased need for lay staff to provide ministerial services means that, compared to fifty years ago, parishes have to raise more money, relative to the average family income of parishioners. Consequently, the average parishioner in the twenty-first century is probably being asked to contribute more (relative to the average standard of living) to the parish than had been the case in the twentieth century. Furthermore, the need for qualified and adequately compensated lay ministers working in parishes will only increase in the coming years as the numbers of available sisters, brothers, and priests continues to fall.

An honest parish financial narrative should acknowledge and justify to parishioners why expenses for a typical parish in the twenty-first century are more burdensome to the average parishioner than they were in the twentieth century. The increased burden comes because dioceses need to support once thriving parishes that now lack regularly participating or contributing Catholic parishioners. Also, due to a diminished number of sisters and brothers, the financial burden for the average parishioner is heavier. Tuition rates in Catholic schools are higher and the costs of running large programs in religious education are greater as well. Pastors have to cover these expenses, and they turn to the parishioners for help. In our experience, the great majority of pastors are neither greedy nor overly focused on money. Rather, the personnel expenses involved in running a normal modern parish are simply higher than they used to be.

The unfortunate fact that many Catholics are nominal rather than practicing Catholics also makes an impact on parish finances. Because the majority of Catholics do not regularly attend Mass on Sunday, those who do must play a bigger role in covering normal parish expenses.

Finally, both Pope John Paul II and Pope Benedict XVI have made evangelization a priority for the Church. In the United States, this means finding new ways to share the good news of belief in Jesus Christ with those who are open to this message. It also means inviting them to become regular members of a worshipping, praying community that provides loving service.

Whatever the new outreach activities are, they will necessarily involve some expense. This additional expense for growth in evangelization will be modest, but it, too, must be shouldered by parishioners.[1]

Parishes are definitely not corporations. Nonetheless, earlier in this book we argued there is a concept from the world of business that can reasonably be applied to Catholic parishes in the United States. In business, a corporation, firm, or partnership is usually interested in market share. Let's examine what market share means in a parish.

Suppose the Sleek Corporation produces computers. Sleek wants to know the percentage of all computers sold in a given year in a particular geographical region where its product is sold. That is Sleek's market share expressed as a percentage of the whole market. When properly understood in a theological and ecclesial context, market share should concern the Catholic Church in the United States. Attracting people to be regular participants in the life of the parish occurs through a triple dynamic. First, the leadership of the parish structures parish activities so that they both conform to Church norms and are attractive to potential practicing Catholics. That means regular parish activities should be both genuine reflections of the Church's liturgy and belief and also appeal to some deep yearnings for religious fulfillment that modern individuals have. Thus motivated, each parish should have a reasonable schedule of Sunday Masses and a decent array of parish organizations. Second, the parish should have some outreach activities (for example, a hospitality committee or signs outside the parish church) that offer potential parishioners a glimpse of what participation in the regular activities of the parish is like.

These first two components enable the faith community to worship together and can also generate some interest in the parish on the part of some people. The third component is the work of the Holy Spirit, which disposes some people to practice their faith in a parish and avail themselves of the graces offered through a regular sacramental life. But even in this divine initiative, parishes play a role. They do so through the prayers of parishioners that the Holy Spirit will move more people to join the Catholic Church through this local community. In the end, however, Christians come to belief through the work of the Holy Spirit and, also through the action of the Holy Spirit, live out their belief regularly in a local community of believers.

Masses, loving service, religious education, prayer groups, and many other activities of parishes do not take place in a religious market in any normal sense of the word. Nonetheless, if a local church is committed to evangelization and if it is adhering to the principles for institutional success, all other things, including the work of the Holy Spirit, being equal, the parish should be attracting people to its regular services. Planning, proclaiming, and praying are all essential components of evangelization, and it is important for a parish to plan to attract more people and increase the size or breadth of the religious services it offers.

There are some downsides to the term "increasing market share." For one thing, it overemphasizes human activity and underemphasizes the divine initiative. Nonetheless, a strong advantage is that it stresses the importance of planning in the Church, which, while of divine origin, still shares many features of any social organization.

An emphasis on increasing market share may also suggest that any parish that does not increase its numbers is in some way delinquent. Such a conclusion may well be unwarranted for any particular parish. As is the case in any large organization, some parts are contracting even when the overall picture is of solid growth. In a country the size of the United States, it is unavoidable that the number of Catholics in some regions will be growing more quickly than in other regions. In areas where growth in the number of Catholics is negative, over the long run, parishes will have to be closed. But in a vibrant Church, the impact of growing regions should far outweigh the impact of contracting ones.

NORMS

Due to the diminished number of priests, parishes have started to cover larger areas, and some have become more complex because they now encompass what used to be two or more individual parishes. In many places, a parish is now under the direction of a single pastor even though Masses and usually some other services are offered at multiple sites.[2] The increased structural complexity of many parishes makes it important that solid accounting measures are in place and that the parish staff adheres to good financial practices.

Bishops and pastors have a fiduciary responsibility to the faithful to make sure that parish financial transactions can be easily monitored at the local and diocesan level. As noted in chapter 10, in previous centuries, as long as the parish accounts were in the black, pastors were trusted to handle all parish accounts themselves, with minimal review by diocesan authorities. That is no longer a tenable approach. Rather, each diocese should review all parish budgets, income statements, and balance statements. Furthermore, the diocese should have clear norms which are communicated to pastors and pertinent parish staff, and the diocese should also have regular procedures for verifying adherence to these norms.

As part of the diocesan program to ensure conformance with their norms, parish financial data should be submitted to the diocese in a consistent format. This will make it possible for diocesan authorities to understand what is happening during the course of a given year and over time in a single parish, and to make useful comparisons between and among parishes.

Both the pastor and the layperson in the parish responsible for entering financial data must be given sufficient training, and both should be held accountable when someone fails to adhere to diocesan standards. Similarly, the person in charge of day-to-day collections and expenditures must have sufficient training to know what actions should be taken when solid evidence emerges indicating the parish will not meet its projected budget for the year.

A realistic danger in parish finances is the misappropriation of funds. In recent years, many instances of laypeople and priests taking significant amounts of parish (and diocesan) funds for their private gain have been discovered and covered in the press.[3] The possibility for larceny and fraud (embezzlement) is constant, and they can occur in any parish.[4] Nonetheless, a parish can strengthen safeguards that inhibit misappropriation of funds.

Because parishes are becoming more complex financial structures, most parishes should have individual annual audits or compilation reports. This would constitute one important step toward financial transparency at the parish level. Furthermore, these audits should be made available in some appropriate format to all parishioners or at least a group of interested parishioners. An auditor would check to make sure that procedures are in place to prevent fraud by people involved in parish finances. The auditor would also verify parish conformity to diocesan-wide policies. It is certainly true that auditors do not catch all misuse of funds. Nonetheless, auditors make misappropriation more difficult. Parishioners should be confident that the money they donate is being used efficiently for the presumed purposes of such contributions. As recently as twenty or thirty years ago, parishes simply did not worry about having annual audits performed by an outside auditor. That approach is no longer reasonable. In an age when financial transparency is needed in the Catholic Church, the subsidiarity principle indicates that the smallest reasonable unit should take responsibility for contributing to financial transparency. Based on this analysis, investing in an outside audit or at least an outside financial review by an auditor is a wise move for most parishes.

In financial matters, the pastor does well to consult regularly with diocesan officials, with his own parish finance committee, and also with experienced people in his own parish. Norms for good financial processes constantly change, and people who are professionally engaged in financial procedures can give helpful advice. In the keeping of financial accounts and in financial reporting, parishes have to maintain a level of expertise and openness that generates confidence in parishioners and other potential donors.

According to canon law, every parish is supposed to have a finance committee charged with reviewing the financial plans and performance of the parish.[5] One or more members of such a committee should be authorized by the pastor to review particular expenses charged to the parish account by the pastor, parochial vicar, priests in residence, or the staff.

Priests traditionally live in the rectory, and many modern rectories are simultaneously residences and parish meeting facilities. This situation makes it easy for priests to charge what should be personal expenses to the parish. For example, vacation expenses, dinners at restaurants with friends, the expense of automobile maintenance, and costs for alcohol beyond modest amounts of wine or beer all should be paid by the individual priest, not the parish. Some laypeople should be able to review the accounts to verify that these norms were adhered to during the past year. On the revenue side, there should be a careful accounting of the amounts taken in, not only by weekly collections but also by special collections. Carefully crafted protocols should be written up and strictly adhered to. Similarly, large donations made by parishioners to the pastor, in contrast to the parish, should not be allowed. If special circumstances warrant exceptions, the circumstances and amounts of the donations should be subject to review both by a subcommittee of the parish finance committee consisting only of laypeople as well as by the diocese. Even without considering budgetary issues, a parish finance committee can perform a great service to the parish.

Some parishes struggle to meet a bare-bones budget while others regularly generate excess revenues. Diocesan personnel usually know how to evaluate parishes, and they generally make good suggestions about what parishes should do to conserve or expand their resources. However, it is important to note that some aspects of a parish operation may present a picture of organizational health even though the parish is in fact living on borrowed time. Consider an urban parish in a once thriving area of the city where at one time several thousand Catholic families lived and attended Mass. Thanks to strong participation in the parish over many years, the parish may now have two school buildings, a gym, a large convent, an auditorium, and a parish center, many of which are now underutilized. Because of demographic changes over the past thirty years, the number regularly attending Sunday Mass may be less than a third of what it once was. In order to cover expenses, the parish may develop a policy of leasing out its unused buildings. It leases the facilities to respectable community groups or for-profit enterprises, but these groups have little to do with the religious mission of the parish. Thanks to the substantial lease payments on these buildings, however, the parish operates financially well in the black.

The solid economic performance of the parish is good and to be welcomed. However, the parish is living off its former wealth, embodied in buildings. There is nothing wrong with making good use of the buildings by leasing them out. However, the financial performance of the parish may mask the fact that not enough is being done at the programmatic level to restructure activities, to reach out, and to attract new parishioners. So, solid economic performance as measured by the bottom line in some instances is not a good indicator of a robust and healthy parish.

PRACTICES AND BENEFITS

Aside from leasing out unused facilities, two strategies will increase parish revenues: more parishioners regularly attending Sunday Mass, and more realistic donations from regularly attending parishioners. Previous sections have addressed regular Mass attendance; this section focuses on contributions.

Many parishes publish data in the weekly bulletin concerning the amount of money collected the previous week and the amount of money needed to pay the regular bills of the parish. Also, in order to establish a steady revenue stream, the pastor and other spokespeople, as well as parish publications, encourage parishioners to register as parishioners and to use the envelope system in making their weekly donations.[6] In most cases, the envelopes themselves have recommendations about what constitutes an appropriate weekly donation. Despite these data points, parishioners frequently wonder whether they are contributing what they should or, more precisely, whether they are giving too much. While most parishioners understand that the parish needs money to operate and want to contribute, they are not inclined to give more than their fair share.

In reality, as every pastor and dedicated collection counter knows, weekly collections contain a distressingly high number of one-dollar bills! Such dollar contributions are anonymous, which is probably why pastors work so hard to get all regular parishioners on the envelope system or its electronic equivalent. People using envelopes adhere to a regular pattern of giving, and most people try to make all their payments, even if they are away from the parish on vacation. At the end of the year, those parishioners using envelopes should receive a statement from the parish indicating how much they have given, a document they use to justify to the IRS the amount of their deductible contributions.

Pastors understand that all contributions are voluntary. They cannot and do not want to force a parishioner to give a minimum amount. On the other hand, the pastor also knows he needs sufficient funds to make the parish operate effectively. Practically all pastors give guidelines to their parishioners about what they should give. We support their efforts by now presenting our own set of guidelines. In doing so, we hope to achieve the following goals: First we would like to establish a more widely accepted norm for parish giving that practically all pastors could endorse. Second, we want to reassure pastors that the pleas they make for support from parishioners are reasonable. And, finally, we know the Catholic Church needs more funds in order to navigate the challenges of our present day. Our guidelines raise the giving bar to a level that, if parishioners cooperate, makes it possible for the Church to challenge the wisdom of the dominant American culture in certain key areas.

We begin the discussion of weekly contributions by asking two practical questions. First, what is the minimal weekly amount that should be given? Second, what constitutes, when adjusted to individual circumstances, a sufficient, reasonable weekly contribution for allowing the American Catholic Church to weave a more competitive culture?

Each parishioner decides what he or she will give. Some parishioners are in situations which prevent them from giving more than a few dollars per week. As valid as these individual cases are, most parishioners in most parishes are not in this situation. To assist all parishioners, a pastor indicates what he thinks is an appropriate minimum weekly amount to be put in the collection. Presumably this minimum is more than two or three dollars. Some pastors, to make their point, say that a good collection should not contain any single dollar bills. This implicitly states that the recommended minimum is $5 per week.

From our vantage point, a better minimum is related to an optional activity that modern individuals or parents and their children engage in regularly. As the weekly minimum for an individual or a married couple, we propose the cost of a regular movie ticket. For the sake of concreteness, in 2008 this would be approximately $9 or $10, depending where the parishioners live. Since many families allow their child or children in any given week to see a movie or go to a fast-food restaurant for dinner, the price of a movie ticket seems like a plausible minimum. If a family can afford a weekly movie or fast-food dinner for their children, it seems reasonable to assume that giving $9 or $10 per week to their parish would not be a hardship. Were most families to give this weekly minimum, parish revenues would likely increase by at least 50 percent. This guideline also easily adjusts for inflation. As the price of a movie ticket increases, the weekly minimum contribution to the parish would also increase. It is certainly possible to adjust the guideline based on dual income couples or the number of children in the family. However, at this point we think it is better to keep the minimum contribution simple and straightforward: the price of a regular ticket in a typical movie theater. It's a helpful guideline and a prod as donors consider where to locate themselves in the range of weekly parish contributions.

The second important question we pose is "What is a reasonable amount to give?" In our answer, "reasonable" incorporates both the income of the donor as well as the needs of the American Catholic Church to build a strong, competing culture. Clearly, a person making $200,000 a year who has no children should not be satisfied with giving the minimum. (If such a person gave $10 a week for 52 weeks of the year, the annual total amount contributed is $520, which is much less than 1 percent of the person's annual net income, let alone their annual gross income.) Many parishioners are capable of giving more than the minimum, and most want to know what the pastor thinks is a reasonable contribution. Since pastors are the ones who pick the design for the weekly envelopes, the pastors usually adopt the recommendations printed on those envelopes. These often request that people give to the parish each week the value of an hour of their time on the job.

For ease of calculation, let us assume that a person employed outside the home works 40 hours per week, which is approximately 2,000 hours a year. Whatever the hourly salary, if a person contributes the value of 1 hour out of 40 hours, the contribution is 2.5 percent of the salary paid. It is certainly appropriate to make the calculation of the amount to be donated on the basis of the average hourly wage after taxes rather than on a before-tax basis. For example, suppose a person makes, after taxes are deducted, approximately $30 per hour. Such a person has a weekly take-home salary of $1,200 and an annual after-tax salary of $60,000. Pastors ask such a person to donate $30 per week to the parish, which is $1,560 per year. Or if this is the income of a married couple, this is the level at which the couple is requested to give.[7] The value of an hour a week is a reasonable, fair, intuitive guideline. As a person's salary increases, it is easy to know about where it should be pegged in the giving spectrum.

One hour a week is a request and a guideline, not a commandment. Some young families may have many expenses related to their children, mortgage payments might be high at this point in their lives, or tuitions for private elementary school, high school, or college might make big demands on a family for several years. In the end, the family has to decide what is reasonable. For a number of years a family might make smaller payments and then make more generous contributions once the children are out of college. Any pastor realizes circumstances differ from family to family. Nonetheless, contributing the value of an hour a week is a reasonable request for all parishioners and a helpful norm for most.

Parishioners know there are often second collections at Sunday Masses. These donations are usually for Church projects of national or international scope. Earlier we mentioned a very important special collection, the Peter's Pence collection for the Holy See. But there are many others: the Holy Land, Catholic University, Catholic Relief Services, Missions to Blacks or Native Americans, the diocesan seminary, the national effort for social justice (the Campaign for Human Development), communications, the Church in Latin America, Catholic rural parishes, Propagation of the Faith, retired religious, and poor Catholic churches in Eastern Europe. There can also be a special collection for the victims of a national catastrophe, such as a tsunami or a hurricane. Catholics making good decisions about their weekly contributions to the parish will certainly know approximately how much to give for these endeavors. There are about fifteen special collections each year, although the specific number differs from diocese to diocese, since some collections are paired together so as not to overburden the parish.

In the interest of proposing standards that are clear and reasonable, we offer specific numbers which, if adhered to by most, would raise current special collections substantially. If every regular parishioner gave a minimum of $5 (or, to better account for inflation, half the price of a movie ticket) for each special collection, a special collection would be reasonable. On the other hand, each collection would be very good if each person gave on average a third of what they normally give in the envelope each week. In the example given above, the person earning $60,000 after taxes contributes $30 per week, or $1,560 per year. If the person contributed $10 for each of 15 special collections, this would be an additional $150, or a total of $1,710 contributed to the parish or national collections per year. In this scenario, the person would contribute 2.85 percent of his or her after-tax income to the parish, the diocese, the Holy See, and national and international Catholic projects.

Empty nesters whose children are grown and living elsewhere are usually in a position to give more than the value of just one hour per week. Indeed, many parishes rely on the great generosity of these senior givers to assure sufficient revenues to run the parish. Pastors also tell wonderful stories about people of modest means giving substantial amounts of money. In one parish, a retired busman was generous to the parish in his weekly contributions. However, he outdid himself each year in the Peter's Pence Collection, for which he wrote out a check for $1,000. He wanted the Pope to be able to have enough money to do whatever the Pope thought important for the Church. Also, people often respond generously if a missionary makes a personal appeal for money at each of the parish Masses. Seeing directly how the money will be used for the poor or for poor parishes in developing countries generates a great incentive to give.

Our focus in this section has been on financial contributions because they are essential for the ordinary functioning of the parish. Any parish also relies on many parishioners to volunteer to run special events, teach in religious education, serve on committees, and review general procedures and policies. Both contributed services as well as donated funds are essential for a parish to achieve its goals. All members of the community should contribute as best they can along the guidelines suggested above and also be grateful for those parishioners who are even more generous with their time and money.

Over the past several decades, a number of pastors have introduced tithing, an approach that works better in some parishes than others. Tithing is related to the word "tenth" and it means donations equal to a tenth of a person's or a family's disposable income. When presented as a norm for parishes, this is usually interpreted to mean 5 percent goes to the parish and 5 percent goes to other charities. Even this seems excessive for most parishioners, and it is certainly higher than the recommended amount we propose above. But whether it is excessive depends crucially on what one counts as donations. For example, many proponents of tithing tell families they may include among their 5 percent contributions to the parish, tuition paid for Catholic schooling, contributions to special collections, and in some cases, direct financial support for elderly parents or other relatives. Another way to interpret the guideline of 5 percent is as a measure which includes all giving to the parish—that is, both the weekly donations as well as the contributions to capital campaigns either for the parish or the diocese. Capital campaigns do not occur frequently, but when they are under way, people are requested to make "sacrificial gifts" to cover special expenditures for new buildings, renovations, or improvements in basic infrastructure. Certainly a person who is committed to donating 5 percent of his or her annual net income to the parish or diocese will be in a good position to assist in a capital campaign.

The previous discussion should be amplified with appropriate distinctions and nuances. These involve particulars we can only suggest here. For example, consider the particular case of a two-income family in which, after taxes, one spouse earns $40,000 per year and the other spouse $30,000. Adding the two salaries together, the gross family annual after-tax income would be $70,000. However, depending on circumstances, this couple can legitimately adjust this figure downward. In order to make it possible for both spouses to work outside the home, the parents may have to have day care or after-school care for their children, or they may have to use babysitters more frequently than a family in which only one spouse works outside the home. Suppose the cost of these ancillary services is $8,000 per year. In this instance, and not taking tax exemptions or tax credits into consideration, it certainly makes sense for the couple to adjust their after-tax income downward by approximately $8,000, to $62,000. In other words, a couple such as this should be on an approximate par with a couple in which one spouse works outside the home earning $62,000 while the other spouse works in the home so that no or little after-school care is needed. Similar types of adjustments are appropriate when a couple with primary responsibility to care for elderly parents makes a decision concerning the amount of money they should donate weekly or annually to their local parish.

Most pastors do not enjoy asking parishioners for money and would prefer never having to bring up the subject. If donations are generous, parishes can effectively perform their threefold ministry of evangelization, liturgy, and loving service. In parishes where this happens, pastors are more than delighted to thank the parishioners for their generosity. Unfortunately, not every pastor is so lucky. In far too many parishes across most dioceses, average donations do not cover legitimate costs.

Certainly no pastor wants to nag his parishioners for money, returning month after month with appeals for higher levels of giving. Given aversions to frequent requests for money by priests, parishioners can be fairly sure a pastor is under pressure if he repeatedly approaches a congregation for more money. In these situations, the pastor almost certainly is unable to pay bills or cover the parish's ordinary expenses. Such pastors may even have been contacted by the diocesan finance office with a directive to either cut expenses considerably or increase annual revenue. Pastors do not like being in these situations, but depending on the parish, it may be an important service he performs for the local Catholic community. We point this out to clarify a financial reality. If a pastor regularly makes appeals for money, the odds are the parish truly needs it. In most instances, this is the judgment not just of the pastor but also of the diocesan or archdiocesan finance office.

While many pastors are reluctant to address financial issues with parishioners, they need to. Pastors perform a valuable long-term service to the Catholic Church in the United States when they point out financial guidelines for giving similar to the ones we have proposed here. Ours is a nation of immigrants who, for the most part, quickly embrace the American dream and make contributions to the well-being of the United States. In time, the new immigrants will do well financially, as have the prior immigrants. At that point they will be able to give more and will want to give more. If they already understand what the regular, expected level of parish giving is, they will be far more likely to step up to the plate once their income has risen sufficiently. Pastors who regularly find a nice way to remind parishioners of their appropriate giving level will eventually make an impact. It might not happen within the next four or five years in any given parish, but it will happen sometime and somewhere for the Church. If pastors are united in regularly repeating guidance for giving, that impact might be substantial for the Catholic Church in the United States twenty years from now.

WEDDINGS AND FUNERALS

Most parishes either charge a fee or strongly suggest a minimum donation for performing weddings and funerals. Pastors are willing to make exceptions and waive fees in pressing cases, but most people are asked to make the required contribution or payment. What is the justification for this approach, and why is this done with weddings and funerals and not with other religious services?

For those raised according to traditional Catholic teaching, charging for weddings or funerals may appear to be simony, which, according to the Catechism of the Catholic Church, is defined as "the buying and selling of spiritual things" (n. 2121, pp. 514–515).[8] However, simony focuses on a non-approved demand of the individual minister of the sacrament. The priest is not allowed to require a payment that has not been approved by the bishop or the competent ecclesiastical authority. The Catechism of the Catholic Church cites New Testament references to the claim that the laborer deserves his food. The church can require contributions to support the church's ministers. So simony is an issue only if the transaction is considered by the priest or layperson as purchasing a spiritual good or service. The diocese decides the general norms regulating "required contributions" for such things as weddings, funerals, or other semireligious events such as quinceañeras (elaborate celebrations, beginning in church, for fifteen-year-old girls).

In U.S. parishes, why is it that weddings, quinceañeras, and funerals often have significant fees associated with them? There are no payments for Communion, confession, or Confirmation, though there may be payments for educational programs which prepare students to receive the sacraments. The answer involves the one-time occurrence of these events in the life of the parishioner.

Parishes charge both to cover the cost of providing the particular service and also to secure some additional revenue for the parish. The parish charges for large events which, even if there were not a church ceremony, would involve a substantial expenditure. The notion here is that the religious aspect of the event is worthy of support, and exceptional circumstances aside, parishioners are expected to pay a predetermined amount. In our view, a better justification for such expenses relies on the orientation of the couple or their parents to the Church. For a wedding, costs are borne by the couple if the couple has accumulated sufficient financial resources, or more traditionally the parents of the bride splurge on their daughter.[9] The parents' joy in their daughter impels them to celebrate with all their friends. The celebration and the reception are indeed extravagant, but this is intended to be a once in a lifetime event. In their joy for their daughter, in their expectation of the blessings to come through grandchildren, the exuberant parents throw a major party.

Since Jesus himself often participated in banquets and parties and weddings, as Christians we should not shy away from celebrations of this type. Catholics should, however, be careful to make sure such celebrations are done in accord with their fundamental convictions and beliefs.

Ideally, a wedding which takes place in a parish grows out of the faith of (usually) the bride, who has practiced her faith for many years within that parish community. In many cases, the bride grew up in the parish and worshipped there for many years with her parents. The basis of a marriage is love, and splurging is a way to signify that financial resources count as little when celebrating the love parents have for their children (or the love children have for their parents and friends). The form of the marriage celebration is a solemn commitment ceremony in the parish church followed by a party, reception, or dinner.

In our view, love and splurging, partially revealed in exuberant celebration, should encompass the three mainstays of Catholic life: liturgy, evangelization, and loving service. Liturgy is certainly involved, since the wedding ceremony takes place in the church. Splurging in the liturgy is evident in many details: the music, flowers, dresses of the bride and bridesmaids, formal dress for the groomsmen, and the many people attending.

How might splurging in evangelization and loving service occur in a marriage celebration? One way to splurge is to show the parish church how much the faith community of this parish has contributed to the religious and spiritual formation of the bride or groom. A generous financial contribution to the church would signify this. Ideally the contribution should not be considered a payment required by the parish. Rather, it is above and beyond any required payment to the parish. In the spirit of splurging at weddings and wedding receptions, it is a generous contribution so that the parish can continue its mission of evangelizing and bringing the life of Christ to new Catholics as well as those who have practiced their faith for many years in the parish.

Should a pastor and his team decide that this would be a good cultural practice in their parish, it would take some years before the practice became rooted in the community. Of course, the motivation for requesting the couple's donation to evangelization should be explained to the engaged couple. The required general fee, the pastor would explain, covers the approximate cost to the parish of arranging and hosting the marriage ceremony. Beyond this, the couple is encouraged to make an additional contribution to the evangelization activities of the parish. The size of the donation is entirely in the hands of the parents or the couple. We will not shy away from suggesting a numerical guideline for this contribution, but first we wish to consider extravagance in the context of loving service.

In his parables, Jesus frequently spoke of inviting people in from the highways and byways to participate in the banquet of the Kingdom of God. In the great judgment scene from the Gospel of Matthew (Matt. 25:31–46), people are welcomed to heaven because they gave water, food, or clothing to someone whom they never recognized as Christ. At a time when he or she is splurging, a Catholic should be sure to include the poor and less fortunate. It should be recommended to the couple or the parents that they directly give money to the less fortunate or make a donation to some group that provides food, clothing, or shelter to the poor or homeless or that takes care of prisoners. The couple should do this not out of fear, but out of their desire to be careful to fulfill the gospel message at this important moment in their lives.

What would be a reasonable contribution? The couple or parents will be the best judges of that, but a few suggestions will assist them in their judgment. The largest contribution should go to the poor, not to the church. Inviting poor people to a wedding Mass and reception would be a wonderful initiative, but most people—poor or not—are comfortable participating in a wedding celebration only when they know the couple. Still, it is useful to think of inviting some of the least advantaged to the wedding ceremony or reception. By concentrating on the reception, as many couples do, the first component of a financial guideline emerges—the approximate cost per person of having an additional person at the reception. The next step is figuring out about how many poor people will be invited to the banquet. A reasonable and yet generous approach would be to increase the guest list by 5 percent and earmark these extra invitations for the poor. If, for example, there were 100 people at the reception, this would mean inviting five more guests. If the cost of each additional person were $100, one could either have five poor people from the neighborhood attend the reception or make a contribution of $500 to some charitable group.

The level of contribution to the evangelizing efforts of the parish church could be derived from the level of contribution to the loving service. Half the amount contributed to the group supporting loving service would seem about right for the contribution to evangelization. If the contribution to the loving service were $500, the contribution to the parish church to promote its evangelizing activities would be $250.

None of these suggestions are hard and fast rules for all couples. Rather, they are attempts to insert the parish church into the framework of an exuberant celebration by drawing general consequences for the three activities of liturgy, evangelization, and loving service. The local church requires some payment to cover expenses for the liturgy. In addition, the priest or whoever organizes wedding services could recommend that the couple or the parents make a donation to loving service and to the evangelizing efforts of the parish.

Analogous observations could be made about funerals. Because at a funeral there is a desire on the part of loved ones to remember and honor the life of the deceased, an important way to do this for a parishioner is to wrap the celebration in the threefold context of liturgy, evangelization, and loving service. For example, by making a generous contribution to some charitable group that helps the poor, as many families do, a family highlights the commitment of the deceased relative to the needs of the less fortunate.

MONEY AND EVIL

Money is, of course, a danger as well as an opportunity. Generating financial resources in parishes should be closely related to their core activities, namely, evangelism, liturgy, and loving service. Commitment to the parish and its needs, nonetheless, can lead to an accentuation of those needs and actually move the parish away from its mission. In his first letter to Timothy, St. Paul says, "the love of money is the root of all evil, and some people in their desire for it have strayed from the faith and have pierced themselves with many pains" (1 Tim. 6:10). This danger exists both for individual Christians and groups of Christians in parishes. With the best of intentions of having financial resources available for the Christian community in future times, a parish may seek to develop substantial endowments or savings. This may make sense in some circumstances, but Jesus also warned his followers "not to store up for yourselves treasures on earth, where moth and decay destroy, and thieves break in and steal, but store up treasures in heaven, where neither moth nor decay destroy, nor thieves break in and steal. For where your treasure is, there also will your hearts be" (Matt. 6:19–21).

Sin and self-deception can blind pastors, staff, and dedicated parishioners to appropriate attitudes toward annual resources and long-term endowments. For this reason, it is appropriate for the pastor to ask prayers from the parishioners that the parish be guided by the Holy Spirit in the pursuit and use of resources and to regularly embed money issues with requests for seeing things in the light of Christ.

MONEY AND INFLUENCE

The Catholic Church seeks to influence its faithful and also those who are at the edge of the Catholic community. It exercises this influence predominantly at the local level, through the parish and its various institutions. Financial resources are needed for these institutions to prosper. The primary thrust of this chapter has been to justify the financial needs of parishes and suggest common appeals for support from the laity.

The Catholic Church also seeks to influence those at the national level, including both Catholics and non-Catholics. Through evangelization, individual bishops in the United States as well as the Conference of Catholic Bishops try to persuade people that the Catholic message is worthy of careful consideration. But the bishops of the United States also seek to influence all people of goodwill, whether or not they are religious. They do this through public policy statements—the subject of our last and final chapter.

NOTES

1. Effective outreach activities can be spearheaded by the diocese, but such activities almost always require strong participation by parishes to be effective. In chapter 10, we described an initiative to promote vocations to the priesthood and to religious life; we recommended that young men and women volunteer a year of service to the Church. Such a program would involve expenses at both the diocesan and parish level. Hence, "evangelization expense accounts" can usefully be created at the diocesan as well as at the parish level.

2. In a recent survey of young priests ordained between five and ten years ago, over 40 percent of them reported to be either in charge of or serving in a parish with two or more churches. See Dean R. Hoge, *Experiences of Priests Ordained Five to Nine Years* (Washington, D.C.: National Catholic Educational Association, 2006).

3. The reported incidents constitute only a small fraction of all parishes in the United States. Nonetheless, because so much money is collected and spent in the parish, apart from direct diocesan oversight, the potential for fraud is great.

4. A recent survey undertaken at Villanova University indicated that 85 percent of parishes surveyed had experienced some significant financial impropriety during the past ten years.

5. See canon 537. For context and a discussion, see *New Commentary on the Code of Canon Law*, ed. John P. Beal, James A. Corriden, and Thomas J. Green (New York: Paulist Press, 2000), 710–711.

6. Private firms now provide financial services to parishes that allow parishioners to make automatic monthly payments to the parish at a level chosen by the parishioner. The parishioner need not use envelopes, since he or she can make the payment via credit or debit card or by the automatic bill payment feature offered by many banks. This service typically increases the amount of money collected by a parish, in large measure because people freely make payments in this system even if they do not happen to attend Mass on a given Sunday or during a vacation period.

7. Comparisons with actual contributions across various religious congregations are available. Dean R. Hoge, Charles E. Zech, Patrick McNamara, and Michael J. Donahue in *Money Matters: Personal Giving in American Churches* (Louisville, Ky.: Westminster John Knox Press, 1996) present extensive data from 1992 on giving patterns according to religious denominations. For example, average annual giving in 1992 to the Catholic parish per household was $386. Comparable data for Lutheran, Presbyterian, Baptist, and Assemblies of God are respectively $746, $1,085, $1,154, and $1,696.

8. The current code of canon law stipulates a penalty for simony, although it does not define simony. See canon 1380 and *New Commentary on the Code of Canon Law*, 1587–1588.

9. The motivation behind the large expenditures on quinceañeras can be considered in a similar way to the analysis of marriage.

13

Politics and the Witness Community

The public square is alive with policy discussions that impinge on morality and ethics. Religious as well as secular voices are engaged in rigorous debate about what we should value and what policies we should adopt. Unfortunately, what emerges when these voices are lifted is more cacophony than chorus, because no coherent and commonly held understanding of morality is shared in American society.

The Catholic Church is a vigorous participant in these discussions as it seeks to both teach its own about faith and morals and offer broader-based moral guidance. It offers its input at a time when secular culture increasingly shies away from accepting, let alone invoking, religiously grounded ethical positions. Today, major nonsectarian institutions such as corporations, governments, and media enterprises aspire to moral neutrality. Hoping to offend no one, these institutions are reluctant to embrace even such basic principles as obeying parents, being faithful to a spouse, or never lying, cheating, or stealing. They have found that too much particularity in these matters gets them in trouble.

The society is also inundated with the laissez-faire morality prevalent in the public media. With no generally agreed-upon moral framework in the United States, most important human issues are discussed in terms of feelings or personal convictions. And if they are evaluated at all, evaluations tend to be political. Because feelings and convictions are deemed personal, fixed, and impervious to influence by rational argument, they are not subjected to critical review, either by individuals or by the media. They are just accepted in the spirit of tolerance. It is true that people are often inclined to do what is good in particular circumstances. However, many lack a moral tradition in which they can evaluate their inclinations critically. They do not have a set of prin-

ciples that would indicate whether their feelings should be accepted and reinforced on the one hand, or managed and massaged on the other. Similarly,
they are unable to evaluate the feelings and sentiments of others.

This lack of a moral framework and the tendency to evaluate all moral
positions in political terms raises a serious question for those interested in
moral inheritance. How can a moral heritage be maintained or necessarily
refined if people do not speak about its principles in public or use them to
arrive at policy positions?

Despite these factors, which we assume will only intensify over time, religion still plays an important role in public discussion. That is particularly
true when the discussion concerns moral issues with policy implications.
Discussions about abortion, embryonic stem cell research, condoms for
teenagers, traditional marriage versus civil marriage, the legitimacy of preemptive war, capital punishment, immigration, the sufficiency of presenting a Darwinian approach to creation in the classroom, and other issues engage people with a variety of religious beliefs and convictions as they
wrestle with religious issues.

One of the chief responsibilities of bishops is to teach their flock, namely,
the Catholics of their diocese, with respect to faith and morals. Related to
this responsibility is their duty to provide education and formation for the
faithful in reading and interpreting Scripture and in applying ethical principles to important issues in society. In order to fulfill this duty, bishops
provide necessary resources and rely on an array of pastors, educators, and
writers both in and outside their dioceses. They also have the responsibility
to clarify faith and moral issues that are contested.

Local parishes, in union with their bishops, play an educational and leadership role in formulating and promoting general and particular moral
stances. In doing so, they rely on the wisdom that comes from centuries of
experience and a set of principles and coherent values. These principles and
values provide a framework for "building a just society and living lives of
holiness amidst the challenges of modern society."[1] The topics in this chapter address this important role, focusing particularly on issues with practical political consequences for the general public and the Catholic Church.
How such issues are resolved by various levels of government can produce
beneficial, modest, or deleterious effects on people in society. This is certainly the case with abortion, war, torture, poverty, hunger, homelessness,
unemployment, and a host of other issues. For this reason, it makes sense
for bishops to provide some moral guidance on these issues.

NARRATIVE: REASON AS THE BASIS FOR NATURAL LAW

A bishop's first responsibility as a teacher is to Catholics in his own diocese.
In exercising this responsibility, bishops rely on a developed system of

teachers to articulate and reinforce the Church's central teachings. They also rely on pastors to teach the faithful about their moral and ethical responsibilities. Catholics do live in secular society and may share some secular viewpoints. Consequently, the bishop has to be attentive to broader trends and issues in society. On major social issues, the bishops in the United States often find it helpful to unite their voices in common statements. A unified statement receives more attention in the national media and it communicates to Catholics that the bishops are of one mind about the issue.

Not every social issue demands a statement by the bishops of the United States. Nor does every important social issue require a policy recommendation. Teaching effectively and persuasively requires bishops to tread a fine line. If they speak too frequently and with too much specificity on too many political issues, Catholics may begin to tune them out. If, however, they remain silent in the face of direct public challenges to the Church's most basic moral principles, they will confuse both Catholics and the broader community. Bishops can be most effective in persuading those committed to reason of their responsibilities in determining just policies if they speak to a limited set of broad civic concerns. In that way they can make a national contribution and clarify the responsibilities of Catholics.

Catholics are free to vote for the political candidate of their choice, and bishops know that. Consequently, they are careful to address issues and not recommend candidates. No bishop wants to publicly endorse or reject a candidate for political office. Because any candidate has views on a wide variety of issues, bishops are also well advised to focus whatever criticisms they have on policies, not people.

When a bishop speaks or the bishops speak in unison, they are merely presenting their convictions as religious leaders. Their viewpoint can be accepted or rejected by the body politic. The more effective a bishop's argument, the more likely he is to persuade. In their public arguments, bishops teach and try to persuade. They never coerce. Catholics must seriously consider the guidance of their bishops, because of their teaching office and their authority as the leader of a diocese. However, Catholics will only vote in accord with Catholic moral teaching if bishops are persuasive in presenting that teaching.

Catholic moral teaching relies heavily on natural law, which is based on "a core of universally binding moral precepts that can be discerned, at least in principle, through human reason."[2] Since it appeals to reason, natural law is not something "owned" exclusively by the Catholic or even the Christian tradition.

The principles of natural law are fairly general. One succinct and at least approximately adequate formulation of the principles of the natural law highlights seven fundamental or human values: life (including health), friendship (including love), knowledge (including truth), beauty, playfulness, religion, and practical reason. The values are distinct and only one is more fundamental than any other. The most fundamental one is life, since without life a person cannot pursue the other fundamental values. Natural law says a country's economic system should be structured so that people have adequate resources to pursue the values, and that people should never act to undermine the fundamental values. Examples of undermining values are the following: killing, including capital punishment, is against life; adultery is against the friendship of marriage; lies undermine truth and knowledge; deformation of nature is contrary to beauty and life; a killjoy is against playfulness; prohibiting religious expression is against religion; being willfully obstinate is against practical reason.[3]

The fundamental values point to what activities should be promoted. However, it is also possible to derive from them actions which should be prohibited because they undermine the fundamental values or are directly contrary to them. Linked to these values are two organizational principles: the principle of solidarity and the principle of subsidiarity. In simple terms, solidarity means that we are responsible for each other, and subsidiarity means we should not ask others to do things we are capable of doing ourselves. In terms of social policy, solidarity requires that we organize society in such a way that all people, not only Americans, can pursue the fundamental values. For this reason, U.S. Catholics cannot be indifferent to some First and Third World realities: poverty, hunger, disease, global warming, unsanitary water, AIDS, slavery, lack of education, oppressive governments, refugees, unemployment, environmental hazards, lawlessness, the plight of women and children, homelessness, and so on. These problems do not have to be resolved this year or next. However, Catholics are expected to support reasonable programs that limit or lessen the obstacles which keep people from participating in the fundamental values.

The principle of subsidiarity preserves freedom in society by bringing decision making and the provision of services as close as possible to those directly affected by them. Subsidiarity means that the smallest feasible group of individuals should be allowed to take responsibility for the issues directly affecting them. For example, how public schools are funded is decided by local towns in which those schools are located. Education at the elementary and secondary level could be regulated nationally. But if local responsibility leads to effective results, such a system conforms to the principle of subsidiarity. For a similar reason, giving urban dwellers of a certain zip code responsibility for public education would not promote the best educational policy. It would probably lead to significant inefficiencies, either because cities could have several different school districts, each with its own policy with respect to students and teachers, or because in rural areas the zip code would cover too large a geographical area. On the other hand, the power to sign treaties and levy tariffs belongs to the federal government, not state or local governments. Poverty, too, should be confronted at the level where it can most effectively be addressed.

Subsidiarity locates primary responsibility with the group closest to the issue, but it does not absolve all other parties from any responsibility. If a poor country is unable to address its dire circumstances effectively, the next nearest body or group that has the capacity to provide necessary resources must get involved to improve the welfare of their disadvantaged neighbors. People automatically invoke this principle when there is a major national disaster. Those closest to the disaster pitch in immediately, and then neighboring regions or countries also provide resources. More generally, if poor countries need assistance in improving the welfare of their citizens, both solidarity and subsidiarity require wealthier countries, such as the United States, to provide some type of effective assistance. This is part of traditional Catholic social teaching.

These are the basic principles that define Catholic morality. There are some qualifications, however, about how they are applied in society. First, not everything that is immoral must also be declared illegal. Catholic moral teaching supports good order, and it teaches that good laws must be enforceable, otherwise they will be ignored and possibly encourage contempt for the law. A society may also confine the area of law enforcement to activities undertaken in the public realm. For example, according to the principles of natural law, a society, even a predominantly Christian one, need not criminalize adultery. Since for the most part sexual intimacies take place in the private sphere and because citizens want to respect the privacy of individuals, they may not want to criminalize adultery, even though there is broad agreement that adultery is contrary to natural law.

Citing the distinction between private and public acts should not be a warrant, however, to allow actions which cut short human life. If the life of an individual or a class of people is threatened in important ways, laws should protect them. For this reason, the state usually classifies the physical abuse of a wife or a child to be a criminal deed and authorizes the public authorities to intervene. If there is good reason to think a person is in danger, preemptive intervention is considered reasonable. Also, because a person has to be alive to pursue the fundamental values, natural law requires that, as a way to protect people, murder, violence, and violent threats against others should be criminalized.

According to Catholic moral teaching, Catholics and others who adhere to the natural law approach can have significant differences of opinion about what actions should be criminalized in society and which offenses against natural law should be tolerated. Nonetheless, natural law implies a strong protection for life and the wholeness of life, since without life one cannot pursue the fundamental values. Even if life is only diminished by physical injury or psychological harm, this impairs the ability of the person to pursue the fundamental values.

It is also true that when faithful people apply the principles of Catholic morality to particular social issues, there is little chance they will come up with the same policy solutions. Consider an example close to home. Some U.S. citizens may be convinced that low taxes for the wealthy and middle class benefit the poor because low taxes generate much economic activity. Other voters may endorse moderately high taxes for the wealthy and middle class to generate sufficient tax revenues to run special programs for the poor that give them enough resources to pursue the fundamental values. Well-motivated Catholics can have legitimate reasons for endorsing one view rather than the other. Similarly with respect to subsidiarity, there are many contested issues in the United States. For example, some people may feel that only the federal government can undertake large, important research projects, while others would leave these to the states and private initiatives. Because the natural law lacks specificity and is tolerant of a variety of views, Catholics can legitimately differ about how its principles should be applied in particular circumstances.

PRACTICES AND BENEFITS

Given some clear requirements of Catholic moral teaching and a fair amount of indeterminacy with respect to many proposed or actual policies, what is a prudent approach for bishops and pastors to take with Catholics and non-Catholics when addressing important social issues? We suggest three things:

- Effective programs that educate Catholics about natural law and how to apply its principles should be developed.
- Bishops should consult laypeople with expertise on a particular issue before they endorse specific policies.
- Informed laypeople should be on the front lines of policy debates.

EDUCATING ABOUT NATURAL LAW

Bishops rely on natural law in evaluating social policy. They expect Catholics to do the same. Unfortunately many Catholics lack even the most basic understanding of natural law and the principles that define Catholic moral teaching. It is therefore up to bishops to address this problem. They must make sure there is a carefully thought out program of instruction in the principles of Catholic moral teaching and natural law widely available in their dioceses. These programs can best begin in a formal way in high school and then continue at higher levels of education. They should be designed to help interested Catholics achieve some facility in handling and applying moral principles by the time they are adults. Some teaching can also take place in the parish via talks and church publications. Whatever the specific components of the program designed by the bishop and his advisers, it should be one which touches a good number of Catholics.

Natural law has important general principles which should be learned by interested laity. However, modern American society attends to what is au courant and emphasizes specialization. Therefore, natural law education and formation programs should eventually focus on areas related to burning policy issues and target adult Catholics with specialized expertise. To teach the general principles and the specific applications, bishops might wish to structure their teaching programs in different ways. General programs could be taught at the local level, while highly technical offerings should be advertised to the national audience of Catholics so as to attract a sufficient number of participants. For example, bishops might encourage some Catholic colleges, universities, health systems, or research institutes to offer succinct programs on particular social issues such as world poverty, environmental issues, medical ethics, immigration and refugees, and ethical issues related to marriage and education in public schools. Laypeople from a broad geographical region or even from across the United States would be encouraged to participate in one or more such programs. On the other hand, a single diocese or contiguous dioceses might organize some general sessions on the basic principles of natural law or a discussion of which types of moral issues need not be enshrined in statutory law. Such introductory sessions could be offered and advertised at the local level.

Strategy 1: Effective programs that educate Catholics about natural law and how to apply its principles should be developed.

LAYPEOPLE WITH EXPERTISE

Policy recommendations often require careful analysis of both intended and unintended consequences of new approaches. Estimating and understanding such impacts may require extensive knowledge of a particular discipline. Therefore, bishops should be wary about addressing political or social issues in which they have no particular expertise. The better approach is for bishops to consult laypeople with particular knowledge in the pertinent area before taking a public stance. Also, rather than take the lead in formulating policies, bishops can fulfill their episcopal responsibilities in other equally effective ways. They can point out to Catholics and others important social issues which cry out for resolution. Bishops can do this forcefully without specifying a particular policy approach. When they proceed this way, bishops acknowledge the complexity of the issue. At the same time, they encourage the faithful to push for effective solutions that are also authentically Catholic.

Strategy 2: Bishops should consult laypeople with expertise on a particular issue before they endorse specific policies.

LAYPEOPLE AND POLICY DEBATES

A bishop or bishops should develop his or their own Catholic "think tanks" to make policy recommendations. Laypeople well trained in the principles of Catholic morality and natural law and with requisite expertise should be tapped. Bishops can organize groups of such laypeople and ask them to outline potential policies consistent with Catholic social teaching. These groups should also identify policies that violate or come close to violating Catholic moral principles. In order to avoid giving the impression that the committee's report is endorsed by the bishop, it is wise to have the lay group publish their recommendations and analysis in their own name, possibly in some diocesan or national publication. This is important because other lay groups may form to challenge the position taken by the original group. If this occurs, it is up to the bishop to decide how to go forward. It might make sense to endorse one approach over another. Or it might be equally fruitful to avoid identifying perspectives taken by one of the groups as the definitive Catholic approach. Rather, depending on the issue, the bishop could prudently encourage further discussion.

Catholic writers and speakers can provide important contributions in the application of general ethical principles to specific situations or policies. In fact, the more specific the application, the more informed some laypeople are, and the more closely bishops should attend to the points they make. Bishops have authority and expertise in stating and explaining the Church's position on a variety of issues relating to social justice and public policy. However, as proposed legislation becomes more specific, well-informed and dedicated Catholics may still differ in their interpretation about how general ethical principles apply to the specific legislation. By reason of their office, bishops have no special knowledge, expertise, or mandate to apply general moral principles to particular political situations.

Many issues discussed and debated in regional or national politics neither offend against moral principles nor are required by them. They are indeterminate with respect to these moral principles.[4] That is, individuals can either support the proposed policy or legislation or oppose it and still be fine Catholics. It may be that traditionally the Catholic Church in the United States has adopted a certain approach to a particular topic, such as unions. However, times change, as do the unions themselves and the context in which unions operate. Catholics can oppose aspects of the traditional formulation and still conform to all the pertinent moral principles. Carefully formulating reasonable policies that reflect Church teaching on specific issues is certainly an important contribution. It is one to which laypeople who understand natural law and also are well informed about their own area of specialty are often more suited. Sometimes they are in a far better position to recommend policies than even informed bishops. In the Catholic Church, bishops retain the final word for Catholics in their diocese. That does not mean bishops should be speaking the first, second, or even the third Church words on important subjects.

By giving prominence to the views of informed laypeople, bishops also convey an important message to Catholics: namely, many policies are morally acceptable for Catholics. The impression that there is such a thing as *"the* Catholic policy" on all issues is neither true nor helpful in most policy discussions. On life issues such as abortion, embryonic stem cell research, and capital punishment, there is only one acceptable approach, namely, to defend life in all its forms. But there are other political issues which are not so clear cut.

Consider a "Catholic policy issue" which is more ambiguous. In 2006, controlling the flow of immigrants across U.S. borders became a divisive topic, more divisive than it had been in the recent past. Some U.S. citizens endorse a high fence along the U.S.-Mexican border and a much more effective presence of border control agents to intercept those who would try to enter the United States illegally. This group wants U.S. borders secured first before there is any discussion of comprehensive immigration reform. Others think it is shameful that the United States does not have a better method for allowing Mexicans to come to the United States, perhaps obtain citizenship in a fairly easy manner, and move back and forth rather easily between Mexico and the United States. Some want to stanch illegal immigration first and only then discuss comprehensive immigration reform. Others reject the notion of a fence and want to work out some system whereby Mexicans can obtain citizenship or at least easily stay in the United States or Mexico for a protracted length of time without worrying whether they will be turned back at the border when they try to enter the other country. Succinctly put: some want control first and others want amnesty now.

Is there a "Catholic policy" on this issue? We claim there isn't and there should not be. Yes, there are many Mexicans, most of whom are Catholic, in the United States. We are delighted to have Mexicans filling our parish pews. Whether they are here legally or not, they are here and we want them to participate in the local community of Catholics. Catholics should respect Mexicans and want them to prosper, whether they have citizenship here or not and whether or not they are documented.

Catholics should have nothing but goodwill for Mexicans living in the United States. But there are no principles in natural law that prohibit a fence or require easy naturalization of illegal immigrants. One can be a very good Catholic, thinking with the Church in all significant matters, and be either diametrically opposed to a high, imposing fence along the border or staunchly supportive of such a barrier. One can be a Catholic Democrat and lament the plight of Mexicans in Mexico as well as Mexicans in the United States. Alternatively, one can be a Catholic Republican and also lament the status of Mexicans in the United States or in Mexico. One can be very open to welcoming immigrants, provided they adhere to the legal process. It is not a question of whether fence opposers are more Christian than fence supporters. Policy should be based on principles of national stability and security as well as on principles that enable many people to pursue the fundamental values.[5] Catholics are free to take the political position they think best suits the circumstances of the United States and its position in the world. Whatever position a Catholic takes, he or she should assume goodwill toward immigrants by those citizens who take a contrary view.

Natural law is not permissive with respect to all situations. As we noted above, according to natural law, Americans cannot be indifferent to those who are poor, with inadequate resources for food, education, or health care, or whose lives are in danger. This is true whether the people are U.S. citizens or not, whether or not they are living in the United States or outside our boundaries. To cite a particular example, the Catholic Church and many others adhering to the natural law are opposed to any policy, whether articulated or not by the U.S. government, which promotes Mexicans dying at the U.S.-Mexico border. Furthermore, the intent of U.S. policy, whatever it is, should not be to sunder Mexican families by trapping parents in one country and children in another. That should not be the intent or the impact of our policies. On the other hand, people should not violate American immigration laws and thereby put their families at risk of being separated.

The two authors personally support a policy that creates both a guest worker program and a path for all nondocumented workers currently in the United States to become naturalized citizens. We are also adamantly opposed to building a high fence. Ours is a Catholic position, but it is not the only Catholic position. Catholics can legitimately support creating a fence on the border. Those who are against constructing a fence must be willing to admit that other Catholics can take a contrary position. Even as we vigorously disagree with their position, we have to respect them and assume they have good motives.

Bishops should stay out of the specifics of this discussion, because there is no decisive Catholic issue. The bishops should urge Catholics to be compassionate toward Mexicans in the United States or Mexico and encourage ways to improve their well-being in both places. However, once specific legislative solutions are advanced, in our view it is better for the bishops to remain neutral. Catholic moral principles allow a country to have secure borders; they also encourage providing employment to those willing to work to improve the welfare of their family. But Catholics and others of goodwill can legitimately differ in how the moral principles are applied and which policy they endorse.

Numerous additional examples of positions taken by the U.S. Conference of Catholic Bishops can be cited, but the previous example makes the point clearly.[6] Bishops should reserve their collective voices for the most important moral issues facing the United States and other countries. Those appropriate for episcopal comment would certainly include protecting the unborn and working against capital punishment, international matters of death and life, war and peace, hunger and prosperity, slavery and freedom, and trafficking in women and children. Issues that impact the family and anything that pertains to the ability of the Catholic Church and its organizations to operate effectively in the United States would also fall into this category. In all of these cases, however, it is best for the bishops to address the principles and issues, indicate any effective policy requirements, and then allow informed laypeople to propose recommendations about specific legislation.

If a bishop is doubtful about whether Catholic moral teaching prohibits a certain approach, he should err on the side of silence. At the very least, he should allow different groups of laypeople to write and discuss the issue before he makes any public statement. Bishops should not be first to the microphone in matters which are detailed and require citizens to weigh many different aspects of the natural law.

Bishops should boldly and frequently speak out on life issues. However, we feel that their other statements on important public issues will carry more weight if the bishops follow two guidelines. First, the bishops should generally curtail the number of public statements they make about social policies. When they do speak in the public forum, at least Catholics will more likely pay heed and follow their wise counsel. Second, bishops will be more persuasive in their arguments about important international, national, or local policies if they have involved laypeople in developing position papers on relevant issues. In short, bishops should refrain from addressing specific legislation about large social concerns. Instead, for specific political proposals, they should regularly use well-informed laypeople to develop acceptable policies and to identify unacceptable policies. To the extent the bishops adhere to this approach, they will speak more forcefully and persuasively on central Catholic issues.

At the current time in the United States, important discussions are taking place with respect to the following topics: embryonic and non-embryonic stem cell research, preemptive war, abortion, capital punishment, the role of gays in society, free trade, taxes and deficit spending, the definition of marriage, global warming. With respect to many of these issues, the bishops have endorsed or criticized certain approaches. Their doing so suggests all positions other than the ones they endorse are morally objectionable. That is certainly not the case, but this impression of exaggerated specificity undermines the Church's moral teaching.

A more helpful approach would be for bishops to designate two groups for each policy issue, each group composed of one or more persons who are well versed in natural law and Catholic social teaching. One group would identify most strongly with the Democrats and the other with the Republicans, which would help clarify that the Catholic Church does not endorse or identify more strongly with one political party over another. Each group would provide the other with progress reports, but for the most part their deliberations should be separate. The process itself would be informative for most of the people involved in the deliberations. Not only would they bring their own professional expertise to bear on important policy issues, but they would also have to make themselves more familiar with Church teaching and the natural law.

What about the outcomes? An ideal outcome for each specific topic would be considerable overlay between the two groups about those policies which are incompatible with natural law and Catholic social teaching. In the absence of such overlay, some people would claim that the process just leads to confusing claims by various groups of informed Catholics. However, if the reports were written in a helpful, respectful style, even in the absence of considerable agreement on forbidden policies, the process would have benefit. The groups would emphasize that the study team is providing their best professional opinion, even as they acknowledge their own political dispositions. If the bishops disagree with some position taken by one or both the groups, they can state their disagreement. If the bishops can agree with practically every result of the study commission, the bishops know they have a group of well-informed laypeople on a particular issue. Since much of public policy consists of persuasion, by supporting experts in the field, the bishops will be more persuasive.

At the university level, faculty members identify with their own individual department, such as English, physics, or sociology, rather than with the liberal arts in general or sciences in general or undergraduate education in general. In our modern world of national and regional policy, there are very few generalists. We are a world of many specialists and specialties. By establishing standing groups on particular public issues, the bishops would promote thinking about natural law morality and Catholic social teaching, and they would also purchase some good social capital for their own pronouncements.

Strategy 3: Informed laypeople should be on the front lines of policy debates.

COMMUNION OF THE FAITHFUL
AND THE PERCEIVED UNFAITHFUL

A recent document issued by the U.S. Catholic Bishops addresses the preparation Catholics should make to receive the Body of Christ.[7] In this document, the bishops included a paragraph addressing prominent people, including politicians, who do not support teachings of the Catholic Church with respect to faith or morals:

> When a person is publicly known to have committed a serious sin or to have rejected a definitive teaching and is not yet reconciled with the Church, reception of Holy Communion by that person is likely to cause scandal for others. This is a further reason for refraining from receiving Holy Communion.
>
> To give scandal means more than to cause other people to be shocked or upset by what one does. Rather, one's action leads someone else to sin. "Scandal is an attitude or behavior which leads another to do evil. The person who gives scandal becomes his neighbor's tempter."[8]

There is an important footnote to the second sentence that references the encyclical *Ecclesia de Eucharistia* in which Pope John Paul II states: "The judgment of one's state of grace obviously belongs only to the person involved, since it is a question of examination of one's conscience. However, in cases of outward conduct which is seriously, clearly and steadfastly contrary to the moral norm, the Church, in her pastoral concern for the good order of the community and out of respect for the sacrament, cannot fail to feel directly involved."

The U.S. bishops address here a thorny issue which arises when prominent Catholics, especially politicians, espouse political policies that appear to be at variance with Catholic teaching. The specific issue is usually whether a bishop or pastor should deny Communion to a prominent Catholic who has repeatedly taken public positions in apparent opposition to the teaching of the Catholic Church concerning abortion. The statement of the U.S. bishops avoids this specific issue and says, instead, that the prominent Catholic himself or herself should accept the fact he or she is not in communion with the Church on an important matter of faith and morals and, therefore, refrain from approaching the priest at Mass to receive Communion.

This appears to be a deft way for the bishops to handle an awkward issue. On the one hand, the teaching of the Church is affirmed. On the other hand, it sidesteps any appearance of coercion by putting the ball in the politician's court.

The important point, however, is whether expecting the prominent Catholic to take the initiative and not approach the altar for Communion reflects the teaching of the Church. We claim the position of the bishops reflected in the statement above is a good, strong position, but it still does not address the issue in a clear and unambiguous manner. There is something appealing about letting the politician choose, but there is also the very real possibility that the politician will not choose wisely or well.

In our view, the standard principles of natural law provide politicians with wiggle room they may genuinely use to promote Catholic teaching in the contested area. Unfortunately it is also possible that politicians will use the wiggle room simply to avoid censure by the bishop. We do not claim to know which situation is more likely and we do not claim to be able to read hearts, much less consciences. Therefore, following the general admonition of the Gospel, we give the politician the benefit of the doubt.

According to the natural law, any person has a responsibility to take reasonable measures to prevent evil from occurring. This is true whether or not the person is prominent nationally or locally. If, for example, it is possible to prevent a car from hitting a child by simply yelling at the driver who might be backing up or yelling at the child to move, we are obliged to do so. We do not have to put ourselves in danger, however, and need not take extraordinary means to prevent some bad thing from occurring to someone else. Nevertheless, we should take reasonable steps to prevent bad things from happening. If we pass by someone's house and see a fire in the yard, we should ring the closest fire alarm, call 911, or ask someone else to make the call. Unless we are firefighters, we do not have to run into a burning building to rescue someone. However, we all have to take reasonable means to promote life and prevent deaths.

The politician is expected to pass just laws which promote the welfare of all the people. According to the natural law, a politician is not allowed to endorse a law, for example, that would be unjust to other people. A politician cannot approve a law which allows some citizens to kill innocent people. In fact, neither politicians nor voters nor citizens nor noncitizens are allowed to back a law that would result in the direct killing of innocent people. Absent special circumstances, a prominent person who publicly endorses such bills on a consistent basis would be causing scandal.

Everyone has a responsibility to protect defenseless life. Politicians who regularly endorse pro-choice legislation appear not to do so. This is true for any politician, and especially for Catholic politicians who have the help of the sacraments to follow the will of Christ. Surely pastors and bishops would meet privately with these Catholic politicians to explain why it is important for them to take a position consistent with Church teaching. If, despite this pastoral approach, these politicians maintain their public position in opposition to the Church, denying them the right to receive Holy

Communion might seem justified. These political figures appear to be committing a grave sin or a serious moral wrong, and because of their public prominence as Catholics their stance causes scandal.[9]

The difficulty for bishops and pastors is that Catholic pro-choice politicians may be operating in good faith and within some narrow confines show support for the Church's position. In the situation we are considering, at the very least, this support is ambiguous, since on a fundamental issue of life, the bishop or pastor is having trouble perceiving an endorsement of the Church's position. Furthermore, politicians can certainly claim that their personal convictions are with the Church even when they do not take a strong public pro-life position. Politicians can be reticent because they are convinced the public will not go along with the Church's position. Hence, as a measure of prudence they take a gradualist approach which, depending on the particulars, may be consonant with natural law.

When it comes to morality and political action, much depends on the interior dispositions of politicians, the political strategies they pursue, and the relation of both of these to the actual legislation the politicians support. Once again we consider the specific issue of abortion. Catholic politicians can point out that, even though they think the electorate is wrong, most Americans do not yet support strong laws against abortion. The politicians might add they are not going along with the electorate when they support pro-choice legislation, but rather they are trying to move them to see abortion for the evil that it is, while working to minimize the number of abortions taking place in the United States. Catholic pro-choice politicians might also point out that, while they vote for bills that appear to be contrary to life, the bills are more pro-life than current law. In fact, they might claim, they are trying to limit the number of abortions.

Pro-choice politicians can find refuge in strategy. It may be a legitimate refuge or it may not. Regardless, it is a strategic one. Their claim is that they agree with bishops and pastors on the goal of reducing abortions; they merely have different strategies. Whether these claims reflect a true interior disposition is something bishops and pastors most probably cannot know. On the other hand, if Catholic politicians are not willing to publicly state that they are personally opposed to abortion and consider it seriously wrong, then there is little doubt these politicians are in fundamental disagreement with basic Catholic teaching. In this case, a bishop or pastor can legitimately withhold Communion from such politicians. But even in this case, doing so could be problematic.

Pastors and bishops realize they must be very careful in how they handle this type of situation. They should only identify public figures as acting in a grave matter contrary to natural law or Catholic teaching if the danger of scandal is great and if they are virtually certain that the politicians are acting contrary to natural law and in bad faith. After all, if pastors and bishops are wrong about the interior disposition of politicians, they will commit a grave injustice against these individuals. Similar to American criminal law, according to which a suspect is innocent until proven guilty, pastors and bishops have to have an extremely high level of confidence that individuals are indeed promoting something contrary to the natural law in a grave matter before publicly accusing them and barring them from receiving Holy Communion. Even then, this approach is risky. On the one hand, a strong stance by the bishop could clarify some of the issues in the mind of the faithful. On the other hand, the politicians could well become sympathetic characters in the eyes of other Catholics who are quick to see hypocrisy in strong condemnations by bishops. Certainly a pastor or bishop has a pastoral duty to meet and talk with pro-choice politicians to try and convince them they should take a public stance more supportive of life issues. But if the politicians are not convinced by the bishop and they speak convincingly and publicly about their commitment to the faith and their personal opposition to abortion, the bishop and the Church can seem cranky, picky, or vengeful.

This clearly is a difficult issue. In an individual case, a bishop may be persuaded that a particular politician has publicly rejected natural-law teaching about some life or death matter. That in turn might lead the bishop to think he must speak out, saying the particular politician should not receive Holy Communion. If this happens, rightly or wrongly many Catholics will sympathize with the politician. Also, rightly or wrongly, pro-choice politicians might be inclined to adjust their rhetoric in order to slip through any loopholes the bishop's statement creates.

IT'S THE GOOD NEWS!

Jesus preached the good news of salvation. Catholic bishops understand they have a sacred responsibility to make sure that good news echoes again and again throughout the Church and the world. Unfortunately, in many of their high-profile public statements, the bishops appear more focused on bad news than good news. There is no question that the Church and her bishops must stand foursquare in support of human life and dignity and against any policy that mitigates against them. And the Church must clearly condemn abortion, unjust wars, genocide, euthanasia, embryonic stem cell research which makes use of aborted fetuses, capital punishment, pornography, and other dehumanizing actions and activities. We are sinful people living in a sinful society, and the bishops must remind us of this sad reality and challenge us to do better.

As was pointed out earlier, Catholic bishops in the United States run the risk of being tuned out in the United States by speaking too often. They also will be ignored or dismissed if they are perceived only as cultural detractors. The bishops certainly speak positively about religious things. They extol faith and participation in the life of the Church and how they contribute to authentic human experience and happiness. These messages are meant to be encouraging but also can promote a dichotomy in the way Catholics view religion and society. On the one hand, religion is always positive and wholesome and offers all things good; on the other hand, secular society has all these potentially evil things that one should avoid at all costs.

What is missing for many people in the bishops' public statements is an accent on the positive, exciting components of American society. At this point, many Catholics and at least some non-Catholics would breathe a sigh of relief if the bishops came out and endorsed something, anything particular to American society and culture that many of us enjoy or think is worthwhile. Such an announcement would convey to a public anxious to hear it that there is at least some development in modern society that the bishops do not greet with suspicion.

At the end of the Eucharist Prayer IV are the words: "Then, in your kingdom, freed from the corruption of sin and death, we shall sing your glory with every creature through Christ our Lord, through whom you give us everything that is good." There are presumably many objects and services manufactured, produced, or promoted in American culture which are correctly used by many people for good purposes. Surely the bishops are convinced this is the case. If so, the challenge for them is twofold. First, to identify and highlight some of these genuinely good things closely identified with American culture. Second, to suggest how they are made available to us "through Christ our Lord" from whom we receive everything that is good.

We are not pressing the bishops to address some favorite positive topic of ours. Rather we are suggesting a strategy that will shake preconceptions and once again rivet attention on what the bishops are trying to convey.

In their public statements, the bishops will certainly not be cheerleaders for secular culture. Instead they will view and appreciate developments through the lens of a Catholic/Christian understanding. In his Letter to the Romans, St. Paul says: "Do not be conformed to this world but be transformed by the renewal of your mind, that you may prove what is the will of God, what is good and acceptable and perfect" (Rom. 12:2). In this vein, bishops can speak of opportunities in U.S. culture to deepen Christian commitment. For example, the bishops might talk about the spirit of entrepreneurship in America and how in the context of Christian belief it can be appreciated and developed. The bishops could emphasize the volunteerism so characteristic of Americans, the pragmatic approach Americans take to solving problems, the way the entertainment industry helps us reflect on many important developments in our society, the positive role that sports play in the lives of people, the technological innovations which make life easier and more enjoyable, the advances in health sciences which provide increased protection from infirmities and contribute to more physically robust lives, the flexibility of the American economy which generates so many jobs, or the great growth in home ownership. Each one of the things we have mentioned has an actual or potential downside, but many millions of Americans currently enjoy many of these goods and services because we have an open society which respects the law and allows significant developments in the way people live and interact.

The good news for Catholics is that there are aspects of American secular culture in which we can rejoice. Even though it cannot rival in importance the good news of the Gospel, this news is welcome. Emphasizing the good in culture reassures the faithful and also offers an appropriate contrast to the divine good in which Catholics participate through their life in the Church. The secular part of human culture offers goods and activities which can wonderfully enrich and deepen our commitment to truth, love, and beauty. Beauty, truth, and goodness are partially realized in secular society, but they find their completion and fulfillment in Christ.

THE PATH OF CHANGE

The focus of this book is Catholic culture at the parish level. Because cultures brush against and interact with other cultures, they constantly undergo change. The change may be incremental and barely perceptible or it may be broad and dramatic. Cultural change often seems rapid to those who are immersed in it, but for the most part, its pace is moderate. Cultures can only change if cultural components—content, symbols, and people—change and each of these changes slowly. Cultural actors certainly change. First of all, in any large culture such as the United States, some cultural actors die every day and every day new actors are born. Also, each new cultural generation assimilates a modern culture that is somewhat different from the one assimilated by previous generations, and they assimilate it more thoroughly. The composition of a culture may well change by several thousand people a day. But in the United States, with a population of 300 million, for instance, it will be some time before this degree of change makes an impact on culture.

The dynamic of changing actors results in at least some cultural change over time. Parishes, as we have pointed out, are adjusting to a dramatic change in cultural actors. Prior to the late 1960s, most of the leading actors in parishes were sisters, brothers, and priests. When the number of these cultural catalysts available for parish work began to fall precipitously around 1965, parishes had to start making cultural adjustments. In the

1950s, parish culture was developing along a path of fairly predictable change that we term an *equilibrium change path*. The changes in the 1960s, 1970s, and 1980s created a new context for parishes, and that new context necessitated a new equilibrium change path. Catholic parishes are in the process of moving toward that new path, but they are not there yet. And until they get there, they will experience heightened levels of cultural change. This cultural volatility certainly involves new people, but it also involves new activities, symbols, and content.

Because parishes are still in the process of making important adjustments, it is difficult to predict what they will look like in the future. Parishes are reacting in various ways as they adjust to the changes in personnel who run programs. The danger in this situation is that the adjustments they make in terms of activities, people, and symbols may fail to attract people to the parish.

An important role of the Pope is to make sure the content of the faith is passed on to the subsequent generation of Catholics and that what is passed on is complete and faithful to what the Church proclaimed and believed at its very beginnings. Nonetheless, the content of the faith as learned at the parish level as well as the form it takes in a parish can change. For good or ill, the faith or practices of the faith as perceived by actual or potential parishioners may appear in a form which does not attract people who are baptized Catholics. Because of his experience in Europe, where Catholic practice is much diminished, Pope Benedict is particularly alert to this possibility, and in his teaching role he tries to present the mysteries of the faith in as compelling a manner as he can. We are happy to highlight the compatibility of our concerns with some of those of the Pope.

This book was written to be a guide for parishes negotiating their way to a new equilibrium change path. It analyzes what we believe are the key areas that define parish culture: Eucharist, the sacrament of reconciliation, prayer, loving service, and education. It also identifies four strategies for cultural renewal that parishes can adopt and apply in each of these key areas. In the history of the American Church, religious sisters were the premier cultivators and transmitters of Catholic culture, and they have left us a rich cultural legacy. The four strategies for cultural renewal we recommend— narratives, norms, benefits, and practices—are taken directly from that legacy. By adopting and adapting them in our own time, parishes can reclaim the cultural legacy of the sisters and reinvigorate parish life. This approach also provides a filter for deciding which practices should be introduced or retained at the parish level. In other words, these four strategies provide a way to evaluate current and proposed new practices.

Much of the book attests to our belief in the importance of specific religious activities for developing vibrant Catholic cultures. Ideally these regular activities can be repeated often. The old Latin proverb tells us that repetition is the mother of learning. When we apply that wisdom to religion, it means that practicing our faith is key. Just as practicing the piano is the best method for learning how to play the piano and appreciate the music, so, too, practice is the best way to cultivate and appreciate our faith. Consequently, in practically every chapter, we have proposed fairly specific religious practices which, according to our lights, fit the circumstances of many parishes and lend themselves to repetition. They are new ways to instruct people in the Catholic faith that also assist them in the regular practice of the faith.

St. Paul spoke of the love of Christ which urged him onward (2 Cor. 5:14) to spread the good news. A similar love pressed thousands of young women religious to develop patterns in worship, prayer, and religious instruction which helped form millions of American Catholics in the nineteenth and twentieth centuries. By their efforts to find ample room for the Gospel in the prevailing culture of their day, the sisters drew upon the wisdom of the Holy Spirit and created a very effective Catholic culture. In recent years, both Pope John Paul II and Pope Benedict XVI stressed the importance of evangelizing. They want the message of the good news to go out, and they want priests and laypeople to find persuasive ways to present our Catholic faith to others. In this book we have looked to religious sisters for the evangelizing principles which made them successful in spreading the faith. When applied imaginatively to our modern situation, these principles provide a way to develop a consistent and compelling Catholic culture that can form committed Catholics and draw others in the ambit of grace which is the Church.

NOTES

1. U.S. Conference of Catholic Bishops, *Sharing Catholic Social Teaching: Challenges and Directions*, www.usccb.org/sdwp/projects/socialteaching/socialteaching.htm (1998).

2. Jean Porter, *Encyclopedia of Catholicism*, ed. Richard P. McBrien (San Francisco: HarperCollins, 1995), 908.

3. For a more extended analysis, see Melanie M. Morey and John J. Piderit, *Catholic Higher Education: A Culture in Crisis* (New York: Oxford University Press, 2006), 139–148.

4. Some use the term "underspecified with respect to the moral principles." That is, the moral principles classify the proposed actions or policies as acceptable, though they may be less favorable to a thoroughly Catholic approach than other policies.

5. In fact, Catholics have a position on this and many other issues. The U.S. Conference of Catholic Bishops maintains a legislative liaison in Congress and regularly endorses or rejects parts of bills being considered by the Congress of the United States. See, for example, the Legislative Report, 109th Congress, 2nd Session, U.S.

Conference of Catholic Bishops, Office of Government Liaison, available at www.usccb.org/ogl/109thCongress2ndSessionInterim.pdf (August 2006).

6. These range from topics of great national importance to fairly trivial topics. For example, the bishops have a position endorsing net neutrality, and positions as well on Cuba, Haiti, Palestine, international debt relief, daylight savings time, farm subsidies, minimum wage, hazardous sites cleanup, housing vouchers, predatory lending, and other issues.

7. See U.S. Catholic Bishops, *Happy Are Those Called to His Supper* (Washington, D.C.: USCCB, 2006). In the apostolic exhortation *Sacramentum Caritatis*, www .vatican.va/holy_father/benedict_xvi/apost_exhortations/index_en.htm (2007), Pope Benedict XVI stresses in paragraph 83 a bishop's responsibility to affirm and promote Eucharistic consistency, that is, the compatibility between the public positions and actions taken by high profile individuals on the one hand, and the endorsement of Church teaching which is the basis for receiving Holy Communion on the other.

8. The quotation is from *Catechism of the Catholic Church*, 2284.

9. If the person is not prominent, few people would be aware that a person has allowed the direct killing of other people. In particular, the local priest would not know this, or if he did, would not want to make it known to others.

Bibliography

Argyris, Chris. *Overcoming Organizational Defenses*. Boston: Allyn and Bacon, 1990.

Argyris, Chris, and Donald Schon. *Theory in Practice*. San Francisco: Jossey-Bass, 1974.

Beal, John P., James A. Corriden, and Thomas J. Green, eds. *New Commentary on the Code of Canon Law*. New York: Paulist Press, 2000.

Beck, Bernice. *Handmaid of the Divine Physician*. Milwaukee: Bruce, 1952.

Benedict XVI, Pope. *Deus Caritas Est*. 2005. www.vatican.va/holy_father/benedict_xvi/encyclicals/index_en.htm.

Bretzke, James T. *A Morally Complex World: Engaging Contemporary Moral Theology*. Collegeville, Mich.: Liturgical Press, 2004.

Brewer, Eileen Mary. *Nuns and the Education of American Catholic Women, 1860–1920*. Chicago: Loyola University Press, 1987.

Catholic Bishops, U.S. Conference of. *Happy Are Those Called to His Supper*. Washington, D.C.: USCCB, 2006.

———. *Co-Workers in the Vineyard of the Lord*. Washington, D.C.: USCCB, 2005.

———. *National Directory for Catechesis*. Washington, D.C.: USCCB, 2005.

———. *Sharing Catholic Social Teaching: Challenges and Direction*. 1998. www.usccb.org/sdwp/projects/socialteaching/socialteaching.htm.

Chittister, Joan. *The Way We Were*. New York: Orbis, 2005.

Coburn, Carol K., and Martha Smith. *Spirited Lives: How Nuns Shaped Catholic Culture and American Life, 1836–1920*. Chapel Hill: University of North Carolina Press, 1999.

Cohen, Eric. "The Ends of Science." *First Things* 167 (November 2006): 27–33.

Contosta, David R. "The Philadelphia Story." In *Catholic Women's Colleges in America*, ed. Tracy Schier and Cynthia Russet (134–135). Baltimore: Johns Hopkins University Press, 2002.

Deacon, Florence Jean. "Handmaids or Autonomous Women: The Charitable Activities, Institution-Building, and Communal Relationships of Catholic Sisters in

Nineteenth Century Wisconsin." Ph.D. dissertation, University of Wisconsin, 1989.

Ewens, Mary. "Women in the Convent." In *American Catholic Women: A Historical Exploration*, ed. Karen Kennelly. New York: Macmillan, 1989.

Finnis, John. *Aquinas: Moral, Political, and Legal Theory*. New York: Oxford University Press, 1998.

Fourez, Gerard. *Sacraments and Passages: Celebrating the Tensions of Modern Life*. Notre Dame, Ind.: Ave Maria Press, 1981.

Gingerich, Owen. *God's Universe*. Cambridge, Mass.: Harvard University Press, 2006.

Gray, John. *Men Are from Mars, Women Are from Venus*. New York: HarperCollins, 1992.

Greeley, Andrew. *Priests: A Calling in Crisis*. Chicago: University of Chicago Press, 2004.

Green, Thomas J. "Sanctions in the Church." In *New Commentary on the Code of Canon Law*, ed. John P. Beal, James A. Corriden, and Thomas J. Green (1529–1607). New York: Paulist Press, 2000.

Gula, Richard M. *Ethics in Pastoral Ministry*. New York: Paulist Press, 1996.

Haught, John F. *Is Nature Enough? Meaning and Truth in the Age of Science*. New York: Cambridge University Press, 2006.

Hoge, Dean R. *Experiences of Priests Ordained Five to Nine Years*. Washington, D.C.: National Catholic Educational Association, 2006.

Hoge, Dean R., and Jacqueline E. Wenger. *Evolving Visions of the Priesthood: Changes from Vatican II to the Turn of the New Century*. Collegeville, Minn.: Liturgical Press, 2003.

Hoge, Dean R., Charles E. Zech, Patrick McNamara, and Michael J. Donahue. *Money Matters: Personal Giving in American Churches*. Louisville, Ky.: Westminster John Knox Press, 1996.

Huels, John M. "The Most Holy Eucharist." In *New Commentary on the Code of Canon Law*, ed. John P. Beal, James A. Corriden, and Thomas J. Green (1095–1137). New York: Paulist Press, 2000.

International Theological Commission. *Communion and Stewardship: Human Persons Created in the Image of God*. 2004. www.vatican.va/roman_curia/congregations/cfaith/cti_documents/rc_con_cfaith_doc_20040723_communionstewardship_en.html.

Jenkins, Philo. *The Next Christendom: The Coming of Global Christianity*. New York: Oxford University Press. 2002.

Lickona, Thomas. *Character Matters*. New York: Simon and Schuster, 2004.

McBrien, Richard P. *Catholicism*. New York: HarperCollins, 1994.

McManus, Frederick R. "The Sacrament of Penance." In *New Commentary on the Code of Canon Law*, ed. John P. Beal, James A. Corriden, and Thomas J. Green (1138–1178). New York: Paulist Press, 2000.

McNamara, Jo Ann Kay. *Sisters in Arms: Catholic Nuns through Two Millennia*. Cambridge, Mass.: Harvard University Press, 1996.

Morey, Melanie M. "Leadership and Legacy: Is There a Future for the Past?" Ed.D. dissertation, Harvard Graduate School of Education, 1995.

Morey, Melanie M., and John J. Piderit. *Catholic Higher Education: A Culture in Crisis*. New York: Oxford University Press, 2006.

Porter, Jean. In *Encyclopedia of Catholicism*, ed. Richard McBrien (908). San Franciso: HarperCollins, 1995.

Renken, John A. "Parishes, Pastors, and Parochial Vicars." In *New Commentary on the Code of Canon Law*, ed. John P. Beal, James A. Corriden, and Thomas J. Green (673–724). New York: Paulist Press, 2000.

See, Holy. *Catechism of the Catholic Church*. Vatican City: Libreria Editrice Vaticana, 2000 [1997].

——. *Lumen Gentium*. 1964. www.vatican.va/archive/hist_councils/ii _vatican_council/documents/vat-ii_const_19641121_lumengentium_en.html.

——. *Constitution on the Sacred Liturgy*. 1963. www.vatican.va/archive/hist _councils/ii_vatican_council/documents/vat-ii_const_19631204_sacrosanctum -concilium_en.html.

Stark, Rodney. *The Rise of Christianity: How the Obscure, Marginal Jesus Movement Became the Dominant Religious Force in the Western World in a Few Centuries*. San Francisco: Harper Collins, 1996.

Stark, Rodney, and Roger Fink. *Acts of Faith: Explaining the Human Side of Religion*. Berkeley: Unversity of California Press, 2000.

Wall, Barbara Mann. *Unlikely Entrepreneurs: Catholic Sisters and the Hospital Marketplace, 1865–1925*. Columbus: Ohio State University Press, 2005.

Weber, Max. "Social Psychology of the World Religions." In *From Max Weber: Essays in Sociology*, ed. H. H. Gerth and C. Wright Mills (287–288). New York: Oxford University Press, 1958.

Wittberg, Patricia. *From Piety to Professionalism—and Back? Transformations of Organized Religious Virtuosity*. Lanham, Md.: Lexington Books, 2006.

——. *Pathways to Re-Creating Religious Communities*. Mahwah, NJ: Paulist Press, 1996.

——. *The Rise and Decline of Catholic Religious Orders: A Social Movement Perspective*. Albany: State University of New York Press, 1994.

Zmora, Nurith. *Orphanages Reconsidered: Child Care Institutions in Progressive Era Baltimore*. Philadelphia: Temple University Press, 1994.

Index

abortion, position on, and Eucharist, 251–54
absolution, prayer of, 104
abstinence, 128, 167–69
accountability, lay ecclesial ministers and, 202
accreditation, sisters and, 27, 55n7
acknowledgment, and Mass attendance, 82
actions, and culture, 7–8
act of contrition, 106
actors, and culture, 8
adapted practices, 49–50; and parish culture, 50; term, 49
administrators, lay, 176–77, 193n4. *See also* lay ecclesial ministers
adoration: of Blessed Sacrament, 26, 84; prayer of, 120
adults: focus on, 76–77; religious education for, 131–51
Advent, 122, 128; fasting in, 167–69
affirmation, and Mass attendance, 82
almsgiving, 128
altar servers, 78, 89n5
amends, making, 216
America, 149
American culture, and Catholic culture, 7

Anderson, Augusta, 29
annulments, 74; cost of, 88n1
Ash Wednesday, 87
audits, 226
Augustine, Saint, 122
authority, 13–14; sisters and, 25, 30–32

baptism, 131
Beck, Mary Bernice, 40
Benedict XVI, Pope, 68–69, 117–18, 154, 216–17, 223, 257–58, 259n7
benefits, 44–45; and Confession, 103–4; and education, 138–40; and financial issues, 228–33; and lay ecclesial ministers, 204–13; and loving service, 157–69; and Mass attendance, 60–61; with other strategies, 47–48; and prayer, 124–28; and social issues, 244–51; term, 39; and vocations, 184–92
bishops: and evangelization, 254–56; lay advisors to, 245–46; and moral guidance, 240; statements by, 241, 246–51. *See also* diocese(s)
Blessed Sacrament: adoration of, 26, 84. *See also* Eucharist
blogs: Catholic, 149; definition of, 151n11

Brewer, Eileen, 32, 46
brothers, 23; recruitment of, x
budgets, 221, 227

capital campaigns, 232
CASAs. *See* Catholic after-school academies
catalysts, cultural, 8
catechism, 131, 150n1
catechists: and Mass attendance, 146; term, 150n2
cathedraticum, 221
Catholic, term, 71n5
Catholic after-school academies (CASAs), 147
Catholic Church: need for reform in, 14–16; and politics, 239–59; precepts of, 71n4; structural weaknesses of, 16–18
Catholic culture: definition of, x; factors affecting, 6–7; lay ministers and, 198–200, 206–7; and parishes, 8–10; sisters and, 23–39
Catholic early summer academies (CESAs), 147–48
Catholic practices: and parish culture, 50; term, 49.
See also practices
Catholic schools, 140–44, 213; current status of, 140; financial issues in, 220
Catholic volunteer program, 187–88, 195n19; and financial issues, 238n1
CCD, 151n9. *See also* religious education
celibacy, 193n9
CESAs. *See* Catholic early summer academies
charity, term, 170n2
chastity, sisters and, 28
children: and Christmas gifts, 163–67; and Confession, 75–76, 102–3; engaging, practices for, 77–83; focus on, 76–77; involving in Mass, 78–80; moral norms for, 205–6, 213–16; and prayer, 123; religious education for, 131–51

Chittister, Joan, 28, 31
choirs, 79
Christian, term, 71n5
Christianity, development of, 63
Christmas gifts, 163–67
citizens, cultural, 8
Clark, Mary Frances, 45–46
cohabitation, lay ecclesial ministers and, 207–8
colleges, Catholic: accreditation of, 27; competition among, 36; and continuing education, 149–50
Commonweal, 149
communication: and Confession, 94, 102; and education, 136; on Mass attendance, 85–87
communities, 14
compensation: for lay ecclesial ministers, 202, 205; for priests, 190–91
competition, sisters and, 35–36, 55n7
compilation reports, 226
complete consent, 99
Confession, 91–110; increasing participation in, recommendations for, 104–9; on Mass attendance, 75–76, 86; seal of, 88n2; term, 92
confidentiality: abuse of, 17–18; in Confession, 107–8
Confirmation, 131
Confraternity of Christian Doctrine, 151n9. *See also* religious education
confusion, on Confession, alleviating, 105–7
congregations of sisters. *See* sisters
conscience, 97–98
consumerism, and Christmas gifts, 163–64
contact, and loving service, 157
contemplative prayer, 121
content, of culture, 8
contingency funds, 221
continuing education, 148–50
contributions, 228–33
contrition: act of, 106; prayer of, 120
corporal works of mercy, 155
Coughlin, Samuel, 32–33

counteractive practices, 50; term, 49
criticism, and priest shortage, 179–80
culture: education and, 131; elements of, 7–8; real versus ideal, 16; and sin, 97; term, 198. *See also* parish culture
curate, term, 21n3

deacons, 10, 194n13
deaneries, 185
deans, 185
desires, 97–98
diocesan priests, 195n22
diocese(s): and financial issues, 11, 221–22; and lay ecclesial ministers, 200–201; and parish financial data, 225–26; and vocations, 182
discipline: lay ecclesial ministers and, 213–16; sisters and, 42–43
displays, of student work, 143
distinguishability, of culture, 8; and Catholic culture, 8–9; and priests, 189; sisters and, 24
divine intervention, 111–29
divorce: lay ecclesial ministers and, 207–8; practices and, 50. *See also* marriage
do and don't lists, for children, 215–16
donations, 228–33
Duchesne, Rose Philippine, 26–27

Easter duty, 110n9
Eastertide, 122
ecclesial ministers, lay. *See* lay ecclesial ministers
education: benefits and, 44; on morality, 239–40; on natural law, 244–45; norms and, 42; practices and, 46; religious, 131–51; sisters and, 23, 27
embarrassment, with Confession, diminishing, 107–8
emotions, 97–98
envelopes, 228
environment: and prayer, 125; and vocations, 180–81
ethical lapses, culture and, 51

Eucharist: and culture, 73–89; development of, 62–63; Easter duty and, 110n9; as living legacy, 61–64; and loving service, 154; and politics, 251–54; and self-knowledge, 67–70; and tipping, 159–60
Eucharistic participation, 5–6; narratives on, 61–67, 69–70; sisters and, 26
evangelization: bishops and, 254–56; and financial issues, 223–24; recommendations for, 256–58
evolution, 113–17

faith, 8
fasting, 128, 167–69
feelings, 97–98
finance committee, 227
financial issues, 219–38; and Catholic schools, 140–41; corruption and, 226, 238n4; in parishes, 11–12; pastors and, 183–84, 194n14; sisters and, 34–35; and vocations, 190–91
First Communion, 88n3, 131; extended, 82–83
First Things, 149
forgiveness, Confession and, 92–95
freedom, 87–88; and sin, 97
free will, 114, 118
full knowledge, 99
full-time staff, 205
funerals, and financial issues, 234, 236

gifts, 163–67
goals, for Confession participation, 104–5
godparents, 80
grace, 115; before meals, 126
grave matter, 99
Greeley, Andrew, 181

health care: and loving service, 158; narratives and, 40–41; practices and, 46; sisters and, 26, 29
heroic witness, sisters and, 28–30, 33
hierarchy, 13–14; sisters and, 30–32

high schools, Catholic, competition among, 36
Hispanic Americans. *See* Latino parishioners
holiness: call to, 68; Confession and, 95–96; lay ecclesial ministers and, 202–3; priests and, 179
homeless people, hospitality for, 161–62
homework, 136; and Catholic schools, 142–43
hope: Confession and, 94; lay ecclesial ministers and, 201
hospitality, 160–63
hospitals. *See* health care
housing, for priests, 192

immigration, policy on, 247–49
inheritability, of culture, 8; and Catholic culture, 9–10; and priests, 189; sisters and, 24
institution, term, 198
intellect. *See* reason
Invitation Sundays, 84–85
irregular marriages, 73–74; lay ecclesial ministers and, 207–9
Isabella, Mother, 33

Jesus Christ: and Confession, 91, 94, 108; and Eucharist, 61–64; and prayer, 111; relationship with, 69–70
job satisfaction, of priests, 188–89
John Paul II, Pope, 223, 251, 258
Joseph, Sister, 34
judgment, 99

knowledge, lay ecclesial ministers and, 202

laity: as advisors to bishops, 245–51; and education, 133; and Mass attendance, 59; and parish finances, 227; and parish leadership, 192–93; and pastors, 183, 186; and priest shortage, 176; support for parishes, 13–14

Latino parishioners: and immigration, 247–49; and participation, 3–5; quinceañeras, 234, 238n8
lay administrators, 176–77, 193n4
lay assistants, 10–11; and financial issues, 223; rewards for, 194n16
lay ecclesial ministers, 197–217; full-time, 205; hiring, 205; roles of, 199; term, 217n1
lay ecclesial movements, 14
leadership: lay, 192–93, 197–217; and prayer, 124; sisters and, 23–38
lectio divina, 121
Lent, 122, 127–28; fasting in, 167–69
Lickona, Thomas, 42
life, value of, 241–43
liturgy: boredom with, 74–75; cycle of, 122, 127–28
love: Confession and, 92–95; Eucharist and, 64–67; extension of, 208; lay ecclesial ministers and, 201; and loving service, 157; prayer and, 117–20; science and, 114–15; self-knowledge and, 67; sisters and, 26; and splurging, 235
loving service, 153–71; term, 170n2
loyalty: abuse of, 18; safeguards on, 19–20

magazines, Catholic, 149
mañanitas, 4–5
Manning, Carmelita, 29
market share, increasing, 12–13, 224–25; sisters and, 32–34
marriage: Eucharist and, 65–67; hospitality and, 162–63; irregular, and Mass attendance, 73–74; lay ecclesial ministers and, 207–9; practices and, 50; preparation for, 65–66
martyrs, 64–65
Mary: and love, 118; Our Lady of Guadalupe, 4–5; and practices, 46; prayer to, 121–22, 129n7; sisters and, 26
Mass attendance, 59–72; and Catholic schools, 143–44; on Christmas,

166–67; cultural expectations on, 4; current status of, ix, 59–60; decline in, causes of, 76–77; factors affecting, 73–89; more than minimum, 83–84; obligation and, 60, 71n4; religious education programs and, 144–46

materialism, and Christmas gifts, 163–64

May Day, 46, 55n10

McNamara, JoAnn, 34

mealtime prayers, 126

media: Church teachings on, 212–13; and materialism, 164; and morality, 239; and sexual abuse scandal, 95–96; and sisters, 13

memorization, 138–40; of moral norms, 215

mental prayer, 121

Mexican Americans. *See* Latino parishioners

money, nature of, 237

Monica, Saint, 122

moral guidance: lack of, 239–40; lay ministers and, 206–16

movements, 14

narratives, 40–41; and Confession, 92–96; and education, 133–34; and financial issues, 219–25; and lay leadership, 198–200; and loving service, 154–55; and Mass attendance, 60–67, 69–70; with other strategies, 47–48; and politics, 240–44; power of, 70–71; and prayer, 112–20; term, 39; and vocations, 177–81

natural law, 240–44; education on, 244–45; principles of, 241–42

nature, 115

new ecclesial communities, 14

news services, Catholic, 149

non-Catholics, and Eucharist, 87, 89n7

norms, 41–43; for children, 205–6; and Confession, 96–97, 102–3; and education, 135–38; and financial issues, 225–28; and homework,

142–43; and lay ecclesial ministers, 200–204; and loving service, 155–57; and Mass attendance, 85–87; with other strategies, 47–48; and prayer, 122–24; term, 39; and vocations, 181–84

nuns. *See* sisters

nursing schools, sisters and, 43

obedience, sisters and, 28, 31

obligation, 60, 71n4, 76, 87–88, 110n9

O'Malley, Seán Cardinal, vii–viii

ombudsman, 19

order priests, 195n22

orphanages, benefits and, 44

Our Lady of Guadalupe, 4–5

pace of life: and education, 136–37; and prayer, 127

parents: and Confession, 102–3; and education, 133–37; and moral norms, 206; and religious education programs, 146–47

parish(es), 3–21; Catholic culture and, 8–10; definition of, 7; diversity in, 5; and financial issues, 220–21; functions of, 11–13; personnel of, 10–11; reconfiguring, 176; selection of, 169–70

parish culture: Confession and, 91–110; current status of, ix; definition of, x; and financial issues, 219–38; lay ecclesial ministers and, 197–217; loving service and, 153–71; Mass attendance and, 59–89; need for renewal, ix–xii; and politics, 239–59; practices and, 50; prayer and, 111–29; priest shortage and, 175–95; recommendations for, 256–58

parochial vicars, 10; term, 21n3

pastors, 10; and donations, 232–33; evaluation of, 185–87; and financial issues, 183–84, 194n14; role of, changes in, 182–83; senior, 186; shortage of, 175–95; training for, 180–82

patience, Eucharist and, 65–66
Penance. *See* Confession
Peter's Pence, 221, 231
petition, prayer of, 120
physicians, sisters and, 30
politics: Church and, 239–59; and
    Eucharist, 251–54
poor people, hospitality for, 161–62,
    235–36
pornography, 51, 209–13
poverty, sisters and, 28
practical reason, 99
practices, 45–47; and Confession,
    103–4; and education, 138–40; for
    engaging children, 77–83; and
    financial issues, 228–33; and lay
    ecclesial ministers, 204–13; and
    loving service, 157–69; with other
    strategies, 47–48; and prayer,
    124–28; selection of, 48–51; and
    social issues, 244–51; term, 39;
    types of, 49; and vocations, 184–92
prayer(s), 111–29; of absolution, 104;
    how to, 120–22; and loving service,
    157; for sporting events, 48; types
    of, 120–21
prepayment plans, sisters and, 30
priests, 23; and Confession, 107–8;
    importing, 176; need for, 178;
    perceptions of, 188–89; recruitment
    of, x, 34; shortage of, 175–95; types
    of, 195n22; visibility of, 191–92
priests-in-residence, 10; term, 21n4
professional norms, and lay ecclesial
    ministers, 201–4
provisional support, principle of,
    19–20
publications, Catholic, 149

question-and-answer format, and
    education, 138–40
quinceañeras, 234, 238n8

RCIA. *See* Rite of Christian Initiation
    for Adults
reason, 97, 99, 110n5, 118; and natural
    law, 240–44; types of, 99

recitation group, 78–79
Reconciliation. *See* Confession
rectories, leasing out, 227–28
religious education, 131–51; current
    status of, 131; financial issues in,
    220; importance of, 132–33;
    programs, 144–48
Religious of the Sacred Heart, 42–43
religious virtuosity, 33, 203, 217n3
responsibility, priests and, 184–87
rewards, 42; for lay personnel, 194n16;
    of priesthood, 181
Rite of Christian Initiation for Adults
    (RCIA), 148
Roman Catholic, term, 72n5
routines, for prayer, 126–27

sacraments, 11; and marriage, 208
Sacred Triduum, 88
saints, prayer to, 121–22, 129n7
school vouchers, 141
science: and Catholic culture, 6; limits
    of, 113–17, 129n2; and prayer, 112
seamen's hospitals, 29
second collections, 230–31
Second Vatican Council, 92; and
    education, 131; and sisters, 24,
    37n3
security, and church visits, 84
Segale, Bladina, 34
self-knowledge: and Confession, 103;
    Eucharist and, 67–70
sentiment, 118; term, 99
service, loving, 153–71
sexual abuse, 217n6
sexual abuse scandal, 14–16; media
    and, 95–96; and priest shortage,
    179; and structural weaknesses of
    Catholic Church, 16–18
sexuality, Church teachings on, 210–12
silent prayer, 125–26
simony, 234, 238n8
sin, 97–102; conditions of, 99; near
    occasion of, 101
sisters: adaptation by, 26–28, 49; and
    Catholic culture, 23–38; criticisms
    of, 51–54; legacy of, reclaiming,

39–55; media and, 13; recruitment of, x, 32–34; term, 37n1
Sisters of the Holy Cross, 29
social issues, Church and, 239–59
sodalities, 46
solidarity, 242
speculative reason, 99
spiritual direction, for priests, 179–80
spiritual practices, of sisters, 25–26
spiritual works of mercy, 155–56
student-teacher Mass days, 143–44
subsidiarity, 242–43
suburban parishes, 5; finances of, 12
Sundays: Invitation, 84–85; theme, 80–81
supplication, prayer of, 120
support for parishes: lay people and, 13–14; provisional, 19–20
symbols, 40; and culture, 8

Tertullian, 65, 155
thanksgiving, prayer of, 120
theme Sundays, 80–81
theoretical reason, 99
tipping, 159–60, 171n4
tithing, 232
torchbearers, 79
transparency, financial, 226
trust, priests and, 184–87

understanding. *See* reason
unity, lay ecclesial ministers and, 203
urban parishes, 5

values, distortion of, 18
vicars, 10, 185; term, 21n3
virtue, 97–98
virtuosity, religious, 33, 203, 217n3
visiting, 47, 83–84; and Catholic schools, 142
vocal prayer, 120–21
vocations, x, 32–34, 175–95; candidates for, attracting, 187–88; self-knowledge and, 68
volunteering. *See* loving service
voting, 241
vouchers, 141

Wall, Barbara, 30–31
Weber, Max, 203, 217n3
weddings, and financial issues, 233–36
witness community, 239–59
Wittberg, Patricia, 31, 33, 36, 37n2
women religious. *See* sisters
works of mercy, 155–56

Zech, Charles, 194n12

About the Authors

Rev. John J. Piderit, S.J., is president of the Catholic Education Institute, a not-for-profit corporation promoting new approaches to the on-going education and formation of Catholics. He received a B.A. degree from Fordham University, majoring in philosophy and mathematics. After completing theological studies in Germany and being ordained there in 1971, he secured his master of philosophy in economics from Oxford University and doctorate in economics from Princeton University. From 1978 until 1990, Father Piderit taught international economics and statistics at Fordham University. His contact with students led him to found Queens Court Residential College, an option for freshman students who wanted a more intentional engagement in the intellectual life on campus and in the city. In 1990 Father Piderit moved to Marquette University in Milwaukee, where he served as Corporate Vice President for three years. From 1993 to 2001, he was president of Loyola University Chicago. Father Piderit is the author of *The Ethical Foundations of Economics*, and, together with Melanie M. Morey, he authored *Catholic Higher Education: A Culture in Crisis*.

Melanie M. Morey is Senior Director for Research and Consulting at NarrowGate Consulting, a division of the Catholic Education Institute. She has worked in the field of education and administration for the past thirty-five years. She received her B.A. from Smith College, a master's degree in religious education from Boston College, and a master's degree in educational administration from the Harvard Graduate School of Education. She has worked primarily as a researcher and consultant to Catholic colleges and universities and religious congregations around issues of governance, sponsorship, leadership, institutional identity, and Catholic culture. She has served on a variety of boards of trustees for Catholic institutions and earlier in her career she worked as a teacher and administrator in Catholic secondary education. Dr. Morey also served as the education director of a Catholic ministry training program and helped administer a medical education program in a teaching hospital in the Northeast. Dr. Morey is a contributor to *Catholic Women's Colleges in America,* and, with John J. Piderit, S.J., she has also authored *Catholic Higher Education: A Culture in Crisis.*